Mosquito Intruders - Target Burma

Mosquito Intruders - Target Burma

The RAF's Daring Low-Level Mosquito Operations

Jeremy Walsh

AIR WORLD

First published in Great Britain in 2023 by
Pen & Sword Military
An imprint of
Pen & Sword Books Ltd
Yorkshire - Philadelphia

ISBN 978 1 39905 265 8

Typeset in INDIA by IMPEC eSolutions
Printed and bound in the England by CPI Group (UK) Ltd, Croydon, CRO 4YY

Pen & Sword Books Ltd. incorporates the Imprints of Pen & Sword Archaeology, Atlas, Aviation, Battleground, Discovery, Family History, History, Maritime, Military, Naval, Politics, Railways, Select, Transport, True Crime, Fiction, Frontline Books, Leo Cooper, Praetorian Press, Seaforth Publishing, Wharncliffe, White Owl and After the Battle.

For a complete list of Pen & Sword titles please contact

PEN & SWORD BOOKS LIMITED
47 Church Street, Barnsley, South Yorkshire, S70 2AS, England
E-mail: enquiries@pen-and-sword.co.uk
Website: www.pen-and-sword.co.uk

or

PEN AND SWORD BOOKS
1950 Lawrence Rd, Havertown, PA 19083, USA
E-mail: uspen-and-sword@casematepublishers.com
Website: www.penandswordbooks.com

Contents

Contents

Foreword

In mid-1942, following the fall of Burma, the Japanese were threatening to advance into India. The Star of the British Empire was under acute threat and much of the British Army in South-East Asia had been defeated or captured. The 'Forgotten War' assembled many combatants from the United Kingdom, its Dominions, the USA and China.

The London Government was attempting to prevent Germany's further domination of both Europe and the Mediterranean. The problem of defeating the Japanese was secondary and dependent upon the Mediterranean and Suez Canal being available for the British to support the Far East theatre. North Africa was the priority to prevent loss of Suez and domination of the Persian Gulf by a rampant German military machine. The Government believed that the loss of Egypt and lines of communication eastward would have signalled a dire position for India.

Physical terrain, jungle and the monsoon season meant that a Japanese invasion of India was difficult so perhaps just enough resource was devoted to ensuring that the Japanese favoured the larger prize of dominating south-east China. Without key bomber and transport aircraft, including the Dakota, a very large measure of air supremacy would not have been possible. Without attack aircraft, including the Mosquito intruder, the progress of the Japanese could have led to the defeat of the British in India.

'Mosquito Intruders – Target Burma' is a compelling account of bravery and organisation. From the absence of global information on weather, mapping and air traffic, it demonstrates the bravery and skill shown by our airmen in just getting the aircraft into theatre, never mind the courage to take the fight to the enemy.

Was it the men or the machines that prevailed? The book's author, Jeremy Walsh, evidences the outstanding courage and persistence of the aircrew as well as those on the ground who endured grim and punishing conditions. He highlights the continuing questions over the Mosquito's structural integrity and the reliability of weapons. These issues must have increased the stress and anxiety for the aircrews, adding to the operational risk they sustained daily.

Japanese logistics were clearly very taught in 1942 and the RAF's Air Land Integration was poor. Nevertheless, by the end of the Burma Campaign, Admiral Lord Mountbatten, General Slim and Air Marshal Baldwin had created the capability in Air Land Integration that led to Slim writing in *Defeat into Victory*:

> 'Our pattern of operations depended almost entirely on a very large measure of air supremacy. Until a degree of air superiority, amounting at least locally to dominance, had been secured, neither air supply, movement or tactical support could be carried on with the certainty and regularity our operations demanded. The fighter and the bomber between them had to sweep the skies and push back the enemy landing grounds; the air battle had to be won first.'

What is also beyond doubt is that the war in Burma was against a ruthless, uncompromising and cruel enemy. Jeremy's account weaves into the chronology of Mosquito operations insidious reference to the consequences for captured aircrew of aircraft failure over enemy territory; a very present danger to the mental well-being of the aircrews and their leaders.

The Mosquito is correctly lauded for its speed, manoeuvrability and capabilities. Its design may have started life as a high-speed bomber with powerful Merlin engines, but such was the flexibility in concept and construction that the Mosquito was rapidly transformed into a formidable multi-role weapons platform.

In 1943 the first Mosquito FB VIs were despatched to the Far East. Even ferrying the aircraft to India proved hazardous and some crews did not survive the ordeal. From May 1943 to the defeat of Japan in Burma in mid-1945, the Mosquito increasingly was seen to be a decisive force in the skies over the Allied campaign. However, delivering the performance was not achieved without compromise. Frankly, the speed with which the aircraft was developed was both an opportunity and a risk. The author's research implies that the opportunity to have a highly flexible and capable multi-role aircraft was key to success in the Burma campaign. It also suggests that the risk to structural integrity for a bonded wooden construction was not well mitigated. This led to airframe failures in a hot, humid and very unstable weather zone, possibly exacerbated by using bombing techniques demanding high 'g' manoeuvres.

As well as a creative and compelling read for all those who are curious about the Mosquito in the 'Forgotten War', this book reveals that, although a Mosquito design weakness was apparent, aircraft crash investigations in India and Burma weren't included in the RAF's systemic investigation. From October 1943 the RAF Accident Investigation Branch were aware of structural failure as a cause of fatal accidents with Mosquitos braking up when performing high 'g' manoeuvres. Yet it was not until early 1945 that the Ministry of Aircraft Production acknowledged that there was an issue. By the end of the war, the RAF Accident Investigation Branch had investigated sixty-nine known aircraft break up accidents but no aircraft accidents from the Burma campaign were included.

From the start of operations with 27 Squadron, under Wing Commander Nicolson VC, the book demonstrates the determination, leadership and bravery required of every young squadron and flight commander. They also demanded much of their aircrew, both commissioned and non-commissioned. Most of these young men were in their early twenties and the author reveals many stories of the heroism, bravery, luck and misfortune as they helped Slim's army make rapid advances against the Japanese invader.

'*Mosquito Intruders – Target Burma*' is thorough and provides a fascinating insight to the lives and deaths of those involved with Mosquito operations. Jeremy clearly shows that it was the ability of the aircrews, groundcrew and the support structure in theatre and beyond that significantly contributed to the rout of the Japanese in Burma. Courage, bravery, leadership and example are evident throughout, resulting in successes in later life as well as their tendency to PTSD. It is a comprehensive and complete, well-researched and balanced account of what must have been a frightening and unpleasant experience borne with dignity and courage by all involved.

Per ardua ad astra.

Air Vice-Marshal Nigel Bairsto
CB MBE FIMechE FRAeS FCMI

For the descendants of everyone who served in
27, 45, 47, 82 and 110 Squadrons
during the Mosquito intruder era in India and Burma

Introduction

The total production of all marks of the de Havilland DH.98 Mosquito was 7,781 aircraft, of which 6,710 were built during the Second World War. The most numerous production variant, with 2,305 built, was the fighter bomber version, the fabled FB VI. As with all Mosquitos, it was crewed by a pilot and navigator and this mark was armed with four .303 machine guns in the nose and four 20mm Hispano cannons under the nose, occupying the forward part of the bomb bay. Even so, it could still carry two 500lb bombs internally and two more bombs (or rockets) under its wings.

Almost as fast as a Spitfire, in its day the Mosquito was a truly formidable and versatile weapon. It was loved by the people who flew it and it could take tremendous punishment. It could also be fragile. Most pilots would agree that they almost 'wore' a Mosquito, rather than sat in one. The controls were light, reactive and beautifully balanced – its response and agility belied its size. Side-by-side, the pilot and navigator acted almost 'as one'. The aircraft was so good that it seemed its capabilities had few boundaries. However, the crews also learned that the Mossie needed to be treated with respect.

Because it was made virtually entirely of wood, the Mosquito did not survive long after the war. Apart from a couple of films in the 1960s, it has fallen from the public psyche. Due to complexity of construction and the cost of rebuilding to airworthy standards, there are very few Mosquitos still flying. Although it arguably transformed British fortunes in the war, the Mosquito has faded from view, unlike its British contemporaries – the Spitfire, Hurricane and Lancaster. It is so pleasing that The People's Mosquito is currently rebuilding one in the UK to return this iconic aircraft to skies over its home.

As the son of a Mosquito intruder pilot, I grew up devouring stories of the daring exploits of Mosquito crews in the Far East. It didn't matter to me then whether they were true or embellished. I believed that Mosquito pilots flew just above the jungle! But, in researching my father's wartime experiences for my first book, *Mosquito Intruder Pilot*, I realised that I had so many unanswered questions. How many aircrew were involved in the intruder campaign? Did the Mosquito really contribute to pushing the Japanese out of Burma? Was the flying daring? Were the operations dangerous? Or was it just propaganda and Government 'hype'?

Some newspaper articles were obviously important to my father, Benjamin 'Benny' Walsh, since he had taped three into his logbook. I have used excepts from one of these articles, 'Mosquitos on the Burma Front – Coming adds to range of daylight offensive', published in February 1944, to introduce some chapters.

To try to uncover the truth, I have used official records, logbooks, contemporary reports and personal accounts of the aircraft, training, conditions and the intruder operations. Where possible, I have cross-referenced. Apart from conforming the presentation of times, distances, heights and speeds, I have reported official records and personal accounts verbatim. For authenticity, in these accounts I have retained terms which were then in common use in the military but are now classed as derogatory.

This book tells the story of the Mosquito intruders' campaign over Burma, often through the words of those involved. Their lives were neither glamourous nor comfortable. They were tightly knit groups of young men, friends who socialised together, who flew to the limit, looked out for each other and lived with death always close. What became clear to me is that everyone – squadron commanders, pilots, navigators, engineers, armourers, catering staff and administrators – deserves our respect and thanks for what they achieved and the conditions in which they did it. No wonder so few wanted to talk about the war for Burma on their return.

Jeremy Walsh
Summer 2023

Acknowledgements

I must first thank the relations of the airmen and groundcrew from the intruder squadrons who have supplied information and photographs to me, including Tom Yanota, Sue Cox, Geoff Pridmore, Nevin Williams, Richard Ewing, Richard North, John Kitchen, Matt Poole, Peter Cox, Penny Hunt and Alan Jenkinson. I must also thank Andy Wright and Graeme Smith for their advice and support.

The Mosquito Aircrew Association archives, held by the Second World War Experience Centre, contain the most important sources of first-hand operational accounts written 'by Mosquito aircrew for Mosquito aircrew' for their journal, *The Mossie*. Other essential sources were the National Archives, the Australian War Memorial and the Commonwealth Grave Commission. Specialist Facebook groups – RAF in Burma India and SEAC, WW2 Burma Research, World War 2 – The Burma Campaign and the various Mosquito groups – have provided information, introductions and guidance.

My special thanks are reserved for:

Barbara Boon, daughter of 45 Squadron pilot Wal McLellan. Barbara has provided critical feedback, advice and encouragement throughout my research and writing.

Alan Brown, who has proofread my drafts. As a retired Army Colonel, Alan has also provided a 'ground' perspective.

Nigel Bairsto, for his excellent foreword. I have known Nigel since we were at the Royal Air Force College Cranwell together in 1976. Memories of a conversation about his challenges of extending the life of the RAF's Tornado fleet made him the obvious choice to write the foreword.

Fiona, my wife. Fi has been hugely supportive throughout another year when virtually every other time I speak relates to events which happened nearly eighty years ago. Not only that, but she has also read through, constructively criticised and provided continual encouragement. I am so pleased that she married me all those years ago.

I must also thank the team at my publishers, Air World, for having faith in me and helping me again through the publishing process: John Grehan, Martin Mace and Ken Patterson.

Finally, I have made efforts to reference the copyright holders of all the sources I have used but some have been untraceable. I will happily include their details in future editions of this book if more information comes to light.

Chapter 1

Ahoy there, Dracula

May 1945

*'The capital city of Rangoon fell to the British Fourteenth
Army today, and the three-year war to liberate Burma from
the Japanese was virtually at an end.'*
New York Times, *3 May 1945, Calcutta, India*

The two wing commanders approached each other. They were senior members of a small specialist group who flew low-level Mosquito intruder operations, however neither had met the other before. The clean shaven one, Arthur 'Soapy' Saunders, had just landed.

A couple of days' earlier, on 30 April 1945, there had been reports of some large letters painted on the roof of Rangoon jail. The Allies knew that this was where the Japanese were holding captured prisoners of war (POWs). The following day, some RAF Thunderbolts and a Mosquito had 'beaten up' the jail, with the pilots reporting that the letters spelt 'Japs gone'. Since the British Fourteenth Army believed that Rangoon was the epicentre of Japanese resistance, the pilots hadn't hung around the area, just overflown it a couple of times at low level.

Both operational imperatives and the monsoon season starting unusually early dictated that there was no time to waste. In the afternoon of 2 May 1945, Wing Commander Arthur 'Soapy' Saunders, the CO of No. 110 Squadron, set off in his Mosquito FB VI from the coastal airfield of Joari to confirm the letters for himself.[1] After a couple of hours flying low across Burma, he reached Rangoon and overflew its centre. He expected the usual hostile anti-aircraft and small-arms fire, but none came. On the roof of the jail, in addition to 'Japs gone', someone had written 'Extract digit'. Soapy knew that it had to be the British who had written that! Even though their radio was playing up, rather than returning to Joari, Soapy decided to gamble and asked his navigator, Flight Lieutenant James Stephen, for the heading to the nearest 'Japanese' airfield, Mingaladon. On arrival, there were no signs of the Japanese, just three people waving a white flag. The runway was clearly full of holes from Allied bombing, but there were usable areas. Soapy approached and landed, slightly damaging his aircraft because the tailwheel failed to come down.[2] There was no going back now!

To Saunders' surprise, the three people with the flag were Indian National Army officers, which he was told had pledged allegiance to the Allies just as soon as the Japanese left the city. With the assistance of Colonel Bashir Ud-In of the INA, Soapy arranged for locals to start filling in some of the craters on the runway. Then he, with 6'7" tall Stephen, hitched a lift with Bashir Ud-In to the city's jail to meet the Allied officer in charge of Rangoon, collecting Japanese officers' swords as mementoes when they entered the city.[3]

Heavily bearded, malnourished and twenty-nine years old, the officer in charge was Australian Wing Commander Lionel 'Bill' Hudson, who had been the CO of No. 82 Squadron until four and a half months previously when he had crashed his Mosquito during his first intruder op.

Having introduced themselves, Soapy explained, 'We saw the Union Jack and your nasty remark on the roof, so I put down at Mingaladon. The Nips had really fooled us on this one. The brass up there are convinced the bastards will be making a last ditch stand in Rangoon. We saw your messages but couldn't take them seriously.'

'You did,' Bill replied.

'Yes, but I'm an idiot!'

'Just the same, they'll believe you if you report that the Japs have pissed off.'[4]

With that, Hudson arranged for Saunders to send a message on the correct frequency on their newly acquired radio transmitter: 'Mosquito K110 landed Mingaladon 1500Z. No enemy in Rangoon – Saunders.' The operator kept repeating the signal, but they didn't receive an acknowledgement. Saunders was worried and decided he had to disclose what he knew about Operation Dracula which was just starting with an amphibious operation to take Rangoon. 'If we don't get word to them, they could be knocking shit out of this place even tonight! You know they are about to go to town on these things. I'd better get a boat and go down river to tip them off,' Saunders proposed, 'Even an hour could make all the difference.'[5] With that, Saunders, Stephen and Bashir Ud-In set off into the dark towards the quay to commandeer a boat.

Before settling down for the night, as a pre-war newspaper journalist, it was second nature for Bill Hudson to record all the key events and conversations he had witnessed in his diary, just as he had every day for the previous two months since he had acquired a pencil and paper.

The Allied assault had started but progress was slow. Due to shallow water, the battle fleet was positioned thirty miles offshore preventing a naval bombardment. The monsoon had started early, a storm of cyclonic fury was hindering the transfer of troops from the invasion force into assault boats and the river was in flood. For twenty-four hours, Gurkha paratroops had been in control of the key defences at Elephant Point at the mouth of the estuary.

In the early morning, from upstream, a sampan approached one of the leading Allied assault craft. Someone onboard was using a torch to flash Morse, 'S.O.S.', 'Do not fire' and 'Friends'.[6] When it was closer, they heard shouts, 'Ahoy there, Dracula. I repeat, ... ahoy there Dracula.'[7] Soapy Saunders had managed to make contact with the assault force to let them know that the Japanese had fled Rangoon on 29 April.

Just after dawn, Bill Hudson arranged for the INA to close off sections of roads with signs saying, 'Don't prang Rangoon', 'Japs evacuated Rangoon' and 'British repairing Mingaladon.' He then set off by car to Mingaladon with two New Zealanders, fellow Mosquito intruder pilot Flight Lieutenant Cliff Emeny and Pilot Officer Eric Osboldstone, as well as Flying Officer Bellingen. The airfield was a mess and they were amazed that the Mosquito crew had managed to walk away from their landing. The INA had already manhandled the aircraft to the edge of the field where it was camouflaged and under guard.[8] Locals told them that the Japanese had mined the airfield, with one saying that he knew where the mines had been placed. The three air force officers volunteered to stay at the airfield and Bill appointed Cliff Emeny as Officer Commanding RAF Station Mingaladon. They set about making it serviceable for Dakotas to land to start evacuating the POWs. Bill then returned to his base at Rangoon jail.

Around 1430hrs, a B-24 Liberator bomber approached Rangoon and headed straight for the city centre. Its bomb bay doors opened. Watching it approach on its bomb run, Bill and his colleagues felt physically sick. Their messages hadn't been received! The Liberator dropped its load directly on the jail – twenty-two containers packed with 'K' rations and one with medical supplies floated gently down to the jail and adjoining street by parachute.[9]

About ninety minutes later a British war correspondent and two official army photographers knocked on the main gate of the jail and were given a very warm reception. One explained, 'We were with the invasion fleet. But our boat was hardly making headway against the strong current in the river, so we jumped off and walked cross-country. Don't tell me we're the first here?' The press men stayed for about an hour before hurrying off to tell the world that Rangoon was British again.

At 1800hrs the sound of marching boots echoed in the street outside the jail. The Royal Navy had arrived. The officer drew his sword and hammered it several times on the jail's wooden gate. 'The Navy's here, the Navy's here,' he yelled. Bill Hudson put his head out of a window, responding with, 'The Navy can fuck off. The Press was here two hours ago!'[10] Even so, the Navy were welcomed into the jail, with one sailor commenting, 'You're a rotten lot. At least you could have let us rescue you. We haven't been able to find one bleeding enemy to shoot at.'

Wing Commander Bill Hudson walked down to the wharf to meet with the navy and army commanders of the seaborne assault. He felt that his reception was a little frosty and assumed that they had probably heard of his welcome message to the Naval party. Major General H.N. Chambers, commander of the 26th Indian Division, said, 'Well, Hudson, you chaps can consider yourself mighty lucky. I only called off the show at 3 a.m. Good job I heard you were here.'

'How did you know, Sir?'

'Some pilot tipped us off. Came down the river in a sampan. Just as well. I was going to give Rangoon a hiding.'

Hudson couldn't resist responding with, 'You know, Sir, the Japs abandoned Rangoon four days ago!'

Chambers glared at Bill Hudson. 'The Fourteenth Army are not here yet, young man. They're stuck in the mud at Pegu and that's thirty, forty miles away. We've beaten them to it. My 26th Division has won the race to Rangoon.'

The Major General started to turn away. Concerned that he was being dismissed, Hudson reverted to his immediate needs, 'Excuse me Sir. We have a lot of very sick boys back in the jail.'

'They'll be alright. We have got a hospital ship out there.'

It was clear to Hudson that Chambers didn't understand the urgency, so he continued, 'Some are on their last legs, Sir. We have a doctor in the jail and he says that they could die if we don't get them in to hospital pretty quickly.'[11]

Bill Hudson then advised the General that he had a party of ex-prisoners out at Mingaladon organising the repair of the runway in preparation for evacuation flights. He asked if he could dictate a signal to the effect that Mingaladon was serviceable for Dakotas and under the control of a party of air force officers, ex-prisoners of war. The General consented and then listened with interest to Hudson's briefing on the situation in Rangoon with the INA and BNA. Obviously now impressed with his recent actions, Major General Chambers walked back to the jail with Wing Commander Hudson to greet the ex-prisoners, as well as taking time to speak to the Indian prisoners in Urdu.

Rangoon was free!

Three Mosquito intruder pilots had played key roles in securing the liberation of Rangoon with minimum loss of life. Surprisingly, just over 230 pilots and navigators created the legend of ultra-low-level fast-striking Mosquito intruders skimming over Burma, day and night.

Chapter 2

Lulus and Rogues

From 1920 to Early 1943

'The development of the Mosquito was a story in itself. Unlike almost every other type of aircraft introduced by both sides, it was not on the drawing boards before the war.'
Associated Press, *India, February 1944*

W hen just twenty-four years old, in 1908, Geoffrey de Havilland designed and built his first aircraft using a 50hp horizontally opposed engine of his own design. After designing aircraft for the Aircraft Manufacturing Company during the Great War, as well as flying with the Royal Flying Corps, Captain Geoffrey de Havilland OBE AFC founded the de Havilland Aircraft Company. He built its early reputation on its Moth training and light aircraft range. In the early 1930s the company ventured into fast, elegant aircraft, enhanced by the success of the DH.88 Comet Racer which won the 1934 Mildenhall to Melbourne Air Race. It then started the development of the DH.91 Albatross, an all-wooden construction airliner targeted at the North Atlantic route.

Meanwhile, with the clouds of war starting to build over Europe, the UK Government issued specifications for two large bomber programmes, B12/36 which resulted in the Short Sterling and P13/36 which delivered the Avro Manchester. This latter specification intriguingly suggested 'the possibility of combining a medium bomber, general reconnaissance and general-purpose aircraft in one design, with a top speed of 275mph at 15,000ft.' Geoffrey de

Havilland, affectionately known to all as 'Capt. D.H.', wondered whether a military variant of the Albatross was the possible answer, creating a 'bomber with fighter speed'. The company's small design team set about creating estimates for twin-engine Albatross-based designs powered by either Rolls-Royce Merlins, Bristol Hercules or Napier Sabres engines. With these completed, on 7 July 1938, Capt. D.H. approached the Air Council through Air Marshal Wilfrid Rhodes Freeman, the Air Member for Development and Production, proposing a bomber of wooden construction, since wood 'is as strong in all but torsion as metal.' Having received a lukewarm response, within a month de Havilland had dropped the idea of a rework of the Albatross and focused on a smaller stripped-down aircraft.

After the Munich crisis, with war now almost inevitable, Capt. D.H. and Charles Walker, his Chief Engineer, visited the Air Ministry to promote their new concept. 'Wood is a good thing – it would save a year in the development phase and, also in war time, employ furniture makers and similar people.' They were rebuffed and asked to make wings for another aircraft manufacturer.

Through early 1939, the team continued looking at the concept of a useful fast bomber and gradually concluded that all defensive armament could be removed if the aircraft's speed and height performance were sufficient. The Mosquito concept was born! On 20 September 1939, de Havilland wrote to Wilfrid Freeman, 'We believe we can produce a twin-engine bomber which will have a performance so outstanding that little defensive equipment would be needed. This would employ the well tried out method of construction used in the Comet and the Albatross and being of wood or composite construction would not encroach on the labour and material used in expanding the RAF. It is especially suited to really high speeds because all surfaces are smooth, free from rivets, overlapped plates and undulations and it also lends itself to very rapid initial and subsequent production.' The Ministry remained sceptical. Could it really be fast enough? Could a two-man crew actually cope?

De Havilland's core design team, which had just relocated to the safety and secrecy of Capt. D.H's home, Salisbury Hall, continued to refine their concept, looking at drag and the impact of adding a two-gun defensive turret. They concluded that an unarmed bomber was the correct path. On 12 November 1939, Capt. D.H. and Charles Walker again met with Air Marshal Freeman to argue that removing armament would result in higher speed, hence most interceptions could be avoided. When asked about the speed, they said that 397mph was achievable. Since this was faster than the current Spitfire, they were challenged to think about other possible roles the aircraft could fulfil and a draft requirement was raised calling for a high-speed, light reconnaissance bomber capable of 400mph at 18,000ft.

A major conference was held on 12 December 1939 to discuss the whole concept. Freeman now championed their cause and the decision was made to order a prototype, and a mock-up. Under specification B.1/40, the Mosquito would be an unarmed bomber with ducted radiators, however the prototype would be a reconnaissance aircraft. Detailed design for the DH.98 Mosquito started in earnest and, on 1 March 1940, as the development progressed, the Ministry placed an order for fifty Mosquitos to replace the Blenheim in the reconnaissance role. In May 1940 the Ministry issued specification F.21/40 calling for a fully armed long-range fighter. As a result, de Havilland were authorised to start building a fighter version of the Mosquito.

The Mosquito was radical in both its design and construction. Led by chief designer, Ronald Eric Bishop (universally known as R.E. Bishop), the team included aerodynamic wizard Richard Clarkson, fuselage designer A.P. Wilkins and wing designer William Tamblin, with Fred Plumb in charge of the construction work. The composite wood structure, combining strength with lightness, was made of spruce, Canadian birch plywood, Ecuadorean balsa, ash, Douglas fir stringers and walnut, using traditional milk-based casein wood glue to bond pieces together. As well as its innovative composite structure, the Mosquito also featured ducted radiators (to reduce drag), rubber block suspension (to minimise manufacture, hydraulics and maintenance) and interchangeable noses for different variants. One of the major manufacturing innovations was the idea of splitting the fuselage down the centreline. Each half consisted of a sandwich shell, formed from an inner and outer spruce plywood skin separated by a core of balsa wood and some wooden formers. Because the two halves were manufactured separately, the internal equipment and services could be installed before the two halves were joined together. The moulds and jigs were designed to facilitate dispersed manufacturing, harnessing the capacity of cabinet makers and carpenters across the country, with much centred around the furniture industry in High Wycombe.

The design and development team worked at breakneck speed on the prototype, designing, manufacturing and testing components to ensure they exceeded the design requirements. Ralph Hare was the youngest in the team and responsible for aircraft overall loads and stressing the wings. He made daily journeys in his 1933 Austin Seven from Salisbury Hall to Stag Lane, Edgware, carrying test pieces to the de Havilland materials laboratory there. 'I must have taken hundreds of panels and specimens for strength testing before the final design decisions were made.'[12] The wing spar booms were made from laminated DTD 36B aircraft grade spruce, glued in jigs under pressure and heated, to speed up glue setting. Initially the front spar boom was three laminates, but in the course of production became ten laminates, saving more wood. Birch plywood was used for the wing skin, made of three plies laid at 45° to each other. One of the final processes was to cover the whole structure tightly with 'Madopolam' fabric before the final undercoat and camouflage. By the late autumn, the prototype was ready to move from Salisbury Hall to Hatfield for flight testing.

Pat Fillingham was one of de Havilland's small team of pilots who tested every aircraft. 'We had just four Test Pilots at Hatfield – the Chief – Geoffrey de Havilland (the son of Sir Geoffrey), George Gibbins, John de Havilland (Sir Geoffrey's youngest son) and myself.'[13] Until the arrival of the Mosquito they were testing Tiger Moths, Rapides and Airspeed Oxfords. In early November 1940, a few weeks after the Battle of Britain had been won, the first Mosquito arrived at Hatfield, watched by Pat, 'There was great excitement when the prototype arrived at the main gate – the fuselage on one lorry and the wing on another – to be reassembled in an old paint shop at the far end of the factory. After two weeks it was out for engine runs and on 25 November, Geoffrey de H and John Walker, the Chief Engine Development Engineer, taxied out onto the airfield. They did a short hop about a foot or so off the ground and taxied back to check the glycol coolant as there was some slight overheating.'[14] Capt. D.H., who was also there, continued, 'The great moment had come after only eleven months from the start of the design of the fastest aeroplane we had ever built – a speed record in itself. The tense excitement of the many watchers showed itself in various ways. We all tried to look and act normally, but I kept walking back to my car to open and shut the door without reason, while others walked off a short way and returned more quickly. It was a great relief when the engines opened up fully with the plane held back by the wheel brakes. The engine roar continued as the brakes were suddenly released. The Mosquito gathered speed rapidly, the power to weight ratio being very high, and lifted easily and was truly airborne on its first flight. As it continued its steady course, the pent-up feelings of awful anxiety gave way to relief and great hopes for the future.'[15] Pat added, 'As all was well, they then took off in a very short distance, the gear was retracted and they flew for about thirty minutes, reaching a speed of about 230mph before coming in for a good landing. All was very satisfactory.'[16]

By this time, Air Marshal Wilfrid Freeman, who had been a strong advocate for the Mosquito, had been moved against his will to become Vice Chief of the Air Staff and Lord Beaverbrook was directly overseeing aircraft production. Importantly, the newly formed Ministry of Aircraft Production placed a second, larger order for 150 aircraft.

Flight testing identified few problems which required only relatively minor modifications to rectify. The first problem was buffet on the tailplane. Wool tufts were stuck on to the prototype with Bostik to show the flow patterns. Pat Fillingham noted in his logbook on 9 December 1940, 'Flew Hurricane P3090 – observing the air-flow tufts on the DH Mosquito at various speeds.'[17] Armed with this information, Chief Designer R.E. Bishop and Aerodynamicist Richard Clarkson visited the Royal Aircraft Establishment at Farnborough where Tom Summerville was in the Aerodynamics Department. 'We developed a wind tunnel model within a couple of weeks and also tested the aircraft within the following two weeks, after which it was suggested the modification was to extend on the nacelle, which subsequently went into production.'[18] This modification, which included splitting the flaps, solved the buffeting problem. Trials continued and, on 16 January 1941, at Boscome Down, the prototype delivered on Capt. D.H's promise to Air Marshal Freeman – it outpaced the Spitfire, giving birth to the Mossie legend! Pat also explained about minor structural change, 'Boscome was a very rough and hilly field with no runways in those days, and unfortunately the tailwheel caught in a rut and cracked the fuselage above the rear door. Hatfield quickly came up with a repair scheme and a strake appeared on the starboard fuselage above the rear door. Every Mosquito built carries this strake and it is hardly noticeable.'[19] This 100" external strake is fixed, through the fuselage, to a far more substantial strengthener between the fuselage bulkheads.

The first flights of the Mosquito demonstrated its outstanding performance, which immediately overcame any remaining opposition in official circles to what was regarded as an unconventional aircraft using outdated production methods. Government orders started to be placed, initially in limited numbers.

The second completed prototype, W4052, the fighter version, was not transported to Hatfield for its first flight. Geoffrey de Havilland and Fred Plumb persuaded the neighbouring farmer to take down a fence and, on 15 May 1941, the Chief flew the aircraft out of a field directly beside Salisbury Hall. W4052 was already fitted with the longer engine nacelles. During the short test flight, among other points, the Chief noted that the throttle and airscrew gates were unsatisfactory, that there was considerable play in both the stick and vertical column, that it flew right wing down and a clearer indication of neutral on the rudder tab indicator was required.[20]

Just a month later, on 16 June 1941, George Gibbins flew the photo-reconnaissance prototype W4051 out of another adjacent field to take it to Hatfield.

Meanwhile, Mosquito production was starting in parallel with development testing. de Havilland had somewhat rashly promised to produce the first batch of fifty bomber and reconnaissance aircraft by December 1941. However, the company was convinced that the fighter version would be required, sooner or later. Within Government circles, the position continually shifted as to the way this initial order should be split between bomber, reconnaissance and fighters. The fighter wing required stronger load factors for the more agile performance. The design team also ensured that the basic design of the bomber fuselage could be arranged to house the machine guns and cannons for the fighter, if required.

Even having taken these factors into account, over half of the first batch of bombers were re-specified as fighters at a late stage in production and had to have their noses replaced. Confidence in de Havilland's capabilities and the Mosquito grew. As flight testing continued, the second order of 150 aircraft was changed to all being the fighter versions.

To allow for volume production of the Mosquito, de Havilland set up the Second Aircraft Group at Leavesden, near Watford and about ten miles from Hatfield. The Mosquito was a unique aircraft in that it had been designed to be manufactured, not in a large single factory, but by large numbers of companies with no previous experience of aircraft manufacture. By May 1941, the initial extensive network of subcontractors had been established. Two former furniture manufacturers in High Wycombe, E. Gomme Ltd and Dancer & Hearne Ltd, were to make wings and spars, whilst Vanden Plas in Hendon were to make wing coverings. These were augmented by the skills and capacity of numerous small manufacturers, including furniture makers, bicycle manufacturers and even a firm that made ecclesiastical ironwork! The task of setting up the manufacturing network was formidable, with many difficulties being encountered and overcome. The challenges that the team tackled included plywood not being to specification, problems with the quality of some of the glued joints and poor production rate for the engine cowlings.

The supply chain and subcontractor network were established in the nick of time. In June 1941, the Government increased the order for fighters to 500, with a production rate of fifty per month.

Every production Mosquito was subjected to test flights before it could be handed over to the ATA for delivery to its unit. The Mosquito test flying team was expanded to all four de Havilland test pilots, as recalled by Pat Fillingham; 'In the early summer of 1941, both John de H and I went solo on the Mosquito. I well remember my first flight – there were no pilot's notes, I was given five minutes instruction in the cockpit, told "to put the that tail trim one division forward and land at 120mph. Watch the swing and don't go too far away." I enjoyed that flight, made an approach over the factory and landed safely.'[21]

With production gearing up, the team developed a flight-test schedule for every new Mosquito. Each test pilot had the 'long roll of paper' of test exercises fitted to their kneepad for the flight. Pat explained the process, 'After take-off, you took all the figures on the climb, went up to 15,000ft. Check the supercharger change over into high gear – up to 30,000ft to check pressure venting. Drop down to rated altitude and did some level speeds, then down to 15,000 to do the stalls. The stall was absolutely first class. It was caused of course by the radiators being inboard of the engines and next to the fuselage and gave you a perfect wing-root stall. There was never any trouble with the stall.

'A few aerobatics were done to test the ailerons, a dive to VNE to check the stick forces and the tailplane incidence then on to land. It took about fifty minutes to an hour. We did a second flight of about twenty minutes to check the snags. A third flight of about ten minutes and the aircraft was off test. Sometimes we had an aeroplane with no snags at all and this was called "A Lulu" – one with a lot of snags was called "A Rogue"'.[22]

On 10 July 1941, before the first Mosquitos had reached any squadrons, a letter from the Ministry stated that output had to increase to 150 Mosquitos per month, of which eighty were to be built at Hatfield, thirty were to come from the Second Aircraft Group in Leavesden and the other forty to come from a new production line to be established in Canada!

Production planning was almost impossible for the team at de Havilland, since the Ministry's production requirements were changing faster than they could put the plans in place. By 8 August 1941, they had been advised that the 150 per month from July should be increased to 160 per month, and that they should prepare for 200 per month. After much pestering from de Havilland, they were finally given a letter from the Contracts Department confirming the need for 150 aircraft per month, including those built in Canada. This at least enabled them to place orders for raw materials.

de Havilland DH.98
Mosquito FB VI Cockpit

It was clear that the Mosquito was a hugely versatile weapon platform – effectively the first multi-role combat aircraft. The Ministry identified a requirement for a fighter-bomber for intruder strike operations. In 1942, based on the F Mk II day fighter variant, de Havilland started the development of the new FB Mk. VI version, which completed its first flight later in the year. Stripped of the F II's air interception radar, the FB VI retained the formidable armament of four Browning 0.303 in machine guns in the nose and four Hispano 20mm canon in the belly. Importantly, it retained a bomb bay behind the cannon, which enabled it to carry two 500lb bombs internally (with fins cropped to fit) and could also carry another two under the wings on hard points. Since it operated primarily at low altitude, the FB VI was unpressurised, and retained single stage supercharged Merlin engines. The FB VI would eventually become the most numerous and widely used Mosquito variant.

As well as training test pilots for Canada and Australia, de Havilland's team tested every aircraft produced at Hatfield and Leavesden. According to Pat, 'I think we did thirty-three aircraft per week.'[23]

On 20 November 1942, the RAF's Accident Investigation Branch convened a meeting at the Ministry of Aircraft production to review possible causes for the four Mosquito airframe failures since it had entered service. They noted possible weaknesses in the elevators and that the undercarriage doors may have opened during manoeuvres. With de Havilland's assistance, strength tests on the fuselage had been completed at Farnborough. Although they couldn't identify any causal link, they suspected the undercarriage doors and recommended tightening the wires closing them. Subsequently, on 25 January 1943, Vernon Brown, the Chief Inspector, released his report, classified as Secret, in which he recommended:

> 'It would appear desirable, therefore, that before any modification action is put in hand, an attempt should be made to assess the loads on the doors in high-speed flight.'[24]

The first squadron to be equipped with the FB VI variant was No. 418 Squadron, an RCAF intruder squadron based at RAF Ford on the Sussex coast and commanded by Wing Commander James 'Jimmy' Hayward Little DFC AFM. The first aircraft were delivered in April 1943, with the squadron being fully converted from Douglas Boston Intruder IIIs to the Mosquito by the end of June 1943.

On 11 June 1943, Jimmy Little and his navigator, Warrant Officer Douglas 'Dougie' Hamilton Styles DFM, flew the FB VI's first operation, returning at 0300hrs the following morning. Later that day, they prepared A for Able (HJ733) for the next operation, with a short test flight. It would be Dougie's hundredth op. It was also a hot afternoon. At the end of the runway, it seemed like Jimmy held for a lengthy power check. The Merlin engines were prone to overheating and fouling the spark plugs on the ground if the pilot was not careful. With squadron members watching from the dispersal, finally A for Able started to roll. It didn't climb away normally, failing to gain height. A for Able crashed into a shallow hillside beyond the runway near Arundel, erupting in an enormous ball of fire, killing both Jimmy and Dougie. Although hugely rewarding to fly, it was clear that the Mosquito had to be treated with respect!

Meanwhile, over the previous eighteen months, the war had not been going well for Britain and her Allies in the Far East.

Chapter 3

Situation Report

Early 1943

*'The British Indian Army appeared tonight to have absorbed
the force of a determined Japanese counter-attack and
was moving back against Donbaik, north of Akyab, in the
wake of a punishing naval bombardment that had started
numerous fires in the enemy jungle stronghold.'*
Associated Press/New York Times, *20 March 1943,
New Delhi, India*

Even after more than a year of war in the Far East, in general it was an unknown to the British public. The media coverage was slim, so as not to depress morale and because it was a distant war. It was already classed by some in the armed forces as a 'forgotten war'. Whilst it was becoming clear that the Allies had begun to turn the tide of the war in Europe and North Africa, a very different war was being played out in the vast reaches of the Far East and Pacific theatres. Most aircrew only knew the basics of the conflict, mainly picked up from crew room discussions.

On 7 December 1941, the Japanese started the war in the Far East with their audacious dawn attack on the large American naval base at Pearl Harbor on Hawaii. This not only brought America into the war against the Japanese, but they also joined the Allies against Germany in Europe and the Middle East. At that time, India and Iraq were under the command of General Sir Archibald Wavell, who had been given the responsibility in mid-1941. With the Japanese declaring war, Wavell was appointed Commander-in-Chief ABDACOM (American-British-Dutch-Australian Command), which covered the Far East and Australasia. The Japanese Empire swept through the Northern Pacific and Asian countries at a relentless pace, through French Indochina towards the British fortress island of Singapore. Unfortunately, the ineptitude of the British staff in believing it was an impregnable base and their lack of security with their defence preparations (naively allowing native Malays to copy and distribute their plans to the various units), together with the brilliance of the unorthodox Japanese strategy, including cycling through 'impenetrable' jungle, meant that this critical military asset fell to the Japanese in February 1942. Some units such as the Australian 8th Division took significant casualties in its defence, but the true cost of surrender to the Japanese would only become apparent over time in their brutal treatment of both POWs and civilians.

With the fall of Singapore, ABDACOM was disbanded, and General Sir Archibald Wavell resumed his position of C-in-C India, responsible now for the defence of India and Burma. The Japanese continued their relentless drive towards India, with Rangoon falling into their hands on 9 March 1942. One of Wavell's first concerns was to create air superiority. Until this time, Britain had directed many of its Empire forces to assist in Europe and Africa, leaving it dangerously exposed and ill-equipped to see off the new Japanese menace. The British had defended India and the Far East using obsolescent or obsolete aircraft. Recognising that Japan had clear advantages through its extremely capable Mitsubishi Zero fighter, which had the range to escort bombers, Wavell asked the Air Ministry for long-range fighters for his Command. His request met with some difficulties as, in general, such aircraft did not exist. The only operational British long-range aircraft available at the beginning of 1942 were the Mosquito, which was just entering service, and the Beaufighter, which was in demand in Europe and the Middle East as an interdictor and night fighter. The Air Ministry informed A.H.Q. India, on 21 April 1942, that the Mosquito was experiencing 'teething problems' and 'The need for long-range fighters your command already realised here and ways and means of providing Beaufighters are being urgently considered in consultation Admiralty.'[25]

Only a desperate evacuation up the 'Valley of Death' by the Burma Corporation, during which the British demolished substantial infrastructure, together with the onset of the monsoon, had halted the Japanese army's forward momentum. By May 1942, about 450,000 Allied troops were amassed against 300,000 Japanese in the frontier region between Burma and India, which was inhospitable jungle and mountainous, with few passable routes. Advances by either the Allies or Japanese were hampered by both terrain and logistics. Once north of Kalewa on the Chindwin River, the Japanese had neither rail nor river transport, whereas, having crossed the Brahmaputra River, the Allies had extremely limited ground supply options, with only a single road to the key border base at Imphal.

Lieutenant General Shojiro Iido, the commander of the Japanese Fifteenth Army, consolidated their position in northern Burma. Although pressured by his superiors, he sided with his forward commanders who felt that, even once the monsoons stopped, the challenges of terrain and logistics would make advancing extremely difficult. To the south, in late-June, the Japanese started construction of the Burma Railway, linking Moulmein, south of Rangoon, with Bangkok in Thailand. It was only a short time before the Allies received reports of the inhumane and horrific treatment of the POWs forced to build it.

Iido disbanded the locally organised Burma Independence Army and replaced it with the subservient Burma Defence Army, trained by Japanese officers. The Japanese also prepared to form a 'puppet government' for Burma under Ba Maw. It would have little real power with the Japanese retaining control of most aspects of Burma's administration. Due to the Japanese advance, the demolition by the British during their retreat, Allied bombing and the loss of markets, the Burmese economy was in free fall.

Whilst Mussolini and Hitler were starting to struggle and suffer setbacks, by late 1942 the Japanese occupied most of the Malay Peninsula and consolidated their position in north Burma. Meanwhile, Britain's premature 'scorched earth' policy in Eastern Bengal, the loss of rice from Burma and the impacts of a severe typhoon had started a famine in Bengal. The British were also hindered by the 'Quit India' protests in Bengal and Bihar, which diverted a significant number of troops from the front to keep the peace. Distribution of aid was woefully inadequate.

The Japanese advance was threatening the very heart of the British Empire – India. If they could cross into India, then they could deny the Allies huge swathes of natural resources and manpower. At the same time, China was waging an increasingly desperate war with Japan in the north and needed resupplying just as the Soviet Union had in Europe. India, despite the challenges presented by the Himalayas, was now the only suitable base from which to mount such an effort. The very area of north-east India being threatened by the Japanese, Calcutta through to Imphal, was critical for the Allied war effort. As the 1942 monsoon season drew to an end, G.H.Q. India, under Wavell, initiated a multi-pronged strategy against the Japanese.

On 12 December 1942 the 14th Indian Division of the Indian Eastern Army, under Lieutenant General Noel Irwin, started to advance down the Arakan intent on securing the Mayu peninsula and the strategically important airfield on Akyab Island. Progress was swift during the advance to Rathedaung and Donbaik, just a few miles from the end of the peninsula, where they were held by a small Japanese force equipped with heavy artillery in bunkers. Indian and British troops made repeated frontal assaults without armoured support and suffered heavy casualties. Japanese reinforcements arrived through what the British had assumed to be impassable terrain, hitting the 14th Division's exposed eastern flank, overrunning several units. The British attempted to hold a defensive position south of Buthidaung, even managing to surround the Japanese at one time. Exhausted, they were finally forced to abandon much of their equipment and retreat almost to the Indian border. Lieutenant General Irwin was relieved of his command and replaced by General George Gifford.

Meanwhile, the Allies reinforced the garrison town of Imphal, where there was continual patrol activity and low-key fighting. However, neither army had the resources to mount a decisive operation. Tiddim was at the end of a precarious 100-mile-long supply line and 17th (Light) Indian Division were tasked with holding this town against skirmishing units from the Japanese 33rd Division, which had much shorter supply lines from Kalewa. V Force, an irregular unit raised through G.H.Q. India, also patrolled from Imphal and Tiddim into the areas held by neither side, providing valuable information about Japanese troop positions and the allegiances of the local Burmese population.

During the second half of 1942 Brigadier Orde Windgate assembled and trained nearly 3,000 men, consisting of 77th Indian Infantry Brigade, 13th Battalion King's Liverpool Regiment, 136 Commando Company (men of the former Bush Warfare School in Burma), 3rd Battalion 2nd Gurkha Rifles and 2nd Battalion Burma Rifles, which were known as Long Range Penetration Groups – the Chindits. The intention had been to use the Chindits as part of a larger offensive but, when it was cancelled, General Wavell sent the Chindits into Burma anyway. On 12 February 1943, Operation Longcloth commenced and the Chindits walked into north Burma with the intention of harassing the Japanese and disrupting supply chains. Three months later the survivors returned over the Chindwin River, having walked between 750 and 1,000 miles. It was clear that their achievements had been very costly, with over 800 killed, taken prisoner, or died of disease. Many of the survivors were too debilitated by their wounds or disease to return to active service. However, the Chindits demonstrated that 'behind the lines' guerrilla action could do damage and the morale boost to Allied forces was significant, showing that the Japanese were not invincible.

The final arm of the strategy was ensuring that the Americans could continue to support the Chinese Nationalist government under Chiang Kai-Shek against the Japanese. Having lost their supply base in Rangoon, the only feasible airlift route was from Assam in Eastern India, over the Himalayas. The airlift soon became known as 'the Hump'. Flying the Hump was hazardous. The terrain and weather conditions tested both aircrews and aircraft to the extremes of their performance envelopes, resulting in many casualties. They were also often attacked by Japanese fighters based at Myitkyina airfield in northern Burma. It was evident that the supply route really needed a road. The American's retrained two divisions of Chinese troops who had retreated into India in 1942 so that they could work on the engineering of the Ledo Road to link India with China.

By April, it was evident that the Arakan offensive would not succeed and that the Japanese were on Indian territory, less than thirty miles from the garrison at Imphal. Notwithstanding the still dangerous situation in Northern Europe, it had become obvious to the political and military leaders that something had to be done. Senior commanders knew that better equipment was needed to counteract the threat to the Empire and start the offensive against Japan. Among other things, A.H.Q. India resumed its demands for the Mosquito.

Chapter 4

Weather Testing

April – June 1943

'Now operating in Burma, and – due to its extreme range –
further afield, is Britain's all-wooden de Havilland Mosquito.
Americans call it the "miracle plane"; pilots say it is "the plane
without vices".'
Associated Press, *7 February 1944*

By early 1943, the de Havilland Aircraft Company was
delivering Mosquitos in operational quantities to the RAF.
The Mossie had already demonstrated its capabilities as
a bomber, fighter, night fighter and in long-range reconnaissance,
capable of striking deep into enemy-held territory. Development
of the versatile fighter-bomber variant, the FB Mk. VI, was nearly
complete, with initial deliveries planned to No. 418 (RCAF)
Squadron. However, even before its delivery to the first squadron
in the UK, the development team had been tasked with assessing
any modifications for operations in India. The situation in the Far
East was sufficiently dire that it had been decided to transfer some
of these latest aircraft, together with some experienced crews, to
that theatre of operations with the hope that the inexorable Japanese
advance might be reversed or at least halted.

The first stage of the programme was to complete some 'weather
testing' on a few Mosquitos, with the Mark II fighter variant being
chosen.

No. 27 Squadron was an operationally experienced low–level intruder squadron flying Bristol Beaufighters. The squadron was based at RAF Agartala, about 200 miles north–east of Calcutta, in Assam. The busy airfield was also home to two other RAF squadrons, as well as No. 169 Headquarters Wing, with in total a couple of thousand RAF, army and Indian labourers working on the base. The squadrons' buildings and aircraft were dispersed all around the airfield, with some aircraft in pens with ten–foot–high earth walls on three sides to protect against bomb blast. The facilities for 27 Squadron were on the south–west of the airfield in a number of bamboo 'bashas' for Headquarters, Stores, Maintenance and Armoury. 'A' and 'B' Flights also had buildings close by, near their aircraft on two dispersals and some hardstanding. In general, aircraft servicing was carried out in the open, although there were a couple of bamboo half–hangars offering some protection.

Agartala had only one runway – a 5,500ft long all–weather concrete strip, 150ft wide, running north–east and south–west, which had a nasty 'roller coaster' dip about 1,000ft from the eastern end, making landings from the east more hazardous than from the west. The runway lighting for night operations was provided by 'goose neck' oil lamps. Whilst there was a taxiway running parallel to the runway, there was no parallel 'kutcha strip' for emergency landings. A narrow–gauge railway had tracks right into the dispersals, delivering heavy provisions to the airfield.

Living accommodation for 27 Squadron, known as No. 1 Camp, was about three miles from the airfield and was divided into three groups – officers, NCOs and airmen. Everything was built from local materials – bamboo frame, rush–grass roof and handmade brick floor. Food rations were the same for all ranks, mainly comprising of tinned bully beef, sausages, fish and sometimes local poultry and eggs. Once a week a truck drove the sixty miles to Comilla to collect a freshly killed water buffalo which was immediately cooked to become a somewhat tough curry served with rice. All drinking water had to be boiled. There were no home comforts such as a cinema, pub, bright lights, or the fairer sex.[26] Life at Agartala was very definitely focussed on the war effort!

Wing Commander 'Harry' Daish, the squadron's CO, had been notified in advance of a special detachment to the squadron but had kept the news on a 'need-to-know' basis. David Innes, one of the squadron's Beaufighter pilots, explained, 'Much to the surprise of those at the aerodrome, on the morning of 11 April [1943], a strange aircraft approached and was quickly identified as a de Havilland Mosquito. Mosquito Mk II DZ695 was to be attached to us for weather trials and operational familiarisation, becoming the first Mosquito sent to the tropics for this purpose. The crew, Flight Lieutenants McCullock DFC and Young, had flown the aircraft out from the UK. One week later a second Mosquito arrived, crewed by Flying Officer Fielding and Flight Sergeant Steer, and on 2 May a third, crewed by Flying Officers Dupree DFM and McDonnell, were attached for the same purpose. Their arrival was to coincide with the approaching monsoon season and, no doubt, had been chosen to deliberately expose the Mosquitos to the tropical element.'[27] Mr F.G. Myers, a representative of the de Havilland Company, was attached to the squadron, whilst a Rolls-Royce representative, Mr Waterhouse, also made a short visit. Both were tasked with monitoring the Mosquitos in the new environment. David Innes continued, 'The first reaction of the Beaufighter crews at Agartala was one of reservation, for the Mosquito did not seem to have the airframe strength desirable for low-level attacks where there was always the risk of hitting objects such as trees during attacks.'[28]

On 19 May 1943, Flying Officers Dupree and McDonnell completed the first Mosquito strike operation into Burma. They flew into central Burma and attacked a moving train, which was forced to stop. Ten days later, the same crew carried out the second operation, which was a reconnaissance of Japanese airfields in the Kanguang,

Meiktila, Thedaw and Heho areas. Over Heho they encountered a Japanese Oscar fighter, but they were able to avoid attack by using the speed of the Mosquito at low-level. Unfortunately, during the month both Feilding and Steer were injured when their Mosquito, having suffered an engine failure, overran the end of Agartala's runway when making an emergency single engine landing. Steer fractured his spine in the crash.

In early June, the weather was very bad and only one of the squadron's operations reached its target. The two Mosquitos completed a low-level attack on Kanguang aerodrome, damaging three aircraft on the ground, one of which was claimed as destroyed. Four Oscars were overhead the airfield at the time but they didn't attempt to attack the Mosquitos. The weather deteriorated further during their return. To make matters worse, Dupree's aircraft, DZ696, developed a glycol leak in the starboard engine, which he was forced to shut down. Landing on a single engine at Cox's Bazar, one of his tyres burst, the aircraft became uncontrollable and the port undercarriage collapsed. Luckily, neither crew were injured.

That same month, three Beaufighters suffered significant operational damage caused by the nature of their extreme low-level intruding. One had hit a tree, causing damage to its starboard wing. Another had hit an unseen Japanese 'tripwire', damaging its engine nacelle, exhaust and propeller. The third had collected an iron rod that was protruding from the top of a pagoda. All three aircraft managed to make it back to Agartala. Like many of its aircrew, David Innes valued the resilience of the Beaufighter and remained sceptical about the Mosquito saying, 'One could only surmise what would have happened if the aircraft had been Mosquitos.'[29]

After two months detached to 27 Squadron, successfully demonstrating the Mosquito's intruding potential, interim reports about the Mosquito were sent to A.H.Q. India. The two surviving F II Mosquitos and the three crews were posted to No. 681 Squadron at Dum Dum to continue the aircraft's evaluation with photo-reconnaissance trials.

Meanwhile, in London, on 14 June 1943, the Accident Investigation Branch under Vernon Brown held a second review meeting into the eight structural failures of Mosquitos to that date. They had determined that the failures fell into two classes: the three accidents in which a wing or wings had failed in up-load and the others where the wing had failed in down-load or where there was no wing failure. The minutes, classified as Secret, concluded with two recommendations:

> 'Mosquito aircraft are being used for a variety of purposes and because the factor of safety originally considered suitable for night fighters may now be inadequate it is suggested that it would be advisable to review the position.
>
> 'It is considered that the retrospective embodiment of metal covered elevators and modified undercarriage should have high priority.'[30]

Chapter 5

Passage to India

July 1943 onwards

*'A new Japanese army, suddenly appearing out of the jungles,
has driven 60 miles into India, it was announced today, in the
second invasion disclosed within 48 hours. The new force, hitherto
unheralded, has pushed northward from Burma up the Manipur
River Valley to within 30 miles of the key city of Imphal.'*
Associated Press, *New Delhi, India, 23 March 1943*

During its development, the Mosquito FB VI quickly demonstrated its potential and versatility. The de Havilland team felt sure that they had a winner. For European operations, the 'standard' FB VI version was powered by two 1,610hp 27-litre Rolls-Royce Merlin-21 engines. These twelve-cylinder engines were equipped with a single-stage supercharger, configuring them to deliver peak performance at lower altitudes. Probably through caution of the hotter conditions in the Far East, de Havilland decided initially to fit the FB VI with Rolls-Royce Merlin-23 engines, equipped with a 16psi boost super-charger, delivering 1,390hp to drive high thrust, round-tip 'paddle blade' propellers. The intruder versions were also fitted with exhaust shrouds, to prevent the flare from the engines' twenty stub ejector exhausts giving away the position of the aircraft at night.[31]

Delivering aircraft around the world was challenging, so the RAF set up specialist units to oversee it. The unit initially responsible for ferrying aircraft to the Mediterranean and the Far East was No. 301 Ferry Transport Unit (301 FTU, as it was known), based at RAF Lyneham in Wiltshire. New and repaired aircraft were delivered to various RAF units by the talented men and women of the Air Transport Auxiliary – the ATA. The skill of these pilots should not be under-estimated, since they delivered most aircraft without the use of their navigational aids and radios, usually crewed by a lone ATA pilot. First Officer Peter George, an ATA pilot attached to 6 Ferry Pool at Ratcliffe, recalled his first Mosquito delivery on 14 December 1942. 'I was handed a typed delivery chit. It read "MOSQUITO DZ258 FROM SEALAND TO SHERBURN-IN-ELMET." 9 ATA. Ops had given me the right to fly, solo, the fastest twin-engine aircraft then on offer – without even asking whether I had flown one before. Well, I hadn't! And what's more, had only ever seen one in the air at a distance.

'Driven by road, in silence, the short distance to Sealand, the hangars came into view. I was looking for a first glimpse of Mosquito DZ258 and could have done without the poor weather and industrial haze but decided to take off and have a look.

'How would one best describe a first impression of the Mosquito. Sleek, beautiful, rounded fuselage – Yes! Powerful, purposeful – Yes! Just look at those muscle-bound Merlins – that also look too big for the airframe together with those big spinners. It looks as though it should have a high stall speed, and it does too – 125mph final approach, 112mph stall. It looks as though I am going to have the ride of my life!

'Some might argue that it wasn't a good idea to attempt a first flight without any dual, not even someone to show me around on such a machine, but that is what we had been trained for, and with the help of the condensed ferry pilot's notes, that's what we were expected to do. There's no turning back.

'Squeeze in through the cockpit door, plus parachute, and find a very cosy compact cockpit. Having placed my parachute in the pilot's seat and struggled with the safety harness, it was time to take stock.'

Having completed his pre-flight checks, started the Merlins and let them warm up, Peter waved the chocks away. 'Look around – if all clear, release the brake lever – hiss of air as brakes release. Aircraft moves away with minimum engine power. Easy to taxi, brakes powerful and answers to turn on rudder pedals. Taxi to holding point. Check through ferry pilot's notes carefully once more – placing fingers on each instrument and lever whilst doing so. All well! Final look around the circuit, especially the approach path. All clear – taxi onto runway – straighten – then advance the short stubby throttles.

'It was quickly apparent that a small amount of throttle movement resulted in a large amount of thrust – and that the Mosquito would swing to port if allowed. I soon had the port motor up to maximum power +9 but, to avoid port swing, held back on the starboard throttle. This was only momentarily until the tail was up and the rudder had authority (+12 boost for take-off). It flew itself off quite happily.'

Unfortunately, it was quickly obvious to Peter that the visibility was nowhere near good enough to complete the ferry flight, '... soon finding it was "like flying inside a used milk bottle". This was no time for heroics and I still had to find out what the beast would be like to land so turned back for Harwarden.' Having arrived overhead, Peter chose a wide circuit and reduced speed to 150mph. 'We would now find out whether selection of flaps really did cause a powerful nose up as the pilot's notes warned. Indeed it did! The Mossie rose up like a bucking bronco, and I quickly stopped further flaps down and trimmed to counteract. Nevertheless, the airspeed quickly decreased from 150 to 130-135mph. By now, on long finals, and discovering that once full flap is on, the warning to guard against undershoot is real. It is necessary to add ever increasing amounts of power to bring the Mossie in against those barn door flaps. This resulted in a rather breathless arrival at 125mph over the hedge, with what appeared to be a runway that was going to be too short. However, as soon as we touched down and closed the throttles, the drag came into its own, and the Mossie slowed faster than expected. This, then, was my first Mosquito – one of sixty-nine deliveries.'[32]

The first Mosquito FB VIs destined for India were delivered by the ATA from Hatfield in early July 1943. HJ787 was then handed over to Flight Sergeant John Davis and Sergeant Richard Goodall for 'acceptance tests' and HJ789, which arrived a few days afterwards, was allocated to Sergeants Albert Goldstone and Cyril Watts.

On 24 July 1943, Davis and Goodall were on an acceptance test flight with HJ787 when one of the engines caught fire. The problem could not be contained so John Davis decided that they had to bale out. In Mosquitos, the navigator had to abandon the aircraft first. Richard Goodall baled out of the aircraft but pulled his parachute ripcord too early. His parachute tangled with the aircraft's tail. Both crewmen were killed when the Mosquito crashed near Church Stoke Montgomery in Wales.[33]

With this incident still in their minds, Albert Goldstone and Cyril Watts set off in HJ789 on their ferry transit at the end of the month. On their journey to India, they experienced some form of problem on 1 August 1943, failing to arrive at their destination. No trace was ever found of them or their aircraft.[34]

In late-August 1943, the next experienced Mosquito crew destined for the Far East arrived at 301 FTU. Flight Sergeant Sidney Sims and Sergeant Harry Randall had been posted from 605 Squadron and were allocated their 'factory fresh' Mosquito, HJ812. Nothing was mentioned to them about the fate of the previous aircrews. They started their preparations for posting to India in concert with acceptance testing on their aircraft.

A couple of days after that, Flight Sergeant Benjamin 'Benny' Walsh and his navigator, Sergeant Harold 'Ossie' Orsborn, arrived at RAF Lyneham, having been posted from 418 Squadron. Both were operationally experienced aircrew, having flown intruder ops in

Douglas Boston IIIs before converting to the Mosquito FB VI with 418 Squadron. Neither were very happy with the way that they had been summarily posted mid-tour. Benny had completed almost two thirds of his first tour. Since 418 Squadron was an RCAF unit and, with its first Canadian CO appointed in June 1943, it was clear that he had been ordered to 'Canadianise' the unit. When the request went out for experienced Mosquito intruder aircrew to send to the Far East, they saw it as an opportunity to achieve their goal by posting out the British NCO aircrew and replacing them with Canadians. The first that Benny and Ossie knew about their posting was when they were called in by their Flight Commander, Squadron Leader 'Chuck' Moran RCAF, on the evening of 6 August. Benny's view was that Chuck Moran's actions 'took my life away from me really.'[35] In the following days, several other RAF NCO aircrews with 418 were also told of their abrupt mid-tour posting to the Far East.

The staff at 301 FTU could not provide any additional information to the ferry aircrew as to their specific posting, just that they were to take their aircraft to India. They were all in the same position, spread out by a few days or weeks.

After receiving their vaccinations for India, drawing their personal service revolvers and being issued with new flying boots, Benny and Ossie started acceptance testing their Hatfield-built Mosquito, HJ811. On 7 September they concentrated on air-firing and the wireless. This was followed the next day by fuel consumption (2.78mpg), with more firing and wireless tests. Ossie, as navigator, would be responsible for managing the fuel system, particularly important during the long transit legs. The staff at 301 FTU stressed that they had to use the fuel in the two underwing auxiliary fuel tanks first before starting on the Mossie's six internal tanks. Benny and Ossie completed two more test flights on 11 and 13 September.

Like virtually all ferry pilots, Benny and Ossie had been partnered before arrival and already worked well together. This was particularly important in the FB VI, because it was a real 'team operation' with the navigator just to the pilot's right and a little behind. They had the same field of view. Benny knew that Ossie was an extremely competent and reliable navigator; Ossie knew that Benny, who had lied about his age to enlist early and was still only nineteen, was a good pilot.

As was standard practice, Benny and Ossie were not given a defined route or timetable; further information, maps and provisions would be given to them on the way. They were told that they were to deliver their aircraft to RAF Mauripur, near Karachi, where they would be given details of their specific postings. Benny paraphrased his instructions, 'As the authorities said, "Here's a map, get on your way."'[36]

On 15 September 1943, with full underwing auxiliary fuel tanks and ammunition magazines, Benny and Ossie flew their Mosquito FB Mk VI to RAF Portreath, on the northern Cornish coast. Early the next morning, they were briefed on the weather for the journey to the Mediterranean. The weather was critical since their intruder Mosquito, like most of the others, wasn't equipped with oxygen, so they couldn't fly above the weather. They would be flying all the way to India at relatively low-level. The first sector to Gibraltar would be through hostile airspace with Luftwaffe aircraft patrolling the Bay of Biscay. Benny and Ossie were given the day's radio codes and colours for RAF North Front, Gibraltar's airfield. There were no diversions in case of problems, and it would be over four times longer than either had previously flown over water!

Benny and Ossie each had two kitbags into which they had packed all their belongings to take to India. Everything, including their uniforms, washbag, a few civvy clothes, daggers, survival equipment and machete, was crammed into these bags. As a pure war machine, the FB VI hadn't been designed with any significant storage space so, the same as the previous day, they lashed their kitbags to the bomb racks in the bomb bay. They secured their smaller haversacks containing their caps, revolvers, logbooks and personal documents, together with HJ811's Form 700 service and maintenance record, in the 'picketing equipment' stowage in the fuselage behind the starboard wing. Benny completed the outside checks on the Mossie, whilst Ossie busied himself in the cockpit, putting Benny's parachute into his seat, stowing his own 'observer' parachute in the underfloor compartment, placing his spare maps in the bulkhead nav store and changing the signal flares just under his seat to North Front's colours of the day. Ossie also stored the food rations for the flight where he could reach them during the journey, by the radio behind the pilot's seat. External checks completed, Benny donned his Mae West and climbed into the cockpit first. With Benny strapped into his parachute and seat, Ossie passed up his nav bag, tightened his 'observer' harness and climbed into the cockpit, stowed the ladder and closed the hatch.

This first leg would be at least four hours over water, out of sight of land. Benny taxied their Mosquito towards the runway, surveying the take-off run which ended with the cliff edge. Receiving the green light from the watch caravan, Benny lined up and opened the throttles on the Merlin engines. Established in the climb, Benny banked to return to overhead the airfield so that Ossie could take an accurate fix for their first leg. He trimmed the aircraft whilst Ossie set up his nav table for the flight ahead, then they both changed to full 'ops' mode. Having set a southerly course across the Bay of Biscay, Benny started his continuous scan of the horizon for hostile aircraft, interspersed with regular checks and adjustments to the Mosquito's trim and throttles for maximum range performance. Their Mosquito's Merlin engines did not allow him control of the mixture of air and fuel, but he could adjust the propeller pitch for each engine, constantly striving for that sweet spot of synchronisation between the two propellers. Meanwhile, Ossie would frequently check his plot and refold his map to match his estimated position, as well as also scanning for enemy aircraft.

A couple of hours into their leg, the Mosquito's starboard engine started to run a little rough. Benny shared his concerns with Ossie. Not surprisingly, neither fancied spending more time than absolutely necessary over water, away from land, with one engine already starting to run erratically. However, one of the few instructions they had been given in their briefing before the flight was not to fly over 'neutral' Portugal and Spain. Allied aircrew would be interned for the duration if they landed there.

The rough running slowly worsened and Benny decided he had to shorten the route over water which would mean flying over neutral territory to get to the Rock. By switching to an overland route, if the engine deteriorated, they at least had the option of baling out and crashing their Mosquito. Benny knew he would have to defend his decision on arrival in Gibraltar. He banked the aircraft gently to port whilst Ossie got to work with his maps and Dalton computer to confirm their new heading. Benny also made the decision to jettison the now-empty auxiliary fuel tanks to reduce drag and concentrated on nursing his ailing aircraft on their new heading directly towards one of the most difficult landing strips in Europe.

Gibraltar is a peninsular jutting out into the mouth of the Mediterranean. Its most distinctive feature is the huge rock which dominates the territory from every angle and against which the single runway nestles. The Rock had been hollowed out during more than two hundred years as a Crown Colony, a fortress guarding the anchorage and airfield below. Benny had never been to Gibraltar before but had been briefed on the challenges of landing there. In fact, like Ossie, Benny had never landed outside Britain before, and yet here he was nursing a sick aircraft over a foreign neutral country towards the now visible Rock on the horizon.

Benny called the tower at RAF North Front and requested an immediate landing from the north-west. He started his descent hoping that his sick engine wouldn't fail, since a single engine landing, after a long and draining flight, onto Gib', with a crosswind, was not an attractive prospect. More than five hours after the cliff at Portreath had dropped away from them, Benny banked his aircraft round in a gentle curving approach towards the runway which jutted out into the Mediterranean. He ran his final checks before landing, 'Radiators open … Speed 180mph … Undercarriage down, selector neutral … Prop controls fully forward … Fuel to fullest tanks … Speed below 160mph, flaps fully down.' Seconds later, with the starboard Merlin still running rough, Benny and Ossie felt relief as the two mainwheels touched the runway.

RAF North Front was a busy transit airfield between the UK, the Middle and Far East. It was also a key base for defence of the Western Med. Benny was guided to a parking bay on the pan where he shut down the Mosquito. As soon as they were out of the cockpit, he explained the problem with their engine to the local groundcrew and handed over the aircraft for them to rectify, service and refuel. Then, Benny and Ossie collected their personal belongings and kitbags before heading to aircraft operations to complete their paperwork. Benny's declaration that they had been forced to fly over neutral territory was not well received since it required an official apology from the British authorities in Gibraltar to the Spanish. He also reported that he had been forced to ditch their auxiliary fuel tanks and asked for replacements to be fitted, only to be told that there were none in Gibraltar. Their ferry flight would continue with shorter legs than they had hoped.

After breakfast the next day, 17 September, Benny and Ossie sought advice on their route across North Africa. They took off from Gibraltar for the relatively short flight south-east across the Mediterranean to Oujda in French Morocco, with strict instructions to avoid overflying the Melilla promontory, part of neutral Spanish Morocco. Oujda, about twenty miles inland from the coast, was on a plateau at about 1,500ft above sea level and their first, albeit brief, taste of North Africa. It was Benny's second day ever outside the UK. Prior to joining the RAF he had never left Lancashire. At Oujda, the groundcrew pumped fuel by hand from large storage drums into the Mosquito. Once completed, Benny and Ossie continued eastwards for about ninety minutes along the coastal strip towards Maison Blanche, near Algiers, where they would rest overnight. They had decided to only fly in daylight on their journey to India. Although this reduced some of their workload, the Mosquito's cockpit still reverberated with the incessant thunder from the two Merlins and also acted like a greenhouse in the sunshine. At least de Havilland had fitted Punkah Louvres to feed cool air into the cockpit.

On 18 September they first flew about 400 miles along the coast to Tunis, where they refuelled. Then they continued a further 300 miles to Castel Benito, an airfield just to the south of Tripoli. Their total flight time for the day was three hours fifty-five minutes. Once again, Castel Benito had no replacement auxiliary fuel tanks.

The next day, Sunday, Benny and Ossie flew on for a couple of hours to Marble Arch, a somewhat bleak desert refuelling base effectively in the middle of nowhere, near Ra's Lanuf in Libya. It was dominated by the Arch of Phila Eni, a huge monument beside the Via Balbia, the coastal road in Libya between the provinces of Tripolitania and Cyrenaica. This monument had only been officially unveiled just over six years before at a night ceremony attended by Benito Mussolini. It was another overnight stay, this time in tented accommodation.

The following morning, 20 September, they checked out their Mosquito for the 800-mile leg to Cairo. It would be their longest flight without auxiliary fuel tanks, with the first hour across the Mediterranean, followed by a lengthy desert crossing towards Cairo. The navigation would be challenging because, apart from wadis and the occasional oasis, the maps were relatively featureless. They decided to treat the desert leg the same as flying over water. Ossie used 'positive error' navigation, where he gave Benny a heading that would take them to the north of Cairo, then their airfield would definitely be on their right when they reached the River Nile. After more than two hours of flying, when they were in the middle of their desert crossing, the Mosquito's starboard engine started to run rough again. It was the worst possible place since there were no diversions. Unfortunately, the problem didn't clear. As they crossed the Qattara Depression, still with 150 miles to go, Benny decided that he had to close the engine down. Once again he asked Ossie to revise their route, to shorten their flight. Benny shut the engine down and feathered the propellor to minimise drag. He retrimmed the Mosquito and then flew it for about forty minutes on only one engine until Cairo started to appear out of the haze and dust. Having identified RAF Cairo West, Benny was on the radio to the tower asking for an 'immediate landing'. Their approach to the airfield took them almost directly over the Pyramids of Giza. Then Benny focussed on the potentially tricky single-engine landing ahead and maintained his approach speed 30mph higher than usual and only selected 15° of flap. He lowered his undercarriage and, leaning across to the right, pushed the starboard propellor's 'feathering button'. With the additional drag from the undercarriage and a windmilling propellor, he knew that they didn't have enough power with just one engine to overshoot. They were committed now. After over three and a half hours flying, Benny landed his ailing Mosquito safely on the runway on a blisteringly hot afternoon.

Benny and Ossie had four days for some sightseeing in Cairo whilst their aircraft was serviced, during which Benny's pilot's watch was stolen from his transit accommodation. He reported the theft but the officer told him not to say anything because, given the political tensions at the time, the Egyptians were not to be upset. Benny's watch was immediately replaced at the stores.

On Saturday, 25 September, Benny and Ossie set off for RAF Habbaniya beside the Euphrates in Iraq. This was another long leg, about 780 miles, but with good navigation fixes for Ossie along the route. Having climbed away from Cairo, Benny headed their Mosquito north-east crossing the Suez Canal near The Great

Bitter Lake. Then they continued across the North Sinai desert heading towards Palestine and the Dead Sea, until they picked up the oil pipeline, which was easy to follow east across the desert. Unfortunately, the starboard Merlin engine gave them problems again! This time it lost its oil pressure when they still had more than 200 miles to go and were over one of the least habited parts of the Iraq desert. Once again, Benny made the decision to shut it down. He retrimmed the Mosquito for asymmetric flight and flew the last hour of the leg on just one engine. By now Benny was becoming pretty experienced at flying the Mosquito with one engine. On sighting the airfield, he called Habbaniya watch tower for another 'immediate landing.' After three hours and thirty-five minutes flying, Benny settled their 'Rogue' Mosquito safely down on the runway and taxied on its one running engine to their hardstanding.

Whilst the groundcrew started to work on the engine problem, Benny and Ossie collected their belongings and reported to the transit centre to sign their aircraft in. There they were told that Sergeant Sim's Mosquito had crashed in Bahrain a few days earlier. Their aircraft, HJ812, had crashed on take-off and burst into flames, killing Sims and his navigator, Randall. Benny wrote in his logbook, 'Have heard of Sgt Sims – Barein [sic] – Crashed.' The loss of Sims and Randall, together with the distance from home, really affected Benny.

During their short stay at RAF Habbaniya, much to Benny's shock and disbelief, his service revolver and ammunition were stolen. Loss of a personal weapon was extremely serious in the military; it was a courts martial offence. Benny immediately reported the theft, but he somewhat naively accepted the advice that it would be replaced when he arrived at his new posting. With hindsight, he realised that he should have sorted out the replacement there and then.

On Monday, 27 September, with the aircraft serviced, Benny and Ossie continued their journey to India and, as temperatures increased, they started flying in their lightweight tropical Beadon flying suits – 'Zoot' suits. This next leg would be about 650 miles to

Bahrain Island in the Persian Gulf. They flew south down the fertile Euphrates River valley, past the town of Basra on their right-hand side, until they reached the Persian Gulf near to the settlement of Kuwait. They then followed the western coast of the Gulf until they reached the island of Bahrain. Before they had set off, they had been briefed about its challenging approach and landing, as the runway jutted out into the sea at both ends, making it difficult to judge height on the approach. With thoughts of Sims and Randall, they landed at Bahrain for another overnight stay.

The next day, Benny and Ossie completed their passage to India. After take-off, they headed east across the northern tip of Qatar and along the Persian Gulf, making landfall on the Arabian Peninsula at the small fishing settlement of Dubai. With the Straits of Hormuz to their north, they flew over the mountain range and then crossed the Gulf of Oman towards RAF Jawaani, on the coast of North-West India. It was very hot and humid there and the insect life, being next to a mangrove swamp, was 'pretty active'. After refuelling they immediately flew 330 miles east, following the coast, to land at RAF Mauripur airfield on the outskirts of Karachi. On landing Benny recalled that both he and Ossie were fumigated with insect repellent, which was far from pleasant but clearly necessary after Jawaani.

Having signed the aircraft in, they then found out about the two other Mosquitos and crews who had not made it from 301 FTU in Lyneham. Of the first four Mosquito FB VIs due to be delivered to India, three had not made it, with their crews killed. Benny later recalled, 'That was a very sad time in my life.'[37] In just the three months to September 1943, at least six young men lost their lives ferrying Mosquito FB VIs to India. The number lost in ferrying through the remainder of the war has not been counted.

Meanwhile, as new FB VIs became available, the other experienced 418 Squadron aircrews also reported to 301 FTU. Flight Sergeant Ball and his navigator, Flight Sergeant Ted Rainbow were first.

Others followed after a brief detachment to 128 AFHQ: pilots, Flight Sergeant Jimmy Kingsbury, Sergeant Billy Gunn RCAF and Sergeant Jackie Blinch, with navigators, Sergeants George Yerby, Bill Luff and Rolf.

Benny and Ossie remained at Mauripur for almost two weeks, 'kicking their heels', pressing for information. They were not impressed that there seemed to be no plan. Eventually, on 10 October 1943, they were instructed to fly HJ811 almost 900 miles across India to RAF Allahabad in Uttar Pradesh. When they arrived, they were separated from their aircraft and given a rail warrant to the Air Transport Pool at Poona. That night they started a three-day train journey, a truly Indian experience!

Twenty-three year old New Zealander Flight Sergeant Cliff Emeny and navigator Canadian Sergeant John Joseph Stephen 'Johnny' Yanota arrived at 301 FTU at the end of October 1943. Cliff's military service was unusual in that he first qualified as both an air gunner and radar observer in July 1940, in time to join No. 264 Squadron and fly in Boulton-Paul Defiant Is in the Battle of Britain. In January 1942 he was selected for pilot training, which he completed in Canada. Back in the UK in 1943, after being initially posted to Blenheim light bombers, Cliff was quickly transferred to the Mosquito and paired with Johnny at RAF Grantham. Johnny was born in Bankhead, Alberta, but raised in Blairmore. After completing high school and training in forestry, Johnny worked in the mine, before he was called up in 1941 and trained as a navigator. On completion of the Night Intruder Course at RAF High Ercall, Cliff and Johnny were posted to India. Although Cliff had completed an operational tour as gunner, he was starting his first tour as pilot.

They had a relatively uneventful ferry journey to India with their Mosquito, taking a slightly different route to Benny and Ossie: 11 November – Lyneham to Portreath, 50 minutes; 17 November

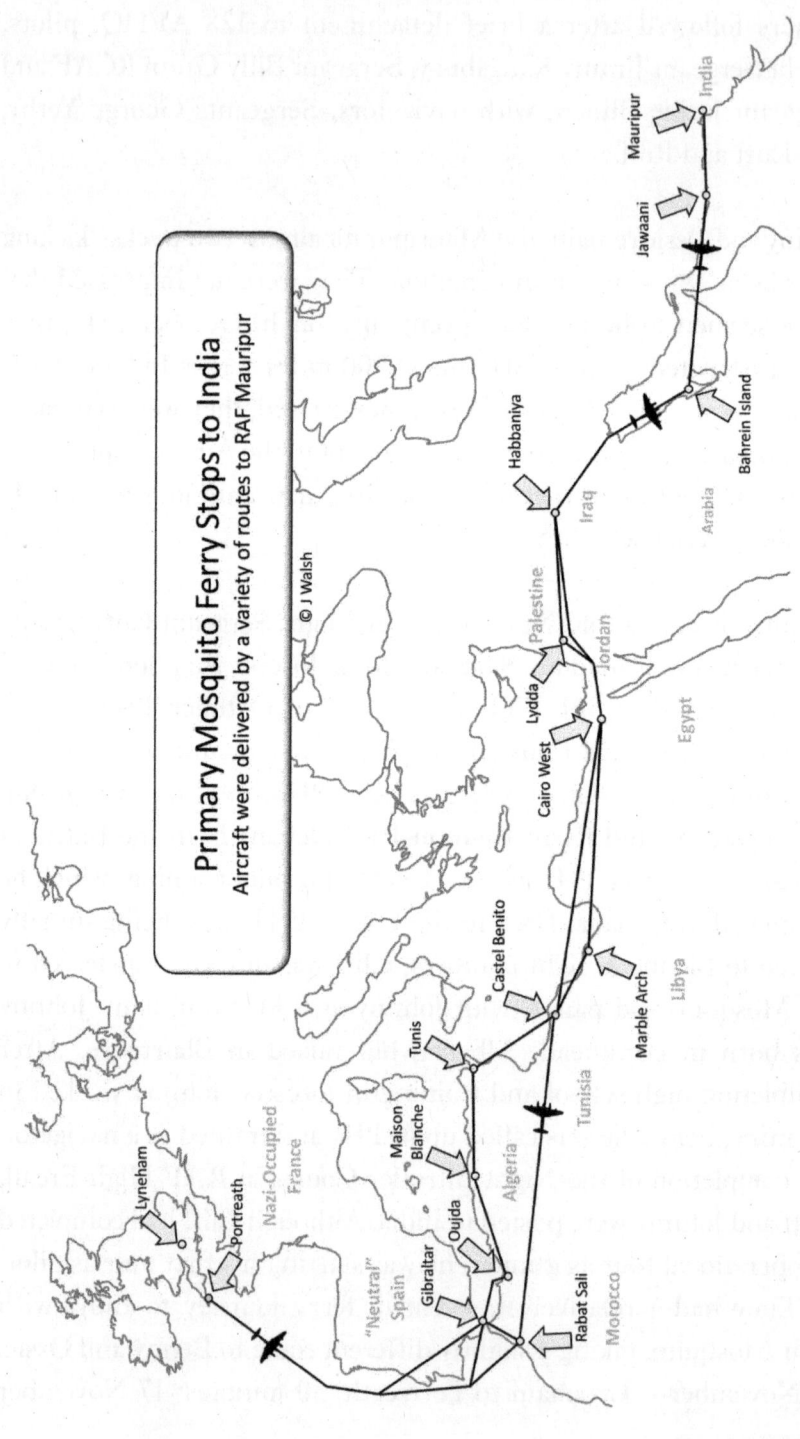

Primary Mosquito Ferry Stops to India

Aircraft were delivered by a variety of routes to RAF Mauripur

© J Walsh

– Portreath to Gibraltar, 4 hours and 15 minutes; 18 November – Gibraltar to Rabat Sali, 1 hour; 22 November – Rabat Sali to Castel Benito, 4 hours and 40 minutes; 23 November – Castel Benito to Cairo West, 4 hours and 40 minutes; 26 November – Cairo West to Lydda (near Jerusalem), 2 hours; and then via Habbinaya, Bahrain Island, Mauripur and Delhi to Allahabad.

Ferrying new Mosquitos to India would be a continual process. Teething troubles on the new aircraft were commonplace, but some problems were more sinister. Most crews ferried the mark that they were intending to fly, although some aircrew were eventually posted to the roles for which they hadn't been trained. Having completed his nine–month navigation training through to being awarded his brevet, Sergeant Alfred 'Alf' Pridmore was posted to No. 8 O.T.U. at RAF Dyce to specialise in photographic reconnaissance. There Alf was partnered with Flight Lieutenant Richard 'Dick' Campbell RCAF on the Mosquito. Soon afterwards, at RAF Benson in Oxfordshire, the pair were allocated a new 'top line' Mk XVI Mosquito designed with a pressurised cockpit and double–glazed windows specifically for long-range high altitude reconnaissance. They were instructed to ferry it to India for delivery to No. 684 Squadron, with their initial reporting point being Karachi.

Dick and Alf took off from RAF Portreath on 26 May 1944. Alf recalled, 'Although we flew the first leg to Rabat at 35,000ft we experienced no problems with icing … [The leg] was completed in 4 hrs for 1,262 nautical miles averaging 315 knots which was not bad for those days. In fact, we took off some half hour after two Beaufighters and landed about 2hrs before them. As we were unable to replenish our oxygen we finished the rest of the journey to India at lower levels, so no icing problems arose.' On the next leg to Tripoli, Dick was feeling rather under the weather following an evening drinking in a bar so Alf, who hardly drank at all, swapped places with him in mid–flight to take over the flying.[38] Changing places inside the cramped Mossie cockpit must have been quite challenging since both men were over 6ft tall! Alf continued, 'On our third leg from Tripoli to Cairo we experienced port engine failure due to loss of coolant and made a single engine landing at Tobruk.' All single engine landings in Mosquitos required skill and concentration. Failure of the port engine added to the pilot's challenges on the approach and landing due to the asymmetric torque from the starboard engine. Even though Dick was a relative novice on the type, he executed it perfectly and they handed the aircraft over for repair. 'An astute engineering officer identified the failure as due to possible factory sabotage on the Packard–built Merlin 72/73. The leaking coolant pipe had identical punched holes at the upper and lower bends which had been filled and painted over, and would eventually leak whichever way the pipe had been fitted to the engine.'[39] Alf and Dick successfully handed over their aircraft to Allied Command South East Asia (A.C.S.E.A.) in India on 6 June 1944, expecting to be posted with it to No. 684 Squadron, a photo reconnaissance squadron at Dum Dum near Calcutta. However, Alf explained, 'On arrival at Karachi we discovered that 684 were more in need of the aircraft than the crew and while waiting to join the squadron we were posted to 143 R.S.U. at Bishnapur as a test crew for repaired Mossies.'[40]

Even towards the end of 1944, when Mosquito transits to India were becoming relatively commonplace, they could still present challenges. Australian pilot Max Howland was tasked with delivering another new Mk XVI to India. On 6 December he and his navigator, Bill, departed Portreath and flew direct to Rabat in North Africa at 27,000ft all the way. After a day's rest, they flew on to Castel Benito, where they spent the following day visiting Tripoli. In his diary Max wrote, '10th – Easy trip to Cairo West. 11th – A day's sightseeing at pyramids, Sphinx and in Cairo. 12th – Off to Habbaniya near the Euphrates. Flew at 10,000ft to save having the masks on. Was tempted to find a phoney excuse to land in Palestine but resisted the temptation. 13th – Off to Bahrein [sic] on an island about halfway down the Gulf. That night it rained and we got flooded out. Stuck here until the drome dries. 17th – I got off pretty quickly before the wet part – about 800 yards. A pleasant high trip to Karachi. [18th] – All set to go and off early too. I selected undercart up and a pipe broke and hydraulic oil smelling like ether or something sprayed all over the place. All over us and our kit. I called up control. The wheels came down OK but to be sure I did a touch and go intending to land off it. She didn't like it and when the bounces increased I went round again, going through the gate. Completed a low circuit without touching the undercart and landed OK. During the emergency had a hell of an argument with control who couldn't get it through their thick heads that I did have an emergency and was coming in to land no matter what they said. There was no one else in the circuit. Later I heard that the engines made such a noise when I went through the gate that the whole station came rushing out. We washed our clothes and gear in petrol, but the boots have probably had it. Went into town in the evening and bought a pair of shoes to use. Expect repairs to take a few days.'[41] After an air test on 21 December, Max and Bill finally reached Allahabad on 22 December 1944.

Squadron or Unit	Mosquito Intruder Operations		Aircrew Losses Operations		Aircrew Losses Training/Other	
	Jul–Sep 43	Total	Jul–Sep 43	Total	Jul–Sep 43	Total
Other Units	0	0	0	0	6	6
Total	0	0	0	0	6	6

Chapter 6

First Forays

November 1943 – March 1944

*'The de Havilland Mosquito, wooden fighter and
reconnaissance bomber which furniture makers and wood
turners in Britain and Canada are helping to produce, is now
operating with the RAF against the Japs in Burma.'*
Associated Press, *India, February 1944*

On 4 August 1943, 26-year-old Wing Commander Eric James Brindley 'Nick' Nicolson VC was given command of No. 27 Squadron at Agartala. Nick had joined the RAF in 1936 on a four-year short service commission. Having completed his pilot training in 1937, he was posted to No. 72 Squadron at Church Fenton, North Yorkshire, where he flew Gloster Gladiators before moving on to Spitfires two years later. In 1939, with war approaching, Flying Officer Nicolson married Muriel Kendall in Kirkby Wharfe, North Yorkshire. Nick was the only Battle of Britain pilot, and indeed the only pilot in RAF Fighter Command, to be awarded the Victoria Cross during the Second World War. The action on 16 August 1940 resulted in Nick suffering burns to his hands, as well as other injuries. In early November, when convalescing at RAF Halton, he sent a telegram to his wife, 'Darling. Just got VC. Don't know why. Letter follows. All my love. Nick.' Later that month, he and Muriel celebrated the birth of their first child, James. After a couple of UK tours, Nick was posted to India in early 1942, then to Air H.Q. in December that year. On his arrival at 27 Squadron, even though he couldn't properly bend his badly burnt fingers, nor use his hands in the normal way, he started as he meant to go on – he flew the Beaufighter that very same afternoon.

Meanwhile, Admiral Lord Louis Mountbatten had been appointed Supreme Allied Commander South-East Asia. Since having his beloved HMS *Kelly* sunk from under him off Crete in 1941, he had filled increasingly important staff roles, becoming the Chief of Combined Operations. That experience of combined arms operations would prove invaluable as he set about raising the morale of the forces under his command, which was not before time for many in the 'Forgotten Army'. Mountbatten journeyed out to the Far East, first visiting General Chiang Kai-Shek in China. He then met with Lieutenant General Slim to review the Burma front and famously told his men, 'I hear you call yourselves The Forgotten Army. Well, let me tell you that this is not The Forgotten Front and you are not The Forgotten Army. In fact, no one has even heard of you. But they will hear of you because this is what we are going to do...'[42]

On 25 October 1943 the Accident Investigation Branch held another meeting in the Air Ministry about Mosquito structural failures. The minutes, classified as Secret, noted that there had been a further three structural failures of the aircraft and reviewed possible contributing factors. They reported that, as requested, the Royal Aircraft Establishment had reviewed the Mosquito's factor of safety:

> *'The overall rate for structural failures for all Marks shows some improvement recently and the overall mean accident rate is 1 in 8,100 flying hours. Four accidents were considered due to high "g" but in each of these another contributory factor has been present and the evidence is considered insufficient to assess the adequacy of the load factor.*
>
> *'This matter is again mentioned because, although the Mosquito is not classified as "fully aerobatic" it is undoubtably*

so treated by many of those who fly it. Moreover, it is perhaps
unfortunate that "test" pilots are among the worst offenders in
this respect in that they set an example to the RAF.[43]

Like all intruder squadrons, 27 had an establishment of twenty-one
aircraft and crews: two Flights, 'A' and 'B', each with ten aircraft and
led by a flight commander, plus the squadron commander's aircraft.
In total there were forty-two aircrew, including the commanding
officer, a mixture of officers and senior NCOs, who worked together
and played together. They were a close-knit group of young men who
accepted the risks in the roles. When it came to flying and operations,
there was no difference between the officers and NCOs. Indeed,
apart from the pre-war commissioned officers, most had started as
NCOs. They did the same jobs and knew each other by first names or
nicknames. They were young and shared a lot of 'banter'. However,
when work finished, they returned to their separate messes, one for
officers and the other for senior NCOs. As the Mosquito pilot and
navigator were usually partnered for a tour, they became a very close
team, instinctively knowing what each other needed next. They flew
together and took their leave at the same time.

Nick had been tasked with introducing the intruder Mosquito
to support the Burma campaign. His plan was to initially convert
A Flight, under Squadron Leader Ernest Bernard 'Bunny' Horn,
to the Mosquito, but first he needed aircraft! Finally, in late
November 1943, four experienced Mossie intruder crews from No.
418 Squadron, Warrant Officers Blinch and Gunn, Flight Sergeants
Ball, Rainbow and Walsh, and Sergeants Luff, Yerby and Orsborn,
were posted to the squadron, bringing with them the FB VIs which
they had ferried from the UK to India.

In preparation for ops over Burma, the new aircrew arrivals to
India were briefed on their enemy, locations where the Japanese
had strung 'tripwires' to bring down low-flying aircraft, the jungle
terrain, weather and, as importantly, their leave. Squadron Leader

Bunny Horn ran through his standard briefing, 'It's a hell of a climate here just before and during the monsoons – twenty-four hours of body drip. You'll all probably get prickly heat, sounds a pretty sort of piddling thing, I know, but I can tell you it's not so bloody funny. When the monsoon's gathering don't try and fly through it. When you see the muck ahead, you may be able to fly under it. But don't get the idea you've come to hell's ugly spot. I'm telling you the worst so you'll find it bloody pleasant by comparison. Bags of leave. You'll probably say now that Calcutta's a pretty lousy spot, but I've had some bloody good times there myself.'[44] The new arrivals were also issued with lightweight flying jackets and trousers, as well as a silk escape map of Burma and 'goolie chits' printed on material, explaining in several local languages that they were allied fighters and requesting help to get them back to friendly forces. Finally, they were issued with some 'blood money', because they would be flying over the lands of the Naga tribes who were reputedly still head-hunters.[45]

With still very few Mosquitos available to train the Beaufighter pilots, Flight Sergeant Ted Ball did many of the introductory conversion flights whilst Jackie Blinch, Benny Walsh and Billy Gunn spent most of December assisting with ground school pilot training. Billy was a 24-year-old Canadian from Toronto and an outstanding college athlete both in football and hockey. He had enlisted in the RCAF in May 1941, being posted to the UK the following year. Billy had flown intruder ops with 418 Squadron, both in Bostons and Mosquitos.

The conversion training for pilots was restricted to just a couple of flights each day scheduled to minimise impact on the operational Beaufighter sorties. Without any TIII dual-control Mosquitos, the converting Beaufighter pilots were just given a short flight in the Mossie's navigator seat with a 'running commentary' explanation from the experienced Mosquito pilot. Additional Mosquitos were collected, at the end of their ferry flights, from the Central Maintenance Unit, No. 1 CMU at Kanchrapara. Once the pilots were conversant with the Mosquitos, they needed to build some hours operating them with their navigators. Sometimes they would fly with their usual navigator, sometimes with one of the experienced ex-418 navs. Of course, it wasn't just the aircrew who needed conversion training. Programmes were also put in place for the groundcrews, armourers and engineers, whilst stores established stocks and their supply chain.

Navigator Arthur Maude was posted to the squadron in mid-December, having ferried a Beaufighter out from the UK. His pilot, Bill Ball, had become increasingly apprehensive or even scared with the torque generated by the two Hercules engines and was having difficulty handling the aircraft. 'The upshot was that a very irate Wing Commander James Brindley Nicolson VC told Ball that he was not welcome on his squadron and that he should go away and learn to fly. As I was a spare body, as it were, I found that I was able to offer my limited expertise to any needy pilot.'[46]

On 16 December, after a couple of weeks of 'working up', the squadron was given a special assignment with their Mosquitos. Squadron Leader Bunny Horn and Flight Sergeant Ted Ball, together with their navigators, flew to Ramu. Then, leaving their navigators behind, Bunny had the privilege of flying Lord Mountbatten, the Supreme Allied Commander South-East Asia, on a tour of inspection of the Arakan front lines. Ted flew another 'dignitary'. They were accompanied by Spitfires from No. 615 Squadron and after the tour landed their VIPs at Dohazari. With their navigators back on board, they then escorted the C-47 transporting Mountbatten as far as Comilla, before returning to base.

The next day, Flight Lieutenant Alexander 'Jock' Torrance and his navigator, Flight Sergeant Jack Shortis, arrived at the squadron. Jock, from Stonehouse in Lanarkshire, was one of the older pilots at twenty-seven years of age. Having joined the RAF in 1939, he had initially flown Hurricanes and helped in the defence of Malta. In 1941, an exploding fuel tank had left him with burnt hands, requiring three months in hospital. Jock then converted to Westland Whirlwind fighter bombers with No. 137 Squadron before being posted to India in October 1943.[47]

The arrival of intruder Mosquitos was really newsworthy and the 'top brass' wanted to announce their presence! It is also likely that Mountbatten had received assurances from Wing Commander Nicolson that 27 Squadron would be flying Mosquito operations over Burma by Christmas, and he made sure that they were, leading from the front! At 0645hrs on Christmas morning, Nicolson took-off on the squadron's first low-level intruder Mosquito operation over Burma. Nick, with his navigator, Flight Lieutenant 'Frankie' Franklin, was accompanied in a second Mosquito flown by Flying Officer Thompson with Sergeant Chippendale. The two aircraft headed for central Burma. 'Flying into Burma meant twice crossing the Lushai Hills, or Naga Hills, or the Arakan Yomas, some of which exceeded 9,000ft, and electrical storms were very much part of the so-called hills and yomas.'[48] They headed for Myingyan, Sagaing and then Thazi, attacking opportunity targets on the railway, putting a goods locomotive and a tanker out of action south of Thazi. Then, near Yegyo, they attacked a truck, killing some of the occupants. However, they received some heavy and close anti-aircraft fire, much to the pilots' surprise, when they overflew the large Japanese airfield at Meiktila.[49] After a very successful first Mosquito FB VI operation, both aircraft landed at Agartala by mid-morning, with the crews back in No. 1 Camp in time for the traditional Christmas dinner, where the officers and senior NCOs served the other ranks with their meal.

The following day the squadron was on 'stand-down' and David Innes recalled, 'In the course of having our own celebrations, Wing Commander Nicolson had a fall which resulted in a broken wrist!'[50] Luckily, Nick was still able to fly with it strapped up and continue with ops. Although some, like Jack Shortis, didn't really care for

Nick, all of 27 Squadron's aircrew would have 'flown down the Valley of Death for him', such was their respect for his leadership, including flying dangerous ops himself.[51]

Between Christmas and the New Year, 'A' Flight continued with their work up on the Mosquitos, with the experienced aircrew getting time for some refresher flying. On New Year's Eve, Bunny Horn chose Ted Ball as his wingman for the squadron's second Mossie intruder op. In this way the flight of two aircraft carried a mix of aircraft type and operational area experience, just not in the same aircraft! This was particularly important for navigation because, away from the coast or rivers, good landmarks in Burma could be few and navigation was difficult; maps were small scale and of variable accuracy. Often the prime means of navigation had to be thorough familiarity with the appearance of the terrain over which they flew regularly.[52] Both aircraft returned safely.

With four Mosquito operational sorties under their belt, the squadron looked forward to increasing the Mossies' contribution in the New Year.

The weather in the first two weeks in January 1944 was not good for low-level attacks, with several sorties aborted. However, most of the Mosquito ops were completed. Having flown for only four hours in total over the previous ten weeks, on 1 January 1944, experienced Mosquito crew Flight Sergeant Benny Walsh and Sergeant Ossie Orsborn flew their first operation over Burma. Benny flew as wingman to Sergeant Clegg, a converted Beaufighter pilot, with his experienced navigator, Sergeant Brinded.

Given the Merlins' tendency to quickly overheat on the ground, especially with the high temperatures in India, as soon as they started their engines, they taxied from the dispersal points to the runway. The two aircraft took off from RAF Agartala at 1345hrs in the heat of the afternoon for their three-hour op. Their aircraft didn't have oxygen systems so they headed east, aiming towards the gap between the Lushai and Naga Hills, near Imphal. Then, as they crossed the front line, they swooped down the eastern side of the Chin Hills towards Kalewa. With a constant look-out for Japanese fighters, they flew low-level, often less than 50ft above the road, from Kalewa to Ye-U looking for opportunity targets. At Ye-U, they picked up the Irrawaddy railway line and followed it, without finding any targets, towards Monywa, where they banked to the north. Finally, the River Chindwin offered opportunities. This is where cockpit design and the close relationship between pilot and navigator came into effect, since they effectively worked hand-in-glove, with the same field of view. Benny strafed from extreme low-level and claimed hits on nine sampans and a raft, all of which seemed to be loaded with tins. Both aircraft then departed back to Agartala, flying back past Imphal on their way.[53]

Immediately after the flight, Sergeant Clegg told the intelligence officer that the area had been 'unusually bare of targets.' He hadn't fired at all. Benny Walsh reported that he only completed the single attack: '1 raft, 9 sampans hit with cannon and m/g.'

The squadron continued with its normal operational rota of 'three days on ops and one day on stand-down'. Each day, the operational commitment alternated between the squadron's two flights, so 'A' Flight and its Mosquito crews were tasked with operations every two or three days. On 4 January, Jackie Blinch, with Sergeant Chippendale as his navigator, flew as wingman to Flying Officer Cotter. Having attacked a couple of serviceable locos, Jackie Blinch attacked another, and his Mosquito was caught in the resulting explosion. A large portion of the starboard propeller was blown off and either this or the explosion itself blew the cockpit door off, slightly injuring Jackie and his nav. Jackie closed down the starboard engine and headed north, with Cotter accompanying the damaged aircraft as far as Mombi before returning to base. Jackie managed to land safely at Tulihal, near Imphal.

A few days later, another Mosquito crew was posted into the squadron, with Canadian navigator Flight Sergeant 'Johnny' Yanota arriving three days before his pilot, the recently commissioned RNZAF Flying Officer Cliff Emeny. The squadron's Beaufighters were now concentrating their activity on the Taungup Pass, which on 11 January cost the lives of Flight Sergeants Britter and Paine. The next day the squadron was tasked with a combined Mosquito and Beaufighter four-ship, led by Bunny Horn, on a night operation back at the Taungup Pass. Billy Gunn, who had been notified the previous week that his commission as Pilot Officer had been confirmed, was allocated HX946, the Mosquito ferried out to India by Cliff and Johnny. The aircraft were despatched at roughly thirty-minute intervals, starting with Bunny Horn at 1750hrs. Bunny found the target but, because the moon wasn't up, didn't attack. Billy and navigator Bill Luff were last seen as they approached the Taungup Pass target at about 2030hrs, but nothing was heard of them again.[54] One of the Beaufighters returned with engine trouble and the other attacked vehicles in the pass, damaging nine of them. Billy and Bill were recorded as 'Missing, believed killed'.

One of the responsibilities of squadron command was writing letters of condolence, so Nick wrote to both Bill's parents and Billy's mother. Billy's father, Platoon Chief Alex Gunn, had been killed in 1941, so Billy's loss would be felt even harder by his mother, two sisters and brother. Billy's death was also a blow to his good friends from 418 Squadron days – Jackie Blinch, Benny Walsh and Ossie Orsborn. Pilot Officer William Gunn RCAF and Sergeant William Charles Luff were the first Mosquito FB VI aircrew deaths during operations in India.

On 24 January, Cliff was tasked with his first intruder op. He, with navigator Johnny Yanota, flew as wingman for their Flight Commander, Bunny Horn, to attack shipping and river communications at Henzada and estuaries to its south. There were rich pickings, with them recording hits on about fifty sampans. At Thabyugyang they scored hits on a 100ft black-painted steamer. They then struck a sawmill, brought a lorry to standstill with cannons and attacked a couple of locos! On their return to base, Bunny's aircraft suffered an engine problem, requiring him to fly on a single engine from Buthidaung to Agartala. Even so, it was a very successful operation.

January was rounded out for 27 Squadron with a three day stand-down. The Mosquitos of 'A' Flight had flown eighteen operational sorties during the month.

Back in London, the Air Ministry made the decision to re-equip twenty-two bomber and strike squadrons in India with Mosquito FB VI aircraft to replace the aging Vultee Vengeance and some Beaufighters. de Havilland was commissioned to produce replacement airframe components in Karachi.[55]

At the start of February, 'B' Flight received a new flight commander, having been without one for a couple of months. Arthur Maude recalled that, 'a most charming Australian Squadron Leader by the name of George Wyndham Nelson Bassingthwaighte arrived without a navigator. He was known not surprisingly by the pseudonym "B16". I was pressed into service right away. At the same time a Mosquito pilot arrived without a valid navigator. This was Freddy Snell. Freddy had flown [Fairey] Battles at the beginning of the war [in the Battle of France], had been awarded a DFC and then gone off to Canada as an instructor. I continued to fly with these two pilots, Freddy Snell on Mosquitos and B16 on Beaufighters.'[56]

The next challenge set by the operation planners was intended to demonstrate to themselves, the press and the Japanese that the Mosquito could disrupt supply lines by strikes as far south in Burma as Rangoon. On 3 February, Jock Torrance, accompanied by his navigator Jack Shortis, was tasked to lead the 'two ship' op. Benny Walsh, with navigator Ossie Orsborn, would be his wingman. Both Mossies were fitted with auxiliary wing tanks to maximise their range. First they flew south to RAF Ramu, just to the east of Cox's Bazar and as near as they could get to the Japanese front line, where they topped up their fuel. A few minutes after taking off from Ramu they were flying low over Japanese-held territory, hugging the western edge of the Arakan Yoma before they turned east to pick up the Irrawaddy railway at Henzada. Then, they flew fast and low along the railway, looking for opportunity targets to attack with their machine guns and cannons. The aircrew called this 'rhubarbing' and it was an important part of most sorties. Jock and Benny continued their search for targets, flying low over Letpandan, Taikkya and Wanetchaung to Dabbin, on the northern outskirts of Rangoon. Following the railway north through Pegu to Nyaunglebin, they attacked the bridge and headed west towards Prome, where Benny attacked sampans on the Irrawaddy. The journey home took them through the Taungup Pass and north along the coastal plain, overflying Ramu on their way back to Agartala. It was a long, exhausting operation, lasting a total of five hours and twenty minutes, with more than four hours flying low-level over hostile territory! On his return, Benny noted, 'No rail traffic. Bridge at Nyaunglebin shot up. Sampans south of Prome attacked – hits scored.'

Associated Press reported this op, 'On Feb 3 fighter-bombers also attacked an enemy camp S of Fort White. On the Malay Peninsula waterways and as far S as Rangoon, single and twin-engine fighters shot up river craft and motor transport. Five sampans carrying troops were also attacked. In all, four large and three small river craft were destroyed and five more damaged.'[57]

On 7 February, the squadron received a signal ordering their immediate move to RAF Parashuram, about fifty miles to the south of Agartala, with help from the Dakotas of No. 194 Squadron. That night an advance party drove to their new home to start the preparations for the move. They reported back that the grass airfield did not have any flarepath equipment, so they arranged for aircraft and crews on night sorties to operate from RAF Feni, which was

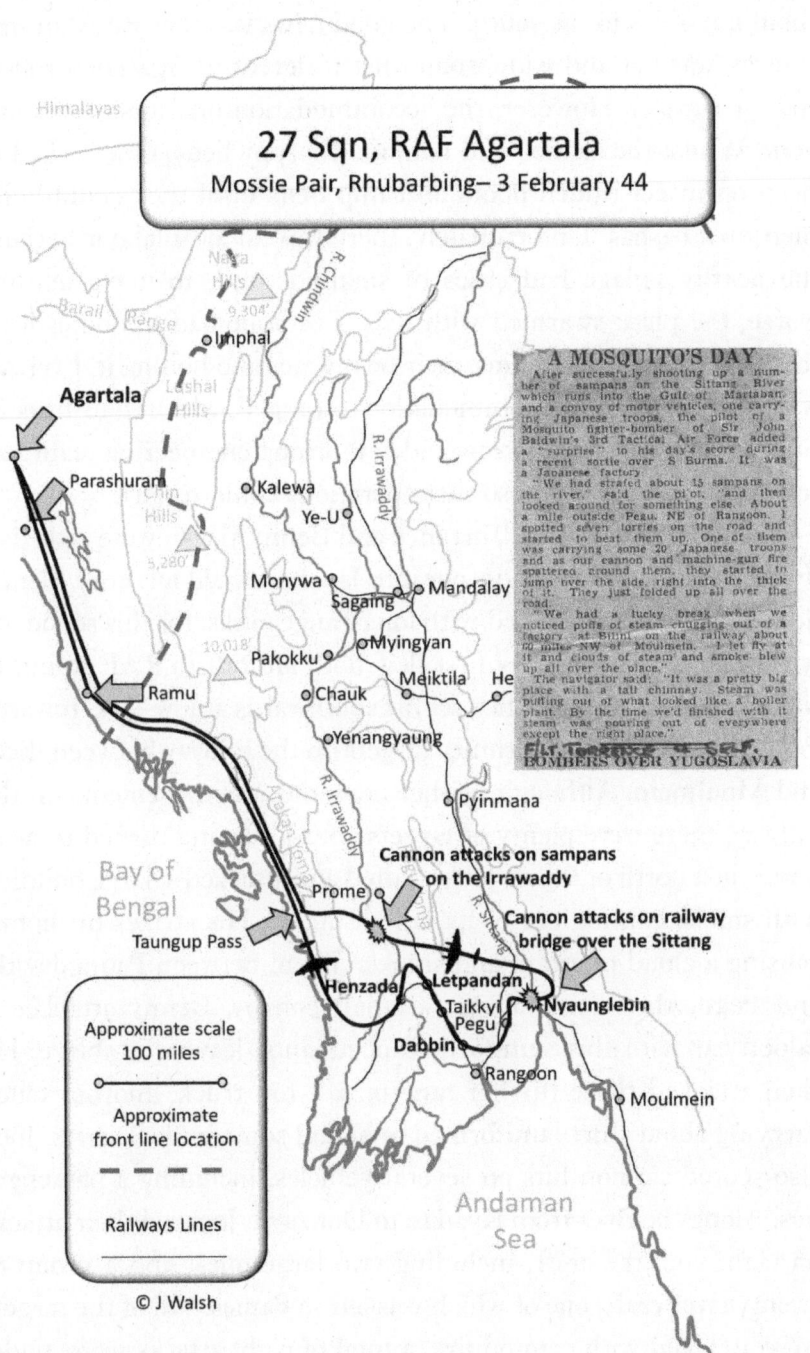

27 Sqn op 3 Feb 44 and article about 12 Feb 44 op

about ten miles to the south. The good news was that Parashuram's runway was flat and wide, somewhat different to Agartala's roller-coaster runway. However, the accommodation quarters were quite poor. Whilst the airmen had bamboo charpoy beds, officers had to sleep on insect-ridden floors on camp beds until they could build their own bashas. Unfortunately, there was no local labour because the nearby village had cases of smallpox and, to make matters worse, the place swarmed with flies. Everyone had to domesticate themselves quickly, fetching their own water and boiling it. Even so, with dispersals and 'accommodation' arranged, within four days 27 Squadron's forty-five aircrew and 150-strong engineering team had relocated to Parashuram so that operations could restart.

On 12 February, Jock Torrance and Benny Walsh were tasked to fly their Mosquitos even deeper into Japanese-held territory. Benny flew K-HX821, again fitted with long-range tanks, for this sortie. As with their earlier op, they first flew both aircraft to RAF Ramu to top up their fuel. Then they set off southwards at low-level towards Pegu to search for opportunity targets on the railway between there and Moulmein. Although neither crew saw any movements on the railway, there were plenty of targets ahead. Having turned to head home, just north of Bilini, Jock spotted and attacked a 'large building with smoke coming out of its tall chimney'. His strikes hit home, causing a cloud of steam and smoke. Then, between Paungdawthi and Pegu, they came across a small convoy. Benny attacked a saloon car with three uniformed occupants, leaving it ablaze. He then attacked three further targets: a 3-ton truck, another truck carrying about thirty uniformed men and some bullock carts. Jock also scored cannon hits on several vehicles, including a passenger bus. Along the river from Kyaikto to Donzayit, Jock led their attacks on eight country craft, including two large ones, and a group of twenty river craft, one of which was left in flames. 'All of the targets were attacked with cannon fire, a total of eight attacks were made, every target was hit.'

Having been debriefed by the intelligence officer after their return to Parashuram, the two crews were interviewed by a newspaper reporter. 'We had a lucky break when I noticed puffs of steam chugging out of a factory at Bilini on the railway about sixty miles north-west of Moulmein,' explained Jock, 'I let fly at it and clouds of steam and smoke blew up all over the place.' Jack Shortis added, 'It was a pretty big place with a tall chimney. Steam was puffing out of what looked like a boiler plant. By the time we'd finished with it steam was pouring out of everywhere except the right place.'[58] Then a photographer took some shots of Jock by his Mosquito.

When the new crews had arrived at 27 Squadron, Bunny Horn had spoken of leave in Calcutta. In general terms, each crew was allocated two weeks leave each year, usually taken at roughly the same time. For Benny and Ossie, their leave time was late February. True to his word, they were given leave and spent it in Calcutta. A perk for aircrew was that they could usually hitch a lift to the nearest airfield on one of the frequent transport and communications aircraft. This saved them enduring many hours of travel by truck, train and ferry.

On 25 February 1944 the Accident Investigation Branch held another meeting focused on structural failures in the Mosquito. In the minutes, classified as Secret, the review group reached a conclusion:

> 'The failure of the airframe structure in four of the five accidents dealt with in this report could be attributed to high accelerations and the evidence suggested that in each case a wing or wings failed first during the pull-out. The start of the trouble was loss of control, and it is becoming increasingly clear that even experienced pilots cannot afford to lose control in a Mosquito since on recovery from an out-of-control dive it is all too easy to break the wings.'[59]

By 8 March 1944, the Japanese had started to lay siege to Imphal, using the now infamous Kohima Ridge as their main vantage point. However, the senior officers at 27 Squadron were assessing the merits of completing the conversion to the Mosquito. 'A' Flight had now completed forty-five operational sorties with their Mosquitos. Was it a suitable replacement for the Beaufighter in the ground attack and intruder role? Was it the right time for 27 Squadron to complete the conversion?

By 9 March they had reached their conclusions. There were concerns that the Mossie's radical wooden construction could not take the heavy punishment meted-out by the Japanese anti-aircraft batteries.[60] Also, the Merlins were 'not as reliable as the radials of the Beaufighter, often returning from a sortie on one engine.'[61] After weighing the range and payload benefits against reliability considerations, Wing Commander Nicolson decided that 27 Squadron should not be the first squadron in India to convert to the Mosquito. Whilst some of the aircrew were happy to return to their reliable Beaufighters, others were disappointed, sharing the opinion of David Bellis, a navigator who had converted from the Beaufighter to the Mosquito. 'Experience of operations with the Beaufighter enable the Mosquito crew to quickly appreciate the unique capability of the Mossie. The Beau was rather like a Mother, solid and respectable who would never let you down. Transfer to the Mossie could be compared to having an exciting affair with a lady which you wanted to last for ever!'[62] All of 'A' Flight's Mosquitos and some of its aircrew were to be posted.

On 13 March, No. 45 Squadron, recently posted to the Mosquito Conversion Flight at Yelahanka, noted that four of its Vengeance crews were to be posted to 27 Squadron and that 27 Squadron would be posting six experienced Mosquito crews to 45 Squadron.[63]

The final part of the review was completed when, on 19 March 1944, a signal confirmed that, having been operational for fifteen months, No. 27 Squadron was to be withdrawn from operations and relocate to Cholavaram.

Squadron or Unit	Mosquito Intruder Operations		Aircrew Losses Operations		Aircrew Losses Training/Other	
	Nov 43 – Mar 44	Total	Nov 43 – Mar 44	Total	Nov 43 – Mar 44	Total
No. 27 Sqn	45	45	2	2	0	0
Other Units	0	0	0	0	0	6
Total	45	45	2	2	0	6

Chapter 7

Working Up

March – August 1944

*'Two pilot-navigators who are interchangeable man the
Mosquito. They are highly trained specialists because in the
Mosquito things happen so fast that split-second decisions have
to be made, calling for the maximum skill, judgement and
stamina, and in low-flying work there is no time for mistakes.'*
Associated Press, *India, February 1944*

Thirty-year-old Wing Commander Harley Charles Stumm
DFC was the CO of No. 45 Squadron. Born in 1913,
Harley was the only son and eldest of four children in
the Stumm family from Gympie, Queensland, Australia. He had
studied Arts Law at the University of Queensland and represented
Australian Universities in rugby union, touring Japan in 1934. In
1935 Harley was awarded a Rhodes scholarship to study law at
Oxford University. On arrival at Baliol College, he joined Oxford
University Air Squadron and gained his RAF pilot's Certificate
of Competency in June 1936. During his time at Oxford, he also
attended the 1936 Olympic Games in Berlin, writing several reports
which were published in a Queensland newspaper. After graduation
in 1938, Harley was called to the English Bar, but he soon returned
to Australia, was admitted to the Queensland Bar and he married
his fiancée, Lorraine Streeter. After the outbreak of war Harley was
called up into the RAF. In September 1943, when commanding
No. 11 Squadron, he was awarded the DFC for 'many operations',

'exceptional leadership' and 'inspiring his unit to the utmost efforts against the enemy.'[64] Throughout the war, he used his spare time to write, with two books, '*After Victory*' and '*A Rifle and Kay*', being published. When the war was over, Harley planned to resume law, before entering politics. He and Lorraine had a 3-year-old daughter when, in 1944, he was given command of 45 Squadron. So that Harley could occasionally see his daughter, Lorraine managed to arrange a job for herself in New Delhi.

Harley was well respected and liked by his squadron, which had a substantial contingent of RAAF aircrew who had been together since the squadron was re-formed in the Middle East. They were operationally experienced, having been equipped with Bristol Blenheims and, more recently, the Vultee Vengeance dive bomber, but the Mosquito and its role were very different for them. The squadron arrived at RAF Yelahanka, near Bangalore, in late February, having been posted to the newly formed Mosquito conversion unit, No. 1672 Conversion Unit. They had a slow start, since their first Mosquito, LR250, was delivered on 29 February and by 5 March they had only three FB VIs to use for demonstration flights for the pilots. On 13 March, Harley Stumm was the first 45 Squadron pilot to actually fly the Mosquito. They keenly awaited the arrival of the Mosquitos and their experienced aircrews from 27 Squadron.

Flight Sergeant William 'Bill' Taylor had been posted to 45 Squadron in mid-February. He had joined the RAAF in November 1941 and completed his elementary pilot training in Narrandera, New South Wales. In June 1942 he embarked on the rather squalid 18,000-ton American transporter, '*Tasker H Bliss*', to cross the Pacific and transit the Panama Canal for Canada. By December 1942 Bill had been awarded his wings and, after crossing the Atlantic to the UK, was selected to fly twins, flying solo in the Bristol Beaufighter on 29 June 1943. With his conversion completed, in early September 1943 his first posting was to ferry a new Beaufighter to India. As with all ferry aircrew, when he arrived in India Bill then reported to A.T.P. at Poona and was eventually posted to 45 Squadron at Yelahanka.

By early April the six experienced Mosquito crews from 27 Squadron had arrived at 45 Squadron at Yelahanka. The conversion unit had also received a dual control TIII Mosquito so that pilots could have one hour of dual instruction before they flew solo on the FB VI. With the Mosquitos also arriving from 27 Squadron, the conversion of the Vengeance pilots and navigators to Mosquitos moved up a gear.

On joining the squadron, Benny Walsh thought that the aircrew were 'cliquey'. However, he didn't realise what they had been through together. Many of the Australian aircrew had been with the squadron since 1942.

The training requirement was substantial since some of the aircrew were flying a twin for the first time, and most had to convert their operational mindset from dive bombing to low-level day and night intruder missions. Flying Officer Walter 'Wal' McLellan was one of the Australian pilots who had been with 45 Squadron since it was re-formed. Wal's views on the conversion to the Mosquito were very clear; 'a pilot's dream compared to the obsolete Bristol Blenheims and the brute Vengeance dive bombers we had flown before.'[65]

Since joining 45 Squadron, Wal had been teamed up with his navigator Jim Vernon and wireless operator/air gunner Jack Nankervis. In Autumn 1942, when 45 Squadron had been virtually 'wiped out', his crew and aircraft were detached to No. 113 Squadron. On 31 October 1942 they had collided with another aircraft on the runway – both aircraft were write-offs. 'Nobody killed but Wal was trapped in the cockpit – Jim and Nank got out but then Nank realised that Wal was trapped by his feet under the rudder pedals with bombs cooking. He ran back to get him out (pretty damn brave!) but meanwhile Wal had managed to extricate himself and with his entire calf muscle hanging down off his leg and no shoes, partly burned side of his body, he was running for the ditch.'[66] Wal was hospitalised and did not return to flying until July 1943, when the same crew was reformed. With the conversion to the Mosquito, it was strictly a two-man operation. Nank applied to retrain as a navigator so that he could remain with the squadron.

Bill Taylor recalled his introduction to the Mosquito at Yelahanka. 'We had a few flights in a Bisley and also flew an Anson for the first time. Two Mosquitos have arrived and we are learning our cockpit drill.' The cockpit made quite an impression on him. 'There is not much room in the cockpit. You have to climb up a ladder and enter through a small door on the starboard side. If you have to bale out, you come out the same way, making sure you stop the starboard engine otherwise you get chopped up. Glad I never had to bale out!'[67]

The initial Mosquito FB VIs for India had been fitted with Merlin-23 engines which only delivered only 1,390hp. However, it was now felt that increased performance from either the Merlin-21 or Merlin-25 engines, with 1,610hp, was far preferable. New deliveries reflected this change. Added to this, there was an increased imperative to move the Mosquitos to the front line. The Battle of Imphal continued to rage, with the Japanese forces threatening to overrun the town. The Allies were holding them off, but the costs were significant.

After only a few weeks at Yelahanka, on 1 May 1944, the squadron transferred to RAF Amarda Road to complete the No. 9 Fighter Refresher Course at the Air Fighting Training Unit. The unit was run by Wing Commander Frank 'Chota' Carey, who had a personal tally of fifteen German and eight Japanese aircraft. That day ten Mosquitos, two Ansons and two Liberators flew from Yelahanka to Amarda Road. To ensure that they had some Mosquito groundcrew available, one was squeezed into each cockpit, along with the pilot and navigator. One of the Mosquitos was HJ811, ferried to India by Benny and Ossie and forcing three single-engine landings due to engine shutdowns. The problems with this aircraft's starboard engine had continued, suffering from a string of technical issues. It was clearly still a 'Rogue'. Engineers had worked on it overnight before it was flown by Flying Officer Arthur Huon RAAF to RAF Amarda Road, 'Two hours after take-off the starboard engine caught fire and at the same time we lost all of the electrically-operated functions. The cockpit of the Mosquito was a pretty tight fit for the pilot and navigator at the best of times. On this occasion we were also carrying a rigger, AC Geoff Dee, as a passenger and I realised that here was no hope of Ced Birkbeck and Dee being able to get at their observer-type parachutes, let alone clip them onto their harnesses. Somehow, we had to land.' Arthur turned and flew back about twenty miles towards a half-completed strip at Rajalmundy, in Tamil Nadu,[68] 'We got down and the undercart collapsed in the process. We left the aircraft in some haste and managed to distance ourselves by some thirty yards before the starboard inner tank exploded. During our short run on the recently laid concrete strip we had marred its pristine surface with a stream of molten metal and burnt rubber.'[69]

With all of 45 Squadron at Amarda Road, on 8 May 1944, the Fighter Refresher Course started. For the pilots, the course consisted of three hours' dual in Harvards and one hour dual in a Mosquito, during which the instructors covered estimation, line, deflection, positioning for attacks and the various forms of attack. They then consolidated this knowledge with between twelve to fifteen hours of practice against either other Mosquitos or USAAF B-25s. The flying was complemented with ground school covering the theory of sighting, care and maintenance of guns, organisation of photo sections, escape and evasion, range firing with rifles, sten guns and automatic weapons, effect of 'g' and medical kits.

On 13 May 1944, just five days into the course, 45 Squadron suffered a significant blow. Wing Commander Stumm had just completed practicing 'quarter attacks' in his Mosquito against a B-25, capturing it on cinefilm. As he approached Amarda Road airfield at about 200mph at 3,600ft with the B–25 and another Mossie, Harley appeared to lose control. His Mosquito rolled and dived between the other two aircraft into a near vertical spin. Then, pieces of the aircraft broke off in mid–air before it crashed into the ground at about 1650hrs. Both Harley and his passenger, Flight Lieutenant Walter McKerracher RAAF, died on impact.

Harley's death affected everyone in the squadron because he was well liked and respected. Fellow pilot Bill Taylor helped recover Harley's body for burial, carrying him on part of the Mosquito's wing.[70] 'B' Flight Commander, Squadron Leader Don Edwards, was given temporary command of the squadron and the training course continued.

Within days the inquiry into the failure of HP939's airframe attributed it to the undercarriage doors having come open during sustained high 'g'. (As early as 20 November 1942, there had been some concern about weakness in the undercarriage doors and Special Instruction R.D.A 428 had been issued calling attention to the need for ensuring that the doors were fully closed when the undercarriage was up.[71])

Flying the Mosquito was still very new to most of 45 Squadron's aircrew. On 16 May, Australian Flying Officer Joe Cartledge managed to get his Mosquito airborne with insufficient flying speed and it sunk back to the ground, bounced heavily and partly buckled his port undercarriage. He and his navigator, Flying Officer Graham Williams RAAF, were unable to either retract or lower it, flying around for two and a half hours trying to resolve the problem. They finally committed to a belly landing on the grass, so as not to block Amarda Road's runway. Graham described their arrival, 'We touched down at 150mph and the right wingtip hit the ground at about 125mph. The undercarriage came through the cockpit under my feet, the propeller straddled the cockpit and went 100ft into the air; the pilot's seat and armour plate broke loose and pinned me in my seat. We spun round and round across the main runway and smashed into the trees.'[72] Incredibly, both Joe and Graham escaped with only bruises, although their Mosquito was written off.

On 28 May 1944 the new CO was appointed. He was 33-year-old Wing Commander Robert James Walker, known universally as 'Johnny' after the whisky. Johnny had joined the RAF in 1937 and, after completing his pilot training, was posted in 1938 to Gloster Gladiators with No. 72 Squadron at Church Fenton, becoming a compatriot of Nick Nicolson. Soon after arriving there, Johnny survived a mid-air collision in which the other pilot was killed.[73] It was also at Church Fenton that he met Margaret Anson and they married in 1939. Johnny briefly served with the squadron on Hurricanes during the Battle of Britain before being posted as an instructor.

Johnny didn't go to Amarda Road but went straight to 45's new base at Dalbhumgarh, a recently completed airfield to the north-west. On arrival it was obvious to him that this airfield had some significant problems, not least the drainage and latrines. Also, since it had never had a squadron based there, there was no established supply chain. The nearby USAAF base at Chakulia agreed to provide some food and rations (which turned out to be far superior) for the first few days, until normal British rations started arriving.

As each 45 Squadron aircrew completed their course, they relocated, with their Mosquito, to Dalbhumgarh to continue their work-up to operational status. It was very quickly clear that the airfield lacked even the basic needs for operational flying. For instance, there was no fire tender and, when it arrived, it was still missing the fire suppressant. Additionally, it was so hot that in the afternoons the Mosquitos were too hot to touch. Johnny Walker changed the squadron's working hours to 0730hrs to 1230hrs, then 1600hrs to 1730hrs.[74]

On 7 June news arrived about the D-Day invasion the previous day. Although pleased, it made them realise how far away from home they all were and that they were fighting a different type of war with a very different enemy. The news from Europe was quickly overshadowed by the lack of spare parts which had grounded many of the squadron's Mosquitos. Only about one third of the aircraft were serviceable and many aircraft lacked replacement tyres or exhausts. Supply of critical aircraft spare parts was not yet in place for an operational squadron. However, the most worrying concern was that the engineers now believed that some aircraft were suffering from a new condition which they had started to call 'wood shrinkage'. They were beginning to think that this could have been the cause for Harley Stumm's aircraft failure. Some of the aircrew had been sceptical of the official inquiry outcome. Warrant Officer Tiff O'Connor recalled his opinion. 'After a quarter attack the aircraft was rolled over and a pull through commenced, as the nose fell the port wing came off and the aircraft spun in. I have always been convinced that it was our first loss due to airframe failure.'[75]

On that same day, in London, the Accident Investigation Branch held another review of Mosquito structural failures. In their minutes, classified as Secret, they noted that there had been eighteen airframe failures until the end of 1943, with eight more in the first three months of 1944. Their conclusions included:

'... most of the accidents were attributed to overstressing, very often preceded by loss of control. Wing collapse has predominated as the primary failure. This may suggest that strengthening of the wings might improve the accident rate, but it is not considered that a great increase in strength will be obtained by any simple modification.'

'Discussions with Mosquito pilots rarely lead to criticism of the aircraft's flying qualities; in fact their whole-hearted approval of its controllability may mean that liberties are being taken with an aircraft which is obviously insufficiently robust to withstand harsh treatment.'

They made five recommendations, including:

> *'Retrospective application of the modification ([Mod]. 638)*
> *to strengthen the bottom wing skin at the front spar should*
> *proceed at a higher priority.'*[76]

At Amarda Road, operational training, especially low-level flying, continued as quickly as aircraft serviceability would allow. However, the flying was challenging and training crashes were relatively frequent. On 14 June, Warrant Officer Bill Tolar suffered a starboard engine failure with HP878 which resulted in a precautionary landing. Unfortunately, the undercarriage failed to lock down and the aircraft ended up on its belly. Even so, his Mossie looked to be repairable, until the crane borrowed from the USAAF to recover it inflicted irreparable damage!

Just over a week later, on 24 June, three aircraft, led by 'B' Flight Commander Don Edwards, took off at 1000hrs on a low flying exercise. Cliff Emeny was flying HP867, with Johnny Yanota navigating as usual. When flying with Edwards near Bishnapur, Cliff strayed so low that he struck a branch of a tree, damaging the mainplane, tailplane and starboard engine, resulting in a partial loss of control. Johnny explained, 'The plane shot up to about 600ft, stalled, then climbed, then stalled three times. As we were over rice paddies, Cliff attempted a belly landing. The plane completely broke up when we hit the walls between the paddy fields. We walked out of the front of the plane as it had completely broken off. I got Cliff out of the sun and under the wing, bandaged his legs and my own and walked about five miles to a village [where I] sent a telegram to base. I got a stretcher party organised and brought [Cliff] out.'[77] Cliff's injuries were such that he needed a week or so in hospital, plus three weeks' convalescence, to recover. Needless to say, with the total loss of an aircraft, the accident resulted in a Board of Inquiry, but it was declared an operational accident.

Throughout June, 45's aircraft serviceability had been dire; tyres and exhausts were in desperately short supply and standard inspections were taking up to ten days. On average, the squadron had only six or seven Mosquitos available. Added to that, the squadron's beer and spirits ration did not arrive, again!

July continued for 45 Squadron with similar challenges. Aircrew were limited in their flying hours due to aircraft serviceability, with availability of tyres causing real problems.

With sufficient moonlight, training focused on low-level night flying. On 8 July, Flying Officer Pete Ewing crashed his Mosquito HP876 at Ondal. Both he and his navigator, Flying Officer Frank Harper, required a few days in hospital to recover.[78]

As Johnny Walker settled in as 45's CO, he became increasing concerned about aircrew numbers. Despite having an establishment for forty-six aircrew, he actually had sixty-six aircrew on his squadron strength. He pointed out to Group that it wasn't a training squadron and so in early July he posted several crews away from the squadron.[79] Johnny gave preference to retaining (and retraining) some of the many Australians and New Zealanders who had been with the squadron a long time, some since 1941. Benny and Ossie were one of only six crews on the squadron who were operationally experienced in 45's new role of day and night low-level intruding and strike in Mosquitos. However, on 10 July 1943, 'More surplus aircrew were posted away from the unit today.'[80] This included Benny and Ossie, who were posted to 82 Squadron, possibly because Benny had been unwell and they hadn't completed the fighter course at Amarda Road.

Johnny had also been outspoken with 231 Group about the problems with spares and Mosquito serviceability. His complaints were heard and group arranged for specialists to provide additional support. On 12 July, engineers from No. 684 Squadron, which flew PR Mosquitos, arrived to help address the maintenance issues. de

Havilland sent their representative, Mr Myers, and Rolls–Royce sent Mr Waterhouse. This support team stayed for five days before returning to Calcutta.

Serviceability slowly improved but spares, especially tyres, continued to restrict operational training. All available aircraft were flown. On 24 July Don Edwards hit a kite hawk during a low–level flight and, suspecting damage to the wing, made a precautionary landing at Kanchrapara where the maintenance unit was based. He left the aircraft there and prepared himself for the long slow train journey back to base.

Whilst 45 Squadron was struggling to reach operational status in Dalbhumgarh, No. 82 Squadron, another Vengeance dive bomber squadron, arrived in July at No. 1672 Conversion Unit at Yelahanka. Conversion to the Mosquito for 82 Squadron aircrew started with twin training in the Anson and Bisley. One of the first experienced crews to be posted into the unit, arriving on 18 July, was Flight Sergeants Benny Walsh and Ossie Orsborn. Then Flight Lieutenant Vivian Robert 'Freddy' Snell DFC arrived from 27 Squadron, to fill the role of 'A' Flight Commander, being subsequently promoted to squadron leader. On 12 August, Arthur Maude, Freddy's navigator at 27 Squadron, arrived to continue that role with 82.

With the change to Mosquitos, on 29 July a new CO was appointed. Wing Commander Lionel Vivien 'Bill' Hudson was an Australian who pre-war had been a journalist with the *Sydney Sun* and little more than two years before had been a sergeant pilot with No. 11 Squadron.[81] 'It was fairly easy to get rank those days as long as you stayed alive and your crimes were undetected. Frankly, I never considered myself as genuine "officer material".'[82] Bill had just completed a year in staff jobs, most recently as Wing Commander Organisation, Air Command South-East Asia, with a wide knowledge of the Allies' top-secret plans. He also believed in running an egalitarian squadron, 'I should make it clear that Allied flyers on a squadron usually regarded rank lightly. The important demarcation was being aircrew. Once in the air a sergeant pilot or navigator could be as equally effective against the enemy as a group captain.'[83]

Flying Officer Ronald Stuart 'Babe' Wambeek joined 82 Squadron in August. Babe was small in stature but was experienced and well respected. He had first flown Beaufighters with No. 219 Squadron from Tangmere before being posted to North Africa with No. 46 Squadron. From there he was posted to India to fly Hurricane fighter bombers in the Battle of Imphal. When he heard that the Mosquitos were arriving, Babe immediately volunteered to transfer to 82 Squadron.

After a check flight with Freddy Snell, his new flight commander, Benny Walsh started working on his bombing techniques. 'They knew we often did not hit the targets – the bombing was atrocious as we did not have bomb sights on the plane.' With the FB VI, pilots only had their gun sight to target their bombs, so practice was essential. Everyone had to learn low-level and glide bombing, but the ex-Vengeance crews were experienced in dive-bombing. The first challenge was bombing from extreme low-level. On 23 August, Benny and Ossie dropped four bombs individually from 100ft with an average error of 27yds. On 26 August, this time flying solo, Benny practiced bombing from only 50ft whilst taking evasive action. Not surprisingly, his average error increased to 44yds. Like the other pilots, Benny would also work on his glide and dive-bombing techniques.

At the start of August, 45 Squadron had been due to relocate to RAF Ranchi for more role-specific training, the Special Low Attack Instruction School (SLAIS). However, they needed to complete some bombing and gunnery practice in the Mosquito first, and aircraft serviceability and scarcity of tyres was hindering their progress. The armourers were complaining about the lack of bomb trolleys and loading hoists. They also needed a mobile crane to lift the Mosquitos into a flying position to reharmonise their guns to focussed them on the 'kill zone'. Even with these in place, the squadron sometimes only had a couple of serviceable aircraft, so progress was slow. In fact, without a proper shipment of tyres, the squadron couldn't fly to Ranchi!

Even with the restricted flying programme, accidents occurred. During an air test of HP914 on 16 August 1944, Pete Ewing experienced intermittent engine problems and then, on landing, brake fade. This resulted in an uncontrollable swing during which the undercarriage collapsed. The aircraft was 'somewhat the worse for wear' but neither Pete nor his navigator, Flight Sergeant Robert 'Pinkie' Pinkerton, were hurt.

It had been a frustrating month, with flying training limited by spares, serviceability and weather. Finally, a shipment of Mosquito tyres arrived! On 27 August, 45 Squadron flew to RAF Ranchi to complete their delayed SLAIS course. Ranchi was a garrison town in Bihar, about 180 miles west of Calcutta and, although the facilities were somewhat better than Dalbhumgarh, they were by no means comfortable, especially for the other ranks.

In London, on 27 August, the Accident Investigation Branch held another review meeting into structural failures in the Mosquito. The minutes of their meeting, classified as Secret, state that they had reviewed ten structural failures which occurred between April and June 1944. Although it wasn't included in their review, they referred to Harley Stumm's accident in India, demonstrating that the information they had received was flawed in at least a couple of important aspects:

> *'In addition to the accidents which occurred in this country,*
> *a few details are available concerning a similar occurrence*
> *in India. The aircraft, No. H.P.939, which was probably a*

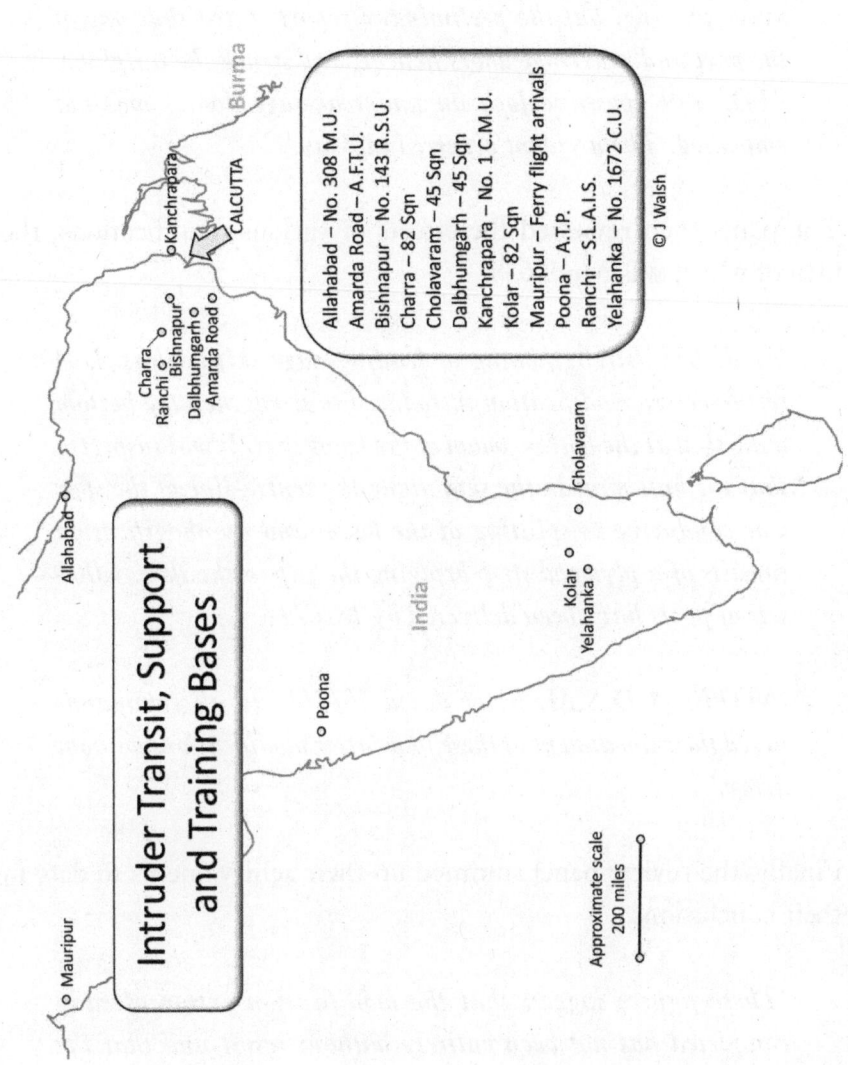

Intruder Transit, Support and Training Bases

Mauripur o

Allahabad o

Poona o

Charra o
Ranchi o
Bishnapur o
Dalbhumgarh o
Amarda Road o

Kanchrapara o
CALCUTTA

Burma

India

Kolar o
Yelahanka o

Cholavaram o

Allahabad – No. 308 M.U.
Amarda Road – A.F.T.U.
Bishnapur – No. 143 R.S.U.
Charra – 82 Sqn
Cholavaram – 45 Sqn
Dalbhumgarh – 45 Sqn
Kanchrapara – No. 1 C.M.U.
Kolar – 82 Sqn
Mauripur – Ferry flight arrivals
Poona – A.T.P.
Ranchi – S.L.A.I.S.
Yelahanka – No. 1672 C.U.

© J Walsh

Approximate scale
200 miles

P.R. Mk. IX or a P.R. Mk. XVI, broke up during a rapid recovery from a dive after the pilot had carried out an aerobatic manoeuvre at a low altitude. The accident was attributed to over-stressing, but the preliminary report stated that one of the port undercarriage doors flew off and struck the tailplane. Mod. 499 (positive lock on undercarriage doors) was not embodied. The accident occurred in May.'

The panel then reviewed the effects of various modifications, the fifth of which was Mod. 638:

'Mod. 638 (strengthening of leading-edge skin) Class 2. A retrospective modification introduced to strengthen the bottom wing skin at the bottom boom of the front spar. It was suspected that the butt joint in the skin along the centre-line of the spar was conducive to splitting of the boom and the modification consists of a plywood strip bridging the gap in the skin. 1,000 sets of parts have been delivered by 18/6/44.

'NOTE: A D.S.M. letter dated 15/7/44 to all commands urged the embodiment of these four latter modifications without delay.'

Finally, the review panel summed up their achievements to date in their conclusions:

'These figures suggest that the modification action already completed has not been entirely without result and that the continuance of structural failures at a rate that has shown little or no improvement in the last year may be due in no small measure to the increase in all-up weight of the Mosquito, to the tendency in C.G. positions to move back in most of the current marks and to low stick forces per "g".'[84]

The much delayed SLAIS course for 45 Squadron, the final part of their work up to operational status, started on 29 August 1944.

Now based in Kolar, 82 Squadron was not experiencing the same serviceability issues as 45, even though they also suffered from tyre shortages. In fact, they flew 503 hours in Mosquitos during August. Group Captain A.E. Whiteley, CO of No. 168 Wing, visited to monitor progress since it was planned that the squadron would come under his command. During his stay he also took a short conversion course on the Mosquito. At the end of the month Bill Hudson reported, 'The first three weeks of Mosquito flying was carried out in August. Enthusiasm was high, serviceability was good and progress better than expected. It augured well for the time when the squadron will be operational on Mosquitos in the near future – we hope.'[85]

Squadron	Mosquito Intruder Operations		Aircrew Losses Operations		Aircrew Losses Training/Other	
	Apr – Aug 44	Total	Apr – Aug 44	Total	Apr – Aug 44	Total
No. 27 Sqn	0	45	0	2	0	0
No. 45 Sqn	0	0	0	0	1	1
No. 82 Sqn	0	0	0	0	0	0
Other Units	0	0	0	0	1	7
Total	0	45	0	2	2	8

Chapter 8

Declared Operational

September 1944

*'Both the fighter and bomber version of this fine British aircraft
are now operating over the Eastern jungles, harassing the Jap
land forces as well as giving battle to Jap aircraft.'*
The Sphere, *4 March 1944*

Finally, 45 Squadron's SLAIS course at Ranchi had started.
Now that 231 Group knew when the course should finish, they
could plan for 45's operational deployment. Johnny Walker
knew that he would soon receive the Movement Order. There was
also pressure because 82 Squadron were working up on the Mosquito
in Kolar and were expected at Ranchi by the end of the month.

The course required all the crews to complete a series of exercises,
practising their skills at low-level. They would cover low-level
reconnaissance, day and night attacks and different section attacks.
Unfortunately, 45 Squadron's progress continued to be hindered
by poor aircraft availability, unlike 82, which was recording good
serviceability with its Mosquitos.

On 9 September, 82's CO, Bill Hudson, flew to Ranchi to make
arrangements for his squadron's course at the end of the month.
His departure did not go to plan! 'The port engine failed near the
end of my take-off run. I aborted and was careering across the
airfield out of control when a crowd of Indian labourers loomed up
dead ahead. I yanked up the undercarriage and we screamed to a

sudden stop in a cloud of dust only yards short of where the Indians were working on a new runway. Only the all–embracing Sutton Harness snug safety belts had saved me from being flung through the windscreen. Then, sitting there thankful for yet another life, I shivered with the strangest feeling. Who put me into my harness? I never wore one.'[86]

That evening 45 Squadron started with their night gunnery and bombing exercises. Whilst taking off, Flight Lieutenant Ron Goodwin could not control the swing in LR304. It careered across the airfield, its undercarriage collapsed and it clipped the wingtip of Bill Hudson's damaged Mosquito, still awaiting recovery.

Just a couple of days later, on 11 September, Flight Lieutenant John Reeves, an experienced RNZAF pilot, with navigator Flying Officer Leonard Prout, lost control of his Mosquito, HP915, during evasive action on Random Range. Failing to pull out of a low attack, the aircraft dived straight into the ground and both airmen were killed. It was a significant blow to morale in the tightly knit squadron aircrew. The two funerals were quickly held and the work up to operational status continued uninterrupted.

Finally, on 13 September, Johnny Walker received the order he had been waiting for!

SECRET
Movement Order No.4/44 Dated 13 September 1944
Intention: To move No. 45 Squadron from RAF Station Ranchi to RAF Station Kumbhirgram. Authority H.Q., No.231 Group Org. Instruction No.21 dated 7/9/44 and H.Q., AC3SEA letter ORG.4/3081 dated 3/9/44.[87]

At last, even though they were not fully prepared and had been frustrated by poor serviccability in their Mosquitos, 45 Squadron were to move forward to the front line and start operations. Johnny

Walker arranged for Jock Torrance to depart two days later for RAF Kumbhirgram, leading the advance party.

That same day, one of 82 Squadron's Mosquitos, HP886, 'crashed unaccountably' whilst carrying out high 'g' quarter turns and attacks on another aircraft at a height of about 5,000ft during training near Mysore.[88] Flying Officer William Clarke 'Tuffy' Tufnell RAAF and Flight Sergeant Victor Abel were both killed. Witnesses said that Tuffy's aircraft disappeared underneath the target aircraft, possibly being thrown upside down. Not surprisingly, because of some similarity to Wing Commander Stumm's unusual crash on 45 Squadron, there were soon suspicions within the squadrons that this could be another case of 'wood shrinkage' causing the Mosquito's airframe to fail.

At Ranchi, 45's SLAIS course was continuing at pace. On 17 September, Bill Taylor, now teamed with navigator Nank Nankervis, landed extremely heavily in his Mosquito, bending the propellers. The aircraft needed checking and repairing. Bill was told to prepare for an enquiry.

The next day, after an arduous four-day journey, Jock and the advance party arrived at Kumbhirgram and started making preparations for 45's arrival. Some of the party already knew the airfield because the squadron had been based there the previous year, with their Vengeances. It was an all-weather airfield on a plain near Silchar and surrounded by jungle. The Manipur Hills to the east and south rose as high as 9,000ft. 'These formidable mountains stretched one hundred and twenty miles eastwards to the upper Burmese lowlands and the mighty Chindwin River.'[89] Pilot Officer Max Levey, with Flying Officer 'Joe' Mears, landed the first 45 Squadron Mosquito at Kumbhirgram that same day. Bill Taylor and Nank Nankervis arrived a little later in the squadron's Harvard, having visited Comilla to make arrangements for the provision of the motor transport the squadron would need.

With the other aircrews completing their course at Ranchi, they prepared to fly the Mossies to their new base. Meanwhile, the groundcrew started packing up all the equipment required to support the 200 or so squadron personnel, as well as its aircraft. Some lucky groundcrew were flown to Kumbhirgram by Dakota when the majority of the squadron's Mosquitos were flown to their new base on 22 September. Having cleaned up the accommodation at Ranchi for the next arrivals, the rear party set off the next day for the railway station at Barkakana with ninety-three cases of equipment and stores in thirty army trucks. There they loaded everything onto a train for the slow journey to the Brahmaputra River, where they unloaded everything and re-loaded it onto the ferry. Once across, they loaded everything onto another train to take them to the railhead at Silchar, finally arriving at 0200hrs on 29 September. The whole journey had been painfully slow and had taken six days, one day longer than planned.

No. 45 Squadron was to form the core of 908 Wing, a long-range striking force as part of the now renumbered 221 Group, which was commanded by Air Vice-Marshal S.F. 'Stanley' Vincent DFC AFC, a veteran of both the First World War and the Battle of Britain. Vincent had been appointed AOC on 17 February 1944 and his tactical use of its squadrons had played a significant part in the defeat of the 15th, 31st and 33rd Divisions of the Japanese Fifteenth Army at Kohima and Imphal. On 26 September, Johnny Walker flew to Imphal to confer with his new AOC, returning later that day.

Even though they were still awaiting most of their equipment and some of the personnel, the next day Johnny Walker and 'A' Flight Commander Squadron Leader Norman Bourke flew to Imphal to take two army officers on an operational recce over north Burma. Unfortunately, the army officers did not turn up, so both crews returned to base that evening.

The following day, 28 September, Norman, in HP941, and Joe Cartledge, in HP884, returned to Imphal. This time the army officers were waiting to sit in the navigators' seats. The pilots were briefed to fly 'offensive recces', taking off at 1515hrs and headed for the Shwebo area before they split up. Norman recce'd the railway line from 50ft towards Ye-U, attacking a rail-canal bridge with two 500lb eleven-second delay bombs. The bombs fell in the water five yards short and 'no damage was observed.' At Tindeinyan, he attacked some rolling stock with cannon from 100ft, saw hits but no damage was recorded. At Chantha, Norman made another attack on rolling stock, with similar results. Meanwhile, Joe recce'd the line from Tangon towards Shwebo. At Zigon he spotted six rolling stock, which he attacked with short bursts of cannon from 50ft scoring hits. Again, no damage was recorded. Norman and Joe, with their army passengers, landed back at Imphal at 1725hrs. 'Recce of special area was completed successfully at heights 2000 – 50 feet.' They had completed 45 Squadron's first ops over Burma.

That same day, 82 Squadron flew to Ranchi to start their SLAIS course.

On 29 September, with 45 Squadron's rear party and equipment at Silchar, where it needed to be unloaded, the CO tasked all hands to help. 'Rain was falling heavily and continued to do so for several hours, but unloading commenced immediately on arrival, all personnel setting to with determination to get the job done as rapidly as possible. Drivers worked unceasingly, as did everyone else concerned, and by 1100hrs unloading of the train was completed. By 1300hrs the last lorry was unloaded at the camp and the rest of the day was spent settling in our new domestic site. Our Messes and Cook-houses commenced operating from midday.'[90]

The next day, with the squadron settling into its new base and no flying, the CO presided over the inquiry into Bill Taylor's heavy landing at Ranchi. Bill received a Red Endorsement in his logbook.

ENDORSEMENT
AUS420480 WO Taylor was pilot of a Mosquito aircraft on 17 September 1944 on authorised flight. On attempting to land the aircraft struck the runway, semi-stalled, very heavily with nose down. The Oleo legs compressed to maximum and the propeller tips scraped along the runway. Aircraft finally came to rest on three points without further damage. Endorsement carried out as instructed in 20/G/C.2004/15/P.1 dated 30/9/44. CARELESSNESS.

R.J. Walker W/CMR O.C. 45 SQN[91]

At the end of the month, although 45 Squadron was operational, it still did not have its full complement of aircraft. Johnny Walker made his frustration clear with his comment in the Operations Record Book. 'Two replacement aircraft arrived today both fitted with Merlin 23 engines and in poor condition, but they were retained because we need machines and replacements are taking about two weeks to reach us after demand. It is expected that they shall be operationally fit in about three days.'[92]

Squadron	Mosquito Intruder Operations		Aircrew Losses Operations		Aircrew Losses Training/Other	
	Month	Total	Month	Total	Month	Total
No. 27 Sqn	0	45	0	2	0	0
No. 45 Sqn	2	2	0	0	2	3
No. 82 Sqn	0	0	0	0	2	2
Other Units	0	0	0	0	0	7
Total	2	47	0	2	4	12

Chapter 9

First Kill

October 1944

'They have yet to find a way of catching it, or to devise a warning system that works fast enough to cope with a fighter-bomber that comes in at tree-top level doing more than 400 m.p.h.'
Associated Press, *7 February 1944*

Whilst 82 Squadron concentrated on progressing through their course at Ranchi, much of which they felt was repeating what they had done in Kolar, 45 Squadron changed to full operational status at Kumbhirgram.

On 1 October, 45 Squadron despatched ten Mosquitos in three different strike operations – a pair and a six-ship operation in the morning and another pair in the late afternoon. The next day, a pair were despatched for a night-time offensive recce of the Japanese airfield at Heho in the early hours, followed by another aircraft to Heho and Aungban airfields before dawn, with a fourth Mossie to two other Japanese airfields. All looked for opportunity targets on the railways and roads on their return.

On 3 October, only two aircraft were despatched, with Flight Lieutenant Proctor and Sergeant Bargh taking off thirty minutes before Flying Officers Arthur Huon and Harry Cargill. The weather was not good, with total cloud cover over Meiktila and Kangdaung airfields. Arthur and Harry returned, unable to locate either airfield. Proctor and Bargh in HP936 failed to return from their sortie, having been last seen by Arthur and Harry at 1639hrs heading 300° at about

50ft. Their colleagues hoped that they had landed safely somewhere and would turn up.

The next day was a stand-down from operations, so the only flights were two cross-countries and three air tests, one of which was completed by 'A' Flight Commander, Norman Bourke. During the air test, he was alarmed to see the wing leading edge of his Mosquito starting to buckle as he recovered from a dive. Not surprisingly, he completed a rapid emergency landing before anything catastrophic happened. The aircraft was allotted to No. 143 R.S.U. at Bishnapur for investigation and repair.

The next flying was on 6 October, when Flying Officers Neil and Hallett were despatched on an op to Heho airfield. They were meant to be accompanied by Flight Sergeants Goodrich and Nessim, but the weather closed in just after their take off, so they went alone. When they arrived at Heho, a Japanese 'Dinah' was taxying out to the runway. After a short burst with cannon, the Dinah exploded and the squadron recorded its first 'kill'. On their return to base, Neil and Hallett scanned for signs of HP936. Nothing was seen. Proctor and Bargh would have to be declared as 'Missing believed killed'.

Four Mosquitos were despatched on offensive recces the next morning and two more in the afternoon. That same day, Squadron Leader Don Edwards flew to Chiringa where he suffered a vulture strike during landing. The impact carried away the starboard undercarriage doors which holed the fuselage, almost causing a serious accident. Luckily the aircraft was sufficiently serviceable for Don to fly it back to base where the damage was repaired. On 8 October they had a rest day due to bad weather. The following day they launched four sorties. The squadron was starting to get into the operational routine.

On 10 October, 45 Squadron sent eight Mosquitos on operations, quite uneventful, apart from one suffered an engine failure and had to return and complete a single engine landing.

That same day, HX821, a 45 Squadron Mosquito FB VI, which had been sent to 143 R.S.U. at Bishnapur for repair, unexplainably broke up in mid-air during an air test. Both crewmen were killed; 21-year-old Canadian pilot Flight Lieutenant Dick Campbell and 28-year-old Flight Lieutenant Douglas William Rimell, 143 R.S.U.'s Chief Technical Officer.[93] Flight Sergeant Alf Pridmore, Dick's navigator, who should have been on the flight, explained, 'Dick was asked to test a Mossie whose exhaust shrouds had been burnt out leaving no shield to the exhaust flames. Dick did not want to fly this, anticipating a fire risk, but the engineering officer wanted to fly in a Mossie and persuaded Dick it was safe and to let him go in my place. I was watching from the ground and saw the wing break off at about 8,000ft and spin into the wild scrub away from the airfield. Subsequent investigation revealed blood and feathers at the point of impact where a kite hawk (a large vulture-like bird) had broken the plywood skin causing the main spar to separate at the joint.'[94] [HX821 was one of the first FB VIs delivered to India and may have been involved in one or both previous incidents, on 24 June when Don Edwards hit a kite hawk and on 4 October when Norman Bourke noticed the leading edge starting to buckle.]

On 11 October, 45 Squadron continued to target Japanese airfields and degrade lines of communication, with six Mosquitos flying sorties. Johnny Walker was forced to return halfway through his sortie with an oil leak. Max Levey, with Joe Mears, who had been flying as the Boss's wingman, became lost. Eventually they realised, due to the sun's position, that their compass was indicating 90° off true, showing 330° when their actual heading was about 240°. They finally landed safely at Chiringa.

The next day, Flight Lieutenant Victor 'Duke' Duclos and his navigator, Flying Officer Keith Botterill, were tasked as part of a Mossie pair with an early morning offensive recce on Kin-U railway to the Japanese airfield at Meiktila. At 0735hrs, having completed

HX821 Airframe Failure
143 R.S.U., Bishnapur - 10 October 1944

© G Pridmore

two strafing runs in HP833 across the airfield at 30ft, on the third run, strafing down the runway, their aircraft was hit on the port side by .50 calibre machine gun fire and Keith was badly wounded. Warrant Officers Wilcock and Maddock in the other aircraft, HP942, immediately took the lead, guiding Duke in his damaged aircraft towards Tulihal, the closest RAF base, near Imphal. Keith succumbed to his wounds on the way. He was left behind for burial at Tulihal and the two aircraft arrived back at Kumbhirgram at 1255hrs.

The next morning, 13 October, Johnny Walker, Duke Duclos, Don Edwards and Eric Sandifer flew to Imphal to pay their respects and represent the squadron at Keith's funeral.

Whilst 45 Squadron were becoming accustomed to their operational role, No. 47 Squadron, which had been flying Beaufighters, became the third squadron to start conversion to intruder Mosquitos. Early in the month, some lucky aircrew flew its fourteen serviceable Beaufighters from their base at Cholavaram to No. 1672 Conversion Unit at Yelahanka, although most of the squadron 'took days making the journey by train.'[95]

The CO of 47 Squadron was 24-year-old Wing Commander William 'Billy' David Loraine Filson-Young, the son of noted journalist, war correspondent, author, essayist and programme advisor to the BBC, Alexander Filson Young. His younger brother, Richard, had also been an RAF pilot but was killed in 1942. Billy was awarded his first DFC in January 1944, when serving as a squadron leader flying Beaufighters with No. 254 Squadron. The bar to his DFC was awarded just a few months later, with the following citation.

'In February 1944, this officer led the squadron in an attack on a medium sized ship which was heavily escorted. In spite of heavy anti-aircraft fire and some fighter opposition the attack was pressed home with great determination and hits were obtained which caused the destruction of the vessel. In this action, Wing Commander Filson-Young displayed skilful and inspiring leadership and played a good part in the success obtained. He has participated in numerous attacks on enemy shipping and his fine work has always been evident.'

Billy was both respected and liked by the people who reported to him.

The conversion training of the experienced Beaufighter crews started immediately, with the format similar to that experienced a year earlier by 27 Squadron. The characteristics of the Merlin-engined Mosquito FB VI were explained to pilots by reference to the Pilots Notes and by demonstration in the air, with the pilot under instruction occupying the navigator's seat. After a couple of short demonstration flights, the pilots went 'solo' with their navigators beside them. It was planned as a general handling flight, to provide the crew with the initial feel of flying the Mossie. However, sometimes it didn't go as expected, as Flight Lieutenant Robert 'Bob' Willis explained:

'Taxying out to the end of the runway, lining up, applying the brakes and then giving the engines a final boost to clear the spark plugs was just routine. The propellor constant speed units were in fully fine pitch, outer fuel tanks engaged, and with 15° flap and a little forward trim we were ready to go. Push the throttle forward, check any swing to port and down the runway you go to reach the take-off speed of 125mph. Much to our surprise the starboard engine failed just as we were lifting off the ground. There was a large crack with the starboard propellor milling around and failing to feather. The starboard engine was still functioning but not driving the propellor. There was no time to speculate. We just had to keep airborne. We just scraped over the airfield buildings ahead. Tommy [Thompson] called down the intercom with some anxiety, "Bob, for God's sake, hold it!" With the wheels and flaps still down I engaged maximum power on the port engine the moment the starboard engine failed. I had my left leg locked stiff on the rudder bar to contain the torque created. Despite activating the feathering button again, the starboard propellor continued to rotate causing extra drag. Climbing slowly I was able to raise the wheels and flaps, and by making a very wide circuit, reach sufficient height to effect a single engine landing. The landing was OK, but it was immediately obvious that the brakes were faulty. As the aircraft ran off the end of the runway a hedge and then the main Yelahanka-to-Bangalore road loomed ahead. Without effective brakes, I swung the aircraft round in a ground loop to halt further progress. The undercarriage collapsed. As the aircraft, now partly through the hedge and over the road, swung round, a propellor caught a male Indian civilian riding in the back of a truck as it passed the airfield. Switching off the ignition, I scrambled out of the cockpit as fast as possible. I could hear the cries of the injured Indian. One of his arms appeared to be severed. There was much blood as we applied a makeshift tourniquet torn from his cotton shirt. To our relief, he was quickly in the care of a British army ambulance team, part of a military convoy travelling on the road at the same time. At the best of times single engine landings are tricky – this is more so when you have never flown the type of aircraft before.'[96]

Bob knew that he and Tommy had been very lucky. Due to its high power-to-weight ratio and wing loading, the Mosquito demanded respect, especially on take-off and landing. To ensure rudder effectiveness with an engine feathered and the other on full power, the aircraft needed to be flying at 170mph. This resulted in a substantial 'no-man's land' between the speed at take-off and this 'safety speed', during which an engine failure was often fatal. Counter-intuitively, below 170mph the pilot had to reduce power on the good engine to prevent the Mosquito from rolling. 'As cynics have said, the only reason to have two engines on a piston-twin is so the good one can take you to the scene of the accident.'[97]

A Board of Inquiry was convened on 16 October 1944 and Bob was exonerated. The brakes were faulty. The constant speed unit and drive shaft to the starboard Merlin had failed on take-off, also making it impossible to feather the propeller and reduce drag.

At the end of the course, 47 Squadron flew their aircraft up to Ranchi. Frank Salt, a sergeant fitter, recalled, 'The remainder of the squadron travelled by troop train which took two weeks for the journey.'

On 14 October only four 45 Squadron Mosquitos were sent on offensive recces since the groundcrew and engineers were preparing for a significant detachment the next day. Again, only four Mosquitos flew operations the next day because eight Mosquitos, led by CO

Johnny Walker, detached to Chiringa in preparation for a large-scale operation against Japanese airfields near Rangoon – Operation Love. Bill Taylor joined them with the squadron's Harvard, in case spares were needed quickly. The groundcrews were flow to Chiringa in Dakotas and, later in the day, the Station Commander, Group Captain Whiteley, also joined them in a Mosquito.

On 16 October, two of the remaining aircraft at Kumbhirgram were tasked with an offensive recce which was aborted due to poor weather. Later in the day, with the weather improving, 'A' Flight Commander Norman Bourke, with Keith Dumas navigating, took off in HP941, with the second aircraft was flown by Arthur Huon with McFadzean navigating. With the sortie almost finished, Norman attacked a target near the village of Kadozeik from which he pulled up to about 400ft, then the aircraft was seen to roll 'to starboard past the vertical and then rolled to port, afterwards losing height, and angle of dive increasing as the aircraft approached the ground. It was not actually seen to crash as trees obscured the view.' Arthur Huon circled the area twice but couldn't see any wreckage. They were convinced that neither of the crew could have survived. 'There seemed to be no attempt to control or right the aircraft and the impression was gained that the pilot had been hit.' However, they didn't see any ground fire so the crash was something of a mystery. They conjectured that a control cable had possibly failed, resulting in loss of control. Norman and Keith were posted as 'Missing believed killed'.

At Kumbhirgram, they had a 24-hour stand-down, during which Duke Duclos assumed command of 'A' Flight.

At Chiringa, 45 Squadron's Mosquitos joined forces with Thunderbolts from 146 and 261 Squadrons for Operation Love. At 0736hrs the first aircraft took off to attack the Japanese airfield at Zayatkwin, near Rangoon, with all the aircraft reaching it at 0930hrs. The Mosquitos strafed it, expending 1,710 20mm cannon rounds and 2,960 .303 rounds. They claimed a Dinah as damaged, as well as the tower, a gun position and a 3-ton truck. On their return they attacked and damaged a factory, a ferry, a sampan and a water tower. During the attack on the water tower, debris and dust was thrown into the air, with a piece of brick lodging in the starboard engine of Johnny Walker's Mosquito. After a couple of minutes, the engine failed and the CO was forced to fly back on one engine, completing a single engine landing on arrival back at Chiringa. After a successful operation, all the Mosquitos and the Harvard were flown back to base except for the CO's. Jock Torrence and Ted Rainbow remained at Chiringa for the Boss's aircraft to be repaired.

As the month progressed, poor weather started causing some delays for 82 Squadron at Ranchi. On 20 October, Flying Officer Babe Wambeek, with his navigator Warrant Officer Brian Mooney, were detailed to practice shallow dive bombing over the range. 'Fortunately, for my navigator and me, the exercise had to be postponed until the following morning because of rain and cloud.[98] Overnight my own aircraft 'P Peter' had become serviceable so I changed over and another crew, Flying Officer Al Parker RNZAF, and his navigator, Flying Officer Maurice D. Randall RAF, were detailed to take the one we had been due to fly. After an early breakfast the four of us went down to the flights on the first transport. We never saw them again. While waiting our turn on the bombing range, a telephone message came through from the range officer; Al and Maurice had 'gone in'. Apparently one wing had disintegrated during the first bombing run and the aircraft rolled over and dived into the ground in front of him.'[99] Ralph Whitworth, an 82 Squadron rigger, added that Al Parker had twice reported an oil pressure fault with the aircraft, but the fitters couldn't find a problem. 'The CO came down and flew the plane and could not find anything wrong. He told Al to get airborne – "That's an order." Al took-off and on the way to the range the wing came off, the aircraft crashed and burned with both

Al and his navigator being killed. The wing that had fallen off did not burn and was brought back to us.'[100]

Arthur Maude, Freddy Snell's navigator, continued, 'Freddy and I were airborne at the time and were waiting for our turn on the range when the Range Control Officer broadcast the information about the incident. Freddy immediately instructed all squadron aircraft to return to base. After landing one of the pilots, Flying Officer Tullett, was walking away from his aircraft when the groundcrew called him back. The leading-edge skin had peeled back leaving a gap. Our engineering officer, after looking at the aircraft, had the skin cut back to the main spar where [a] gap between the main spar and scarf joint was revealed.'[101]

The squadron continued with its investigation. Its record of Al Parker's and Maurice Randall's crash stated that, 'in the course of a normal run up and shallow dive on to the target, half of the starboard wing, outboard of the engine nacelle, crumpled up and disintegrated: the aircraft then rolled to the right, with further disintegration of the wing and crashed into the ground ahead of the target, where it burst into flames. The crew were, of course, killed instantly.'[102]

At the same time, the squadron ensured that their dead colleagues were treated with respect, as Babe Wambeek explained, 'The charred remains of Al and [Maurice] had been placed into two coffins and that evening I found myself with eleven other pilots and navigators, acting as pallbearers again. As we lowered the coffins into the two freshly dug graves each of us was thinking "There but for the Grace of God go I."'[103]

That same day, two of 45 Squadron's Mosquitos were despatched at 0825hrs on an offensive recce but, with 10/10ths cloud from ground to 5,500ft only ninety-five miles east-south-east of base, they aborted. 'B' Flight Commander Don Edwards was flying HP921 OB.O, assisted by his usual navigator, Eric Sandifer, with Flying Officers Neill and Hallett in HJ291. 'Both aircraft returned and were overhead Base at 0923hrs, 320 IAS, 2,500ft, losing height. Everything was quite normal and aircraft HP921 gave the usual order to 'break'. HJ291 'broke' to starboard and within a few seconds saw what was first thought to be a bird falling beneath aircraft HP921. Then larger objects, obviously pieces of aircraft, were seen, followed by the bulk of aircraft HP921 which went down in a spin and crashed 650 yards W.S.W. of middle of the runway. A ground observer states port engine omitting black smoke just prior to accident, followed by breaking away of port mainplane. As far as known, no flames were emitted from the aircraft in the air, but it burst into flames on impact.'[104] Neither of the crew survived. Don's and Eric's bodies were removed from the burnt wreckage in the jungle alongside the strip. They were buried in the afternoon at Silchar.

Johnny Walker wrote, 'This came as another saddening blow to the squadron, particularly as it now meant the loss of two very capable Flight Commanders and their crews.'[105] Duke Dulcos was appointed 'A' Flight Commander and Jock Torrance was given command of 'B' Flight.

The squadron was keen to continue but an investigation was needed. Initially it was thought that it could have hit a flock of kite hawks, but any bird strike should not have resulted in such a catastrophic airframe failure. A.C.S.E.A., particularly their engineering staff, were becoming concerned about the robustness of the Mosquitos.

With two seemingly similar failures on the same day, both the RAF and de Havilland acted with urgency. The next day, as the Mosquitos landed from their operations and training flights, they were temporarily grounded pending inspection. Mr Myers, de Havilland's representative in India, and Squadron Leader Charles J. Chabot, from Base Air Forces South–East Asia, were tasked with investigating the Mosquito crashes at Bishnapur, Ranchi and Kumbhirgram. The engineering officers from both 45 and 82 Squadrons already had their suspicions and were inspecting the aircraft before releasing them for flying. On Sunday, 22 October,

Chabot arrived in his Spitfire at Ranchi to inspect the wreckage of Al's aircraft.[106] He found that Al's airframe had a defective mainplane and, on further inspection, found two others with similar problems. Bill Hudson, 82 Squadron's CO, noted, 'Their findings are still the subject of consideration, but the accident has definitely been attributed to faulty manufacture, and all Mosquito aircraft were grounded pending special inspections.'[107]

After just over three weeks of operational flying, with seven deaths, 45 Squadron had already lost one in six of its establishment of forty-two aircrew. CO Johnny Walker put out an urgent request for another operational Mosquito crew to be posted to his squadron. Having completed their Ranchi programme the previous day, as an operationally experienced Mosquito intruder crew, Benny Walsh and Ossie Orsborn of 82 Squadron were told on 23 October that they were to be detached the next day to 45 Squadron. Luckily, they were still able to attend the much-awaited Sergeants' Mess Dance that evening. The mess members had invited ladies from various institutions in Ranchi to a dance and social evening. They had also invited their officer colleagues. Music was provided by Ranchi's one and only dance band and the mess laid on an excellent buffet and bar. 'The ladies and their chaperones showed considerable enthusiasm for dancing and other delights prepared most painstakingly by the S.N.C.O.s.'[108]

That same day, Mr Myers had met with Squadron Leader Chabot, completed some further investigations and reported their initial conclusions. 'Due to aircraft being left standing for long periods exposed to the weather in the MUs and aircraft parks, the extreme heat has caused the glue to crack and the upper surfaces (of the wings) to lift from the spars.'[109] At the end of their ferry flights to India, the Mosquitos had been stored in the open at Allahabad and Nagpur, where temperatures reached over 40°C in the shade. Their view was that casein glue had not taken kindly to this. All Mosquitos in India now had to be inspected and the future of the aircraft hung in the balance. The task was tackled with urgency, because the grounding immediately impacted 45 Squadron's Mosquitos planned close air support for the Fourteenth Army.

When de Havilland started building the Mosquitos in volume for the European theatre, they had used a traditional milk-based casein wood glue. However, in the spring of 1943, when they realised that this would not fare well in the hot and humid climates of the Far East,[110] they started to introduce a two–part urea–formaldehyde glue to the manufacturing process. The urea was applied to one wood surface, the formaldehyde catalyst to the other and gentle pressure applied. This process made a waterproof bond stronger than the wood itself. Unfortunately, this required a change in manufacturing processes and most of the FB VI Mosquitos in India at this time had been built using the casein glue. It was also becoming clear that the problem was exacerbated by manufacturing quality issues. Whichever glue was used, the quality of the main spar joints sometimes left a lot to be desired. There wasn't time to bring replacement aircraft from Britain, so they had to find a way of keeping as many as possible in operational service. Having discovered this issue, all Mossies were now suspect.

This couldn't have happened at a worse time, because the Mosquito intruder squadrons had a limited window for the offensive against the Japanese. The main campaign period started in late October, since the weather was usually good with less cloud. From March it became increasingly hot and, in the weeks before the arrival of the monsoon, the visibility was often reduced to a thick haze. When the monsoon season started in May, it brought appalling flying conditions for three to four months, with towering cumulonimbus cloud, torrential rains and great turbulence.[111]

By Wednesday, 26 October, the situation had become much clearer. Only eight of 45 Squadron's Mosquitos were assessed as being fit for ops and over the next few days ten 'unserviceable' aircraft were flown to 143 R.S.U.[112] The engineers at Bishnapur, under guidance from de Havilland, were tasked with modifying and strengthening the aircraft.

Linking the various investigations together, the engineers identified what they believed to be the underlying cause of 'wood shrinkage'. The aircrews were then instructed to fly all Mosquitos which had been in the Command for three months, or just one month if they had come from the Middle East, to Kanchrapara for inspection.

Also on 26 October, No. 110 (Hyderabad) Squadron arrived at No. 1672 Conversion Unit at Yelahanka to start their transition to the Mosquito.[113] No. 110 Squadron's CO was Wing Commander Arthur 'Soapy' Saunders. He was an experienced intruder pilot, having commanded 418 (RCAF) Squadron two years previously, when it flew intruder missions in Douglas Boston IIIs from RAF Bradwell Bay, Essex. Like 82 Squadron, 110 had been previously flying the Vultee Vengeance. Their newly arrived Mosquitos were now temporarily grounded, pending inspection.

No. 47 Squadron, with their Mosquitos grounded and still waiting for their groundcrew to arrive at Ranchi, decided to revert to Beaufighters so that they could complete their training at the Special Low Attack Instruction School.

It was clear to everyone that the introduction of the Mosquito FB VI was not going smoothly. Eleven Mosquito aircrew had died during October, but at least 45 Squadron had completed 108 ops.

Squadron	Mosquito Intruder Operations		Aircrew Losses Operations		Aircrew Losses Training/Other	
	Month	Total	Month	Total	Month	Total
No. 45 Sqn	108	110	7	7	0	3
No. 27 Sqn	0	45	0	2	0	0
No. 82 Sqn	0	0	0	0	2	2
Other Units	0	0	0	0	2	9
Total	108	155	7	9	4	14

Chapter 10

Joint Investigation

November 1944

'Striking far beyond the normal area covered by Beaufighters, where road and rail traffic by day is almost at a standstill and where travel by water is fraught with danger to the enemy, the Mosquitos have been presented with tempting targets.'
Associated Press, *February 1944*

The Allied army still forged ahead with its offensive against the Japanese, even though the Mosquitos were temporarily restricted to limited support. On 2 November they had moved into the appropriately named Vital Corner and on 9 November Fort White was regained.

The investigation into the problems with the Mosquito on the frontline at RAF Kumbhirgram continued at pace. Cyril Norridge, 45 Squadron Fitter, recalled 'severe shrinkage in joints in the wood. Main spar joints had, in several cases, opened up to one eighth of an inch and undercarriage attachments were pulling loose from their anchorages. There was also evidence of fracture of metal attachments thought to be due to excessive play.'[114]

On initial inspection of 82's Mosquitos, eight were detached to 1 CMU at Kanchrapara, north of Calcutta, for further inspection of the mainplanes, later to be joined by a ninth aircraft. By 6 November, all fifteen FB VIs delivered to 110 Squadron in Yelahanka for their conversion to the Mosquito had been inspected and grounded. Without any aircraft to fly, Wing Commander Soapy Saunders and his flight commanders even started contemplating returning to the Vultee Vengeance.[115]

On 7 November, Jock Torrence's widely expected promotion to squadron leader was announced. No. 45 Squadron continued with a limited operational programme but, since modified and strengthened aircraft only trickled in during early November, its effectiveness was substantially degraded. Even so, by 8 November the squadron had already completed a total of twenty-seven operational sorties.

On 9 November, 45 Squadron were tasked with a seven-aircraft dawn raid on Meiktila airfield, led by Jock Torrence. Each Mossie was armed with four 500lb eleven-second delay bombs and 'full ammo cans.' The group were meant to rendezvous at Mount Popa at 0620hrs for the attack but, although Jock was there at the appointed time, the other aircraft did not meet up, due to weather and radio jamming by the Japanese.[116] One aircraft went for its secondary target and the others, arriving late, made their attacks separately.

Cliff Emeny and Johnny Yanota were flying their usual aircraft, which they nicknamed 'Zombie 3', and Nick Nicholls, with Bob Barclay navigating, flying as their wingman. Johnny recalled the flight, his seventeenth op, 'We flew a course to the Sittang Loop and then down the Irrawaddy River to Pakokku, Burma. From there, we set course for Mount Popa, roughly thirty miles to the south-east of Pakokku, where we expected to meet up with five other aircraft. Visibility was down to zero because of a storm, so we returned to the river. Joining two other Mosquitos there, we journeyed south around the storm and Mount Popa and set course for Meiktila, in central Burma.'[117] Bob continued, 'The Japs jammed our R/T on all four channels and were therefore expecting us. With 350 IAS we bored in with a quick lift to 100ft to aim our bombs then down again hard as the 20mm and heavy machine gun flak poured up. We thumped our bombs into a group of buildings dead ahead at the same time blasting with cannons and our machine guns.'[118] Cliff and

Johnny then came in over the Meiktila Lake, 'Crossing a lake south of Meiktila town, our Mosquito experienced heavy anti-aircraft fire and took hits in the left engine and fuselage. We attacked at approximately 0635hrs and struck a bomber, a twin-engine Lilly, in a dispersal pen at Meiktila aerodrome. Another bomber, a twin-engine Sally, was taxiing, but it was too late for us to attack it.'[119] Cliff called out over the radio that he had to feather one 'fan' and that the other engine was smoking badly. Bob continued, 'Out the other side we saw that the other Mossie was hit in one engine, when two enemy aircraft bounced on the lame Mossie.'[120]

The enemy aircraft were Oscars from the legendary 64th Sentai, one of the most successful Japanese Army Air Force fighter regiments. The small Nakajima Ki 43 Oscar fighter was renowned for its manoeuvrability and its tight turning circle, which its pilots used to great effect in combat. One Oscar, flown by Sergeant Toshimi Ikezawa, made repeated attacks on Zombie 3. Johnny recalled, 'Bullets passed between me and the armour plate protecting Cliff's seat; some bullets struck his armour plating, sending fragments into my face; and bullets struck the instrument panel.'[121] Bob continued, 'We turned in towards [the Oscars] firing short bursts but missing and in a flash one Oscar pulled a snap loop and jumped onto our tail. We hit 18lbs boost and easily left the enemy aircraft behind.'[122]

Zombie 3 seemed doomed, so Cliff radioed, 'We've had it.'[123] Johnny continued, 'As our port engine was on fire, we had no choice but to crash-land. I jettisoned the door and escape hatch, but my parachute and navigator's bag were immediately sucked out of the plane.' Meanwhile, Bob kept an eye on his compatriots, 'Looking back, I could see the other Mossie make a belly landing with one engine on fire.' Johnny described the crash, 'Approaching impact, I yelled to Cliff to raise his feet up, but he put them down to work the rudder in a successful attempt to miss a tree. After we hit the ground, the Mosquito stopped sliding, and I exited the aircraft, now in flames.'[124]

Cliff added, 'I was momentarily knocked out and came to sitting in a blazing inferno with shells and bullets exploding everywhere. Johnny had already leapt out but I found my legs trapped by wreckage under the instrument panels.'[125] Cliff's foot was trapped by the rudder stirrup and leaked aircraft fuel was now ablaze on the water surface.

As Johnny wondered how to help him, Cliff started freeing himself. 'Quickly thinking, he put his helmet back on to protect him from the flames, and, utilising a hatchet in the escape kit, he was able to work his foot loose.'[126] For Cliff, 'The heat was terrible. Then I lunged for the door, grabbing ... the first aid kit. The blazing wreck of Zombie 3 had fallen into a swamp and the fire had spread over the surrounding water. As I lunged out of the partly submerged door, my head and shoulders went under the water. Weakened by the crash, I struggled to the surface.'[127] Johnny threw one end of his parachute harness to Cliff to use as a lifeline to pull him out. 'Johnny ... now rushed into the flaming water and dragged me clear. We struggled to a dry spot. I had suffered burns to my shoulders and bleeding wounds to my wrist and legs. Johnny remarkably had escaped without any injuries.'[128]

They had survived a crash in the jungle in Japanese held territory and escaped from the burning aircraft. To have any chance of escape, they needed to get well away from the wreckage as quickly as possible. Johnny completed the account, 'We sprinted away from the plane as ammunition "cooked off" in the fire, exploding all around. Heading for the hills through swampy ground, we were soon stopped by a swift river which we could not cross. We managed to keep a first aid kit containing a tube of the topical anti-fungal skin ointment gentian violet, which we used to treat burns on our ears and scalp. Having managed to walk about four miles from the crash site, and quite tired, we crawled into some bushes to rest. We must have fallen asleep, as when we awoke there were Burmese men armed with two spears and a Thompson machine gun.'[129]

Although Cliff and Johnny knew now that they would be handed over to the Japanese army, as prisoners of war, their colleagues who had seen them go down thought that it was unlikely they could have survived the crash. The Operations Record Book noted, 'The loss of Flt. Lt. Emeny and P/O. Yanota is deeply felt by all members of the squadron. Both were most popular and eager and displayed determination at all times.'[130] Cliff's and Johnny's parents were informed that they were 'Missing believed killed.' It was some weeks before the Japanese advised the Red Cross that Cliff and Johnny were prisoners of war.

'Missing believed killed'
Form sent to Johnny Yanota's parents

To   Mr. and Mrs. John Yanota
      I have learned with deep regret that
Pilot Officer John Joseph Stephen Yanota, R.C.A.F.
has been reported missing believed killed.
      The Government and people of Canada join
me in expressing deepest sympathy in your
great anxiety.

                                          H. L. Macdonald
                        Minister of National Defence for Air

© T Yanota

On 10 November, 45 Squadron's Mosquitos were grounded again and all but eight crews were given four days leave. There was much speculation among the aircrews as to whether they might be allowed to fly to 'Blighty' for replacement Mosquitos.[131] On 11 November, at RAF Kumbhirgram, a further round of airframe inspections started focusing on the HR series of aircraft, newly arrived from the UK.[132] This time the team was led by Geoffrey de Havilland,[133] who had come out from England to check and test all the aircraft before they were cleared for flying.[134] Unfortunately, they were not able to provide the assurances that the squadron aircrew so badly wanted.[135] At least fourteen of 45 Squadron's aircraft were found to be defective, with six aircraft being condemned.[136]

Geoffrey de Havilland, with Myers and Chabot, visited the various Mosquito bases. When they visited 82 Squadron at RAF Ranchi, he collected the wing which had fallen off Al Parker's aircraft and sent it back to England.[137] Babe Wambeek watched Geoffrey de Havilland inspecting their Mosquitos during his visit. 'He knew exactly where to look for the trouble. With a fretsaw he cut inspection panels in the wings of all the remaining seventeen squadron aircraft and condemned fourteen of them. Like everything else in wartime skilled labour was in short supply, and the shadow factories constructing Mosquito wings had to make do with relatively unskilled carpenters. Where the scarf joints were imperfectly fashioned the centre sections and outer sections had been set up in jigs and the gaps filled in with glue. The glue filling cracked and crumbled with extremes of temperature. Over dinner that evening [Captain] de Havilland told us that the next nine months' supply of Mosquito wings had already been stockpiled in the UK and that there was little that could be done apart from rejecting those with badly flawed main spars. The invasion of Europe was in full swing, and every possible aircraft was required. This news did nothing to boost morale. Nor did it improve when later it was decided that four of the condemned aircraft could be put back into service after modifications had been carried out to strengthen the wings. All existing aircraft were also to have the same modifications carried out retrospectively.'[138] One of the main modifications to the aircraft was updating them with Mod. 638, which had been 'urged … without delay' four months earlier.

Mr Myers, Squadron Leader C.J. Chabot and the others involved in investigating the causes reported, 'It cannot be definitively stated that these (crashes) are due to faulty manufacture or glue deterioration, but the onus appears to show that there are errors in the shaping of the wood making up the spar assembly. A common fault is that pieces of wood are so shaped that when assembled essential elements do not make surface contact and no adhesion takes place. Under stress the cover skin becomes detached and the modified box section wing assembly collapses. Until a reliable means of inspection and repair can be devised, all Mosquito Mk VI at O.T.U.s will be placed unserviceable.'[139] It is important to note that this grounding order was limited to those squadron's converting to the Mossie and did not affect 45 Squadron, which continued to fly the Mosquito FB VI operationally.

Although the report only mentioned FB VIs, other Mosquitos were affected. On 12 November, No. 684 Squadron, operating F IIs and PR Mosquitos from Dum Dum, noted in their ORB, 'Section of wing-tip splicing on some aircraft found to be defective due to inferior workmanship at the factories building the components.'

On 12 November the order came through to 82 Squadron to ground their remaining Mosquitos until further notice. Their engineering officer, Flight Lieutenant Davidson visited Kanchrapara to be trained on the more detailed methods and standards of inspection required for the mainplanes. On his return to Ranchi, he inspected all remaining seven FB VIs to these standards and placed them all unserviceable! The squadron was pragmatic about their position. 'There was nothing to do but sit back and await events and the month has accordingly been remarkable for its sports and welfare activities which were set in full swing in an attempt to maintain cheerfulness and morale – with some success.'[140]

Like most of the aircrew, Babe Wambeek was concerned, 'In three months of training, we had lost three, and almost a fourth, aircraft due to structural failure – and of the remainder, ten were not repairable and dismantled for spares. To press home attacks against the enemy it is necessary to fly to the very limits of structural strength of one's aircraft. ... Squadron moral went to rock bottom.'[141]

The aircrew were all aware of the problems but felt that the engineers and manufacturer would sort them out. Bob Willis, a 47 Squadron pilot, recalled, 'It became rather obvious that apart from the climate conditions with the monsoon weather and hot sun, some other factor was having an adverse effect on the aircraft structure.'[142] Having identified what was believed to be the problems with the aircraft, ones which could be modified to make them serviceable were flown to 1 CMU at Kanchrapara, as Bob Willis explained. 'On 15 November, following the grounding of all our aircraft, I flew Mosquito HX943 to Kanchrapara. The flight was at a pre-determined speed, with instructions to make no violent manoeuvre and just deliver the aircraft safely. Provided the aircraft arrived in one piece it could be repaired and modified. How great the risk was to the aircrew in flying the aircraft was never spelled out.'[143]

On 20 November 1944 the Accidents Investigation Branch issued a further report, classified as Secret, on Mosquito Airframe Failures. In the introduction they noted:

'Previous reports in this series dealt with thirty-six structural failure accidents involving Mosquito aircraft operating in this country. In addition, brief mention was made to two similar accidents, one in India and the other in Australia. During the period July–September this year there have been a further *fifteen cases of structural failure in this country, fourteen of which were investigated by this Branch. A structural failure accident of a Mosquito Mk. XX which broke up on an altitude test on 26/8/44 has also been reported from Canada.'*

Later, the report continued:

'It will be seen that eight of the fifteen accidents occurred in No. 8 Group (P.F.F.) and involved two Mk IVs, one Mk. XVI and five Mk. XXs, all bomber types with an aft C.G.'[144]

The decision was taken to post all Mosquito ground servicing personnel into new specialist servicing units under a centralised command. Ground support for 45 Squadron would be supplied by 7045 Servicing Echelon with 82's by 7082 Servicing Echelon. This would consolidate the expertise for maintaining the aircraft, enabling the squadrons to focus entirely on operational objectives.

That same day Johnny Walker also received orders from 3rd T.A.F. to detach most of the 45 Squadron's pilots to 221 Group and 224 Group Communications Squadrons where they would fly Sentinel and Tiger Moths in the forward operating areas whilst the Mosquitos were being rectified. The next day, Jock Torrance took some of 'A' Flight to Cox's Bazar to assist with casualty evacuation in the Arakan and Duke Duclos took some 'B' Flight pilots to Imphal. The flying for both detachments was quite hazardous and recorded as 'operations', although it didn't count towards their totals with the squadron. At the same time, Johnny Walker arranged for their navigators to have some additional leave at local tea plantations, which didn't go down well with some of the pilots! 'Though their duties on this detachment will be of little benefit, operationally, to these pilots, it is a most useful form of employment whilst the squadron possesses no aircraft. Hope has not been abandoned for our being permitted to ferry new machines from Britain. The C.O.

W/C R.J. Walker and G/Capt E. Whiteley, DFC, O.C. Wing H.Q., left by air to attend conferences at Comilla and Calcutta concerning our aircraft and the future of the squadron.'[145] It looked as though the squadron might be disbanded. On 24 November 1944 Major Hereward de Havilland (Geoffrey's brother, the managing director of de Havilland Australia), arrived in India on his way back to the UK. He headed up a conference in Comilla on 26 November about the airframe investigation, which concluded that the Mosquitos did have a future in India. Contradicting the earlier assessment by Myers, Chabot and Geoffrey de Havilland, Hereward reported that the accidents were not caused by deterioration of glue but by extensive shrinkage of airframes during the monsoon season.[146] The group concluded that many Mosquitos could be rectified and returned to operations, supplemented with replacements being ferried out. Two squadrons, 45 and 82, would be given priority for rectified and replacement aircraft. No. 47 Squadron would continue its SLAIS course at Ranchi on the Beaufighter and would then start operations on these until Mosquitos could replace them. No. 110 Squadron would have to 'tread water' for the time being and would be re-equipped in due course.

With limited aircraft and only thirty-six operations, there were no fatalities in November, either in operations or training. However, two 45 Squadron aircrew had been brought down in action, survived and taken prisoners of war.

Squadron	Mosquito Intruder Operations		Aircrew Losses Operations		Aircrew Losses Training/Other	
	Month	Total	Month	Total	Month	Total
No. 45 Sqn	36	146	0	7	0	3
No. 27 Sqn	0	45	0	2	0	0
No. 82 Sqn	0	0	0	0	0	2
Other Units	0	0	0	0	0	9
Total	36	191	0	9	0	14

Chapter 11

Additional Strength

December 1944

> '*It was, however, designed and produced in a matter of months
> and full-scale manufacture was more speedy because of its
> unorthodox design: a unique system of hardwood construction
> facilitated Mosquito production over widely dispersed areas
> in Britain and Canada where large supplies of wood are to
> be found. Small firms having no connexion with the aircraft
> industry handle the bulk of the production.*'
> Associated Press, *February 1944*

Mod. 638, as it was known, required a plywood strip to be attached to the wing, sealing the skin across the scarf joint to the main spar. Whilst it altered the aerofoil section of the wing, it did not impact performance. Every Mossie which had not been condemned was updated. Aircraft slowly returned to 45 and 82 Squadrons, having been given priority over the other squadrons which were still converting to the type. The few 45 Squadron crews remaining at Kumbhirgram collected their strengthened Mosquitos and also flew some on ops.

On 4 December, 45 Squadron despatched two Mosquitos to attack bridges and rhubarb the railway and roads close by. They returned safely. The squadron flew four operational sorties the next day, before a stand-down day. On 7 and 8 December they flew two sorties each day. Then, on 9 December, 45 Squadron flew three Mosquitos to attack bridges in the morning, immediately serviced them and flew two again on ops against bridges in the afternoon. The next day and the day after, due to the continuing shortage of aircraft, the squadron again flew two aircraft on ops against bridges, serviced and rearmed them, and other crews flew the same aircraft against bridges in the afternoon. The squadron was maximising the use of its limited resources.

Replacement and modified aircraft also started arriving at 82 Squadron at Ranchi, so that the aircrew could complete their course. Babe Wambeek recalled that their CO 'offered to arrange a posting for anyone who did not want to continue flying Mosquitos. However, he pointed out that anyone who accepted this offer would never again be posted to an operational squadron. None of the aircrew asked for a transfer.'[147] The aircrew just got on with their course.

From 12 December, increased emphasis on Japanese fighter airfields was included in 45 Squadron's tasking. Three aircraft were scheduled to attack Meiktila airfield, but one had problems so only two took off. They dive-bombed the airfield at dawn, with good results. Whilst the first aircraft received little opposition, the second aircraft was subjected to intense and accurate AA fire, being hit by a .50 calibre round.

Later that day, navigator Flight Sergeant Alf Pridmore arrived at the squadron. Although trained on Mosquitos, he would have to develop his low-level navigating skills 'on the job', having previously specialised in high-level photo reconnaissance. His pilot, Dick Campbell, had been killed two months earlier in the airframe failure at Bishnapur.

No. 45 Squadron had nine operational Mosquitos on 13 December and launched five against Meiktila airfield and two against bridges. The next day, three aircraft were again launched at the same bridges, with two being sent to attack a Japanese transit camp at Monywa. With the two bridges still usable, on 15 December, six aircraft again attacked them, led by the CO, Johnny Walker. This time they attacked from a range of heights down to 200ft, using eleven-second delays on the bombs. They were unsuccessful, 'the only claim to the day's work was possible slight damage to one bridge.' It was frustrating. Destroying bridges was really challenging. They were small targets, usually of girder construction, and often the Japanese built one or more 'by-pass' bridges nearby which were approached by small branch lines. The pilots needed to drop their bombs accurately for them to destroy any bridge.

On 16 December the squadron flew ten sorties, six in the morning, with four crews and aircraft flying again in the afternoon. They were tasked with destroying Japanese positions in the village of Gada. In three waves during the day they bombed bashas and strafed troops and vehicles, leaving bashas wrecked, buildings burning and the village covered by a pall of smoke.

That day, the detachments of pilots at Imphal and Cox's Bazar returned to Kumbhirgram to continue the operational scale up.

The next day, 45 Squadron were tasked with attacking the Japanese military camp at Ye-U. Four Mosquitos attacked in the morning, with a further four in the afternoon. In the morning attack, all four aircraft dropped their bombs, with the bombs from the second pair of aircraft overshooting the target. They then all strafed the camp, hitting trucks and locos. Unfortunately, RAAF Pilot Officer Max Levey's aircraft experienced engine trouble and he was forced to feather his starboard airscrew. His navigator, RAAF Pilot Officer Harry Cargill, gave Max the heading to divert to Yazagyo airstrip. Max managed to touch down at Yazagyo but then couldn't control the Mosquito.

Sergeant Ted Daines, RAF Regiment, was there. 'A Mosquito, clearly in distress, crash-landed at the top of the strip. The first we heard was a rough sounding engine, then the noise into a rumble, cum scraping sound of an aircraft on its belly. When we arrived the stricken aircraft was approachable although smoking.' The aircraft had a broken back and the fuselage had twisted so the mainplane and cockpit were upside down and the tail upright. Max's head and arm

Above left: Wing Commander 'Nick' Nicolson VC DFC, RAF, 27 Squadron. (*Internet*)

Above right: Wing Commander Harley Stumm DFC, RAAF, 45 Squadron. (*AWM*)

Above left: Wing Commander 'Johnny' Walker DSO, RAF, 45 Squadron. (*Internet*)

Above right: Wing Commander 'Bill' Hudson RAAF, 82 Squadron. (*IWM*)

Above left: Wing Commander Billy Filson-Young DFC and Bar, RAF, 47 Squadron. (*R. North*)

Above right: Wing Commander 'Soapy' Saunders OBE, RAF, 110 Squadron. (*RCAF PL7839*)

Above left: Billy Gunn RCAF, 27 Squadron. (*J. Walsh*)

Above right: Benny Walsh RAF, 27, 82 & 45 Squadrons. (*J. Walsh*)

Above left: 'Jock' Torrance DFC RAF, 27 & 45 Squadrons. (*J. Walsh*)

Above right: Wal McLellan DFC RAAF, 45 Squadron. (*B. Boon*)

Above left: Bill Taylor DFC RAAF, 45 Squadron. (*S. Cox*)

Above right: Johnny Yanota RCAF, 27 & 45 Squadrons. (*T. Yanota*)

Alf Pridmore RAF, 45 Squadron. (*G. Pridmore*)

Above left: Cliff Emeny RNZAF, 27 & 45 Squadrons. (*Internet*)

Above right: Dick Campbell RCAF, 143 R.S.U. (*G. Pridmore*)

Benny Walsh, 'Ossie' Orsborn and Billy Gunn outside a basha at RAF Agartala, December 1943. (*J. Walsh*)

Flight Lieutenant 'Jock' Torrance, with one of 27 Squadron's FB VIs in early 1944. (*T. Kane*)

HJ811, the Mosquito ferried to India by Benny and Ossie, at a very wet RAF Parashuram in March 1944. (*T. Kane*)

Above left: Ron Pankerd RAF, 110 Squadron. (*Internet*)

Above right: 'Tiny' Lauder RAF, 45 Squadron. (*A. Jenkinson*)

Above left: Jack Nankervis RAAF, 45 Squadron. (*RNZAF Museum*)

Above right: Pete Ewing DFC RAAF, 45 Squadron. (*R. Ewing*)

Above left: 'Tuffy' Tufnell RAAF, Vic Abel RAAF, 82 Squadron. (*Internet*)

Above right: Frank Cox RAF, 110 Squadron. (*P. Jonathan*)

Above left: 'Foo' Howard DFC RAF, 47 Squadron. (*MOD*)

Above right: Rex Garnham RNZAF, 45 Squadron. (*RNZAF Museum*)

Left: Ted Thynne RNZAF, 82 Squadron. (*RNZAF Museum*)

Below: Newly arrived 45 Squadron FB VI HR526, showing 'Snake' marking introduced in 1943 to prevent aircraft intended for India being 'hi-jacked' during transit to another theatre. (*G. White, SWWEC-MAA*)

Strafing sampans on the Chindwin, 45 Squadron, January 1945. (*J. Walsh*)

Administration buildings at RAF Kumbhirgram. (*G. White, SWWEC-MAA*)

Above: 'Freddy' Snell DFC (in 1941), CO of 82 Squadron, December 1944. (*Internet*)

Left: Oil pipeline fire, 82 Squadron, 25 February 1945. (*SWWEC-MAA*)

45 Squadron band, with CO 'Johnny' Walker singing, give a concert at Kumbhirgram. (*G. White, SWWEC-MAA*)

Right: Warrant Officer Freddie Stace with all his jungle flying kit, including Mae West, pistol, kukri and parachute. (*G. Pridmore*)

Below: HR420/OB.C, 45 Squadron. From the left, Jack Nankervis, Max Neill, Ernie Hallett, Bob Barclay leaning against the propeller, Rex Garnham in the slouch hat and Merv Nicholls, with adjutant Herbie Wilson facing them. January 1945. (*Argus Newspaper Collection, State Library of Victoria*)

Time off from Joari for
a swim at Cox's Bazar.
(*G. Pridmore*)

Left: Don Blenkhorne,
Russ Cowley and Doug
Goodrich in the wreckage
of their basha at Chiringa.
(*G. Pridmore*)

Below: With 500lb bombs
under each wing, OB.D,
45 Squadron, taxis from its
dispersal at Kumbhirgram
for a sortie on 7 January
1945. It is likely that this
aircraft was HR409. (*Argus
Newspaper Collection, State
Library of Victoria*)

Damage to the bashas and administration buildings at Chiringa, caused by the severe storm which hit during the night of 12/13 May 1945. (*G. Pridmore*)

Above left: 110 Squadron groundcrew servicing a Merlin engine at Joari. (*T. Kane*)

Above right: Ira Sutherland DFC, 110 Squadron, in the cockpit of his Mosquito at Joari. (*RNZAF Museum*)

Above left: 47 Squadron groundcrew at Kinmagan. 'Taff', Alex Carey and John Bool. (*J. Bool, SWWEC-MAA*)

Above right: Kinmagan airstrip taken on the approach. (*D.A. Bailey, SWWEC-MAA*)

Leaving Yenaungyan, 47 Squadron, 27 March 1945. (*D.A. Bailey, SWWEC-MAA*)

Above: Some of 110 Squadron's Mosquitos at RAF Joari in June 1945. (*J.G. Thomas*)

Right: Ela bridge and bypass bridge, 45 Squadron, 9 March 1945. (*J. Walsh*)

17. 45/187. 9 MAR.

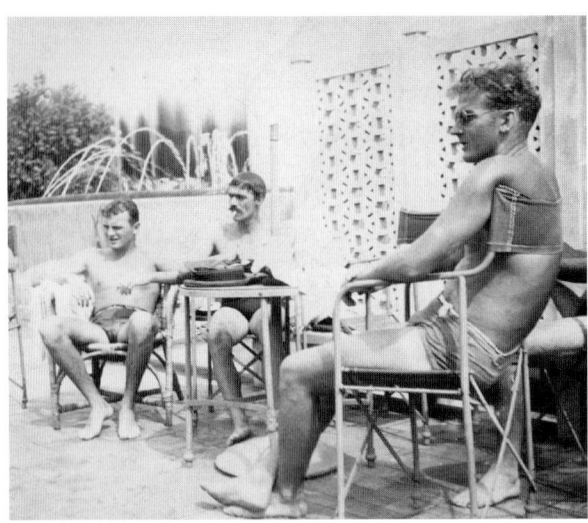

Above: 82 Squadron groundcrew with one of their Mosquitos. (*R.C.A. Barker*)

Left: Don Blenkhorne, Jock Torrance, Bill Taylor of 45 Squadron, relaxing. Location unknown. (*S. Cox*)

Below: Formation of silver painted 45 Squadron Mosquitos, believed to be OB.T, OB.X, OB.N, OB.K and OB.S, probably in April or May 1945. (*G. White, SWWEC-MAA*)

were visible behind the wing's trailing edge and port engine. Harry's body was trapped but his legs were visible. Struggling to release the crew proved futile as they were well entangled. Stripped to the waist, the airmen tried to pull the tail section with the observer clear but to no avail. Ted Daines continued, 'One of the officers spoke to the pilot who was just about conscious and said his feet were trapped in the rudder bar, no way we could do anything, but as the plane began to show signs of bursting into flames the fire wagon rolled up. The tragedy then unfolded, the foam tank was empty, ammo now began to explode, we were forced back and had to watch the incineration of two Australian crew. We arrived back at camp sickened by what we had just witnessed.'[148]

Having completed the SLAIS course at Ranchi, except for the night exercises, 82 Squadron transferred to RAF Charra to await enough Mosquitos to be declared operational. Like many other fliers, Babe Wambeek had some concerns, 'New aircraft from the manufacturers arrived with [the] modifications, and we had little doubt that the problem had occurred in Europe too. Our return to the front was delayed by about six weeks.'[149] Babe's concerns were increased by some repaired aircraft, 'It was decided that four of the condemned aircraft could be put back into service after having modifications carried out to give extra support to the main spars. From that time on, whenever the groundcrew hammered on the wooden cockpit hatch to make it fast before start up, it was difficult to avoid the impression that they were hammering down a coffin lid!'[150]

In mid-December, 82's aircrew, with some Mosquitos, transferred to Kumbhirgram, but the groundcrew remained at Charra. Once settled in, on 19 December Wing Commander 'Bill' Hudson was keen to fly the squadron's first Mossie op.

'My flight into Burma from Assam that day was my own bright idea. It was a journey that was not really necessary. Group operations had no specific target to offer but I was keen and wanted to test-fire my cannon. I should have stayed put and played poker.'

Fellow Australian, Scotty McKenzie, was the CO's wingman. Their two jungle-green Mosquitos took off at 1030hrs and having crossed through the gap between the Naga and Chin Hills, they dropped quickly and flattened out just above the treetops for a low-level rhubarb, seeking opportunity targets. Bill continued, 'We were flirting with the earth a whisper above coconut-tree height, now lifting a wing to check a jungle village, now zooming down over glistening paddy fields, now swerving to miss a gleaming white Buddhist temple. My partner and navigator, Jack Shortis, a Londoner, who had to share my moods, gave me a furtive, quizzical look or two but said nothing. Trusting birds, these navigators.

'The airspeed needle was steady at 250 knots [280mph]. Nothing moved below. Nothing to shoot at. Anyway, it was a beautiful morning. The forest of temples of Pagan, the ancient capital, caught the sun over my starboard wingtip. I knew little about Burma, but at least I was aware that the name had nothing to do with pagan worship.

'Jack gave me a new course – north to Mandalay. Before us was the Irrawaddy River, broad and smooth and lightly veiled in the morning mist. It beckoned. I swished down and skimmed it. Then there was a jolting crash, a jarring note, and a freezing of the music inside my stomach.

'Incredibly we were still airborne and climbing, but my serene and purring Mosquito of a moment before was now vibrating madly. The tips of the port airscrew were curled back and the Merlin motor looked as though it would shake itself out of its bed. I switched the motor off and it seemed to sigh with relief. The starboard motor was still running but it was a struggle to keep straight and level. Anger was my only emotion.'[151]

Bill, with his microphone dangling, yelled to himself, 'You stupid bastard, Hudson.' Jack was effectively a passenger and could do nothing but sit there. Thinking that the coolant coming out of the port engine was smoke, Jack shouted, 'The port engine's on fire.' He swivelled round and pressed a fire extinguisher button.

Bill continued, 'Anyway, we were now dropping out of the sky like a falling leaf ... stick forward or you'll stall ... straight ahead ... land it there ... look for a tree in a wooden aircraft, that instructor in Rhodesia had told me three years before ... put a wing into it ... put the brakes on ... and I'd laughed. A tree came up on cue, dead ahead, and I put the port wing into it.'

They had crashed in Japanese-held territory, near the junction of the Chindwin and Irrawaddy rivers.

'When I came to I was standing there on drying mud in a tangle of control wires, with Jack, slumped a little, alongside me. He was still attached to the armour plating by his Sutton harness. I punched the release and we climbed out of the mess of wires. There was a smell of burning, but I have no idea what happened to the rest of the Mosquito. It seemed to have vanished.'[152]

With their legs lacerated from the crash, as they struggled away from the remains of their aircraft, their enemies were already approaching. At first, the Japanese just stood and stared, but a Sikh INA soldier with them knelt and aimed his rifle at them. Bill Hudson and Jack Shortis were prisoners of war and their first experiences were not good. On their knees, they crawled towards their captors, even though one of Jack's legs was 'mangled'. Without warning, Bill received a kicking. They should be standing with their hands above their heads. Then, with excited chatter, the Japanese realised that Bill was a wing commander. 'Stupid fool ... I had forgotten to take off my wing commander's stripes. Now I was in real trouble. It was a cardinal rule that senior officers put up junior rank while flying over enemy territory.' An open-handed blow caught him by surprise.

They were ordered to march. Jack took one step and crumpled to the ground. Fortunately, Bill got to him first and helped him stand.

Under guard, with Bill's support, they stumbled forward. After a while, they were allowed to rest and sit down, which delivered another challenge for Bill. 'My search for a handkerchief came up with the squadron "Mayfly", a report on the aircraft situation for my squadron – how many were operational and so on. This was unpardonable. Before you took off on an operation you cleaned out your pockets, so as not to be carrying information which would be of use to the enemy if you happened to be captured. I felt sick in the stomach as I palmed the document and prodded it into the soft earth. I looked up and caught the eye of one of the Burmese villagers who had gathered around us. Obviously, he had seen what I had done. He just grinned.'[153]

Bill and Jack would soon be on their way to Rangoon.

Scotty McKenzie reported that he had last seen the CO's aircraft fifteen miles east-south-east of Pakokku. With Bill Hudson posted as 'Missing', Squadron Leader Freddy Snell, 82 Squadron's senior Flight Commander, was appointed to take command of the squadron. Freddy, one of the few surviving Fairey Battle pilots from the Battle of France in 1940, was well liked and respected. His crews would follow him anywhere. As Babe Wambeek commented, 'We could not have had a better leader. From the time he took over, morale improved rapidly.'[154] In due course, Freddy would be promoted to wing commander.

As would be expected, although squadrons at Kumbhirgram co-operated and collaborated, there was a lot of one-upmanship and banter. According to Cyril Norridge, a 45 Squadron airframe fitter, 'There was much friendly rivalry with the two other units which now shared the location. Unprintable jibes at our respective insignia were rife – 45's winged camel and 82's cockerel.'[155]

Ops continued for both squadrons, including on Christmas Day, when 82 Squadron flew two in the morning, back in time for lunch. The cookhouses had somehow managed to prepare traditional

Christmas dinners in the jungle! Later, 45 Squadron flew six night-sorties with aircraft departing between 1826hrs and 2024hrs. No. 47 Squadron, still at Ranchi, and 110 Squadron, at Yelahanka, also enjoyed traditional Christmas dinners. Their COs must have been wondering if and when they might receive Mosquitos, complete their conversion and be declared operational.

On 26 December 1944, four 45 Squadron Mosquitos were tasked with a bombing raid on the Japanese airfield at Heho. Loaded with extra fuel in wing tanks and armed with 500lb bombs fused with eleven-second delays, Bill Taylor, with Warrant Officer Ken Putnam, his navigator, took off in HR447 at 1604hrs.

Bill explained, 'We took off to arrive just after dusk, using up the extra fuel in the wing tanks first to drop them when empty.' It was standard practice to drop the underwing fuel tanks as soon as the fuel was used because they still contained fuel vapour which, if hit, could explode and damage the wing. Having completed their bomb runs, Bill lined the Mosquito up to strafe the airfield. He continued, 'I was number three in line abreast, and we came in at full speed of about 350mph at zero feet. The Japs hit us with everything they had. One gunner got me in his sights and I could see his tracers flying over my starboard wing. I couldn't go up as I would fly into his bullets or go down as we were at zero feet so I just had to keep going. He lowered his sights and hit my starboard engine setting it on fire and we could see a great stream of black smoke pouring out. In a matter of a few seconds I feathered the engine so that the prop edge cut through the slipstream reducing the drag, pressed the fire extinguisher, reduced power on the good engine so the Mossie wouldn't flip over on its back, and cut the switches and petrol to the smoking engine.'

Bill knew that he couldn't get back to base over the mountain range, so he asked Ken for the heading to Kalemyo. At the pre-op

Christmas Menus 1944
Upper: 45 Sqn Officers' Mess - Lower: 110 Sqn Sergeants' Mess

Breakfast.

Cereal, Grape Fruit, Porridge
Fried Eggs and Bacon.
Tomatos, Baked Beans, Fried Bread.
Marmalade, Butter, Rolls, Toast.
Tea,   -   Coffee.

Tiffin.

Asparagus Soup.
Fresh Salad.
Peaches, Pears, Custard.
Tea.   -   Coffee.

Dinner.

Tomato Soup.
Bake Sole,   Tomato Sauce.
Roast Turkey.   -   Roast Pork.
Roast Potatoes, Green Peas, Cabbage.
Stuffing, White Sauce, Apple Sauce.
Christmas Pudding, Mince Pies.
Brandy Sauce.
Blancmange, Jelly, Cream.
Savoury.
Coffee.
Cheese and Biscuits   Nuts and Raisins
Confits   Fruit

© B Boon

"COLD BUFFET"

'SANDWICHES'
• HAM • PORK • TONGUE • COLD MEAT •
SALMON • EGG •

SAVOURIES
CHEESE • LIVER • SARDINE

SWEET
XMAS CAKE • MINCE PIES • ASSORTED PASTRIES
SAVOURY ROLLS

COFFEE   TEA

• • • • •

December 25th 1944

CHRISTMAS DINNER
MENU
SOUP
CREAM OF TOMATO
FISH
BEKTE JULIENNE
ENTREE
FILLET STEAK • CHIPS • GRILLED TOMATOES •
PEAS • GRAVY
JOINT
ROAST TURKEY • SAGE & ONION STUFFING
ROAST POTATOES • GREEN PEAS •
BRUSSELS SPROUTS • GRAVY
ROAST PORK • APPLE SAUCE
BAKED POTATOES • GREEN PEAS •
CAULIFLOWER GRAVY
SAVOURIES
CHEESE AND LIVER
SWEET
CHRISTMAS PUDDING • BRANDY SAUCE
MINCE PIES • TRIFLE • FRUIT JELLY •
PEACHES & CREAM
CHEESE & BISCUITS
TEA   COFFEE
FRESH FRUIT
ASSORTED SWEETS • NUTS
CIGARS   CIGARETTES
BEER AND SOFT DRINKS ?

© A Rendell

briefing, the aircrews had been told that there was now a strip there with night landing facilities. 'In fact, it was the only allied landing strip in Burma at the time. We headed west and, as it was a clear night, we knew we would pick up the meeting of the Irrawaddy and Chindwin rivers. Meanwhile [Ken] and I discussed various options and what could happen on landing. Belly landing and normal landing options both carried their own risks but, as pilot, I made the final decision for a normal landing. Eventually we located the strip and circled, firing off the colours of the period, which changed every six hours. Then we sent off a red one to indicate distress. They signalled back an instruction to wait.'

Bill and Ken continued circling the airfield. 'After a while I could see something like cars, traffic moving up from the base to the aerodrome and I said to [Ken], "These buggers haven't got any lights!" They were moving trucks up to shine on the strip.'[156] Bill continued, 'They parked three trucks diagonally on either side of the strip where we would make our approach, leaving their lights on to indicate where the ground was. They then flashed a green light for us to go in.' Bill knew that it was a short strip built for single engine Hurricanes, so he approached it slightly faster, to ensure better control. 'I knew I would have trouble pulling up. Also, I didn't know whether we had a puncture in the starboard landing gear, so I told [Ken] to keep his hand on the undercarriage handle and be ready to pull the wheels up on landing if I felt any movement to the right. Luckily all went well and I stopped right on the end of the strip.[157]

'When I jumped out of the plane and got up, there was a wing commander standing there and he said, "What are you doing here?" I felt like saying, "What the bloody hell do you think?" He said, "You've done me out of a job. I was supposed to test this tomorrow!"[158] 45 Squadron's pre-flight briefing had been twenty-four hours premature because the airfield wasn't supposed to be ready until the following day.' However, for Bill and Ken it was a life saver, 'It was a mistake that we had been told about it. We would never have got back without it. I received a "Green Endorsement" on my logbook for exceptional flying ability and they flew us back to Kumbhirgram the next day. Everyone at base was saying, "[Bill]! We thought you had gone."'[159]

Sadly, that same day, Flying Officers Ken Dorricott and Hank Wilson of 82 Squadron were not so lucky. They were posted as 'Missing believed killed' when they failed to return from their sortie. Their aircraft, HR394, had crashed near Daungtaung.

With the waxing moon after Christmas, in addition to flying daytime sorties, 82 Squadron aircrews needed to be 'signed off' for night ops. Each day, once darkness had fallen, four or five crews flew circuits one night, then local area flying the next and, finally, completed night sector recces.

On 29 December, six 45 Squadron Mosquitos led by Squadron Leader Jock Torrance were tasked with another dawn dive-bombing raid on Meiktila airfield. Benny Walsh and Ossie Orsborn flew 'M for Mike', HR456, on the operation. 'On a few occasions we would rendezvous with other Mosquitos at the target, usually about six of them, climb to 10,000ft and then one by one we would dive-bomb and strafe the target with each plane peeling off as they completed the raid.'[160] Four of the six would target Meiktila and two would attack the nearby Thedaw airfield. Benny and Ossie would attack Meiktila last when its air defences were most prepared.

The crews made their own way for an hour and a half in the dark over Japanese-held territory before they rendezvoused just before dawn over the Irrawaddy, north of Meiktila. They then climbed to height over their targets before, at about thirty-second intervals, each aircraft dive-bombed in turn from 12,000ft to 3,000ft. When the others had completed their attacks, Benny closed the throttles, opened the radiator shutters and rolled his Mosquito into a steep dive towards Meiktila airfield, with Ossie calling out each 1,000ft decrease. Although the others had meagre AA fire,[161] as Benny positioned his aircraft to release his bombs 'the Japs put up a considerable amount of heavy flak.'[162] Having dropped his bombs, Benny started pulling through 'the squash',[163] unleashing the Merlins' power during levelling off. As Ossie strained to see where their bombs fell, Benny banked to return at low-level to strafe the airfield using guns and cannon on any opportunity target.

Having been the last to attack, as soon as they started climbing away to regroup, Benny asked Ossie to count all their planes to see if everyone was alright. Ossie scanned the dawn skies around them. 'One, two, three, four, five, six, seven, ... eight.' 'What?', exclaimed Benny, 'We have gained two!'

Two Oscar fighters had joined 45's Mosquitos and Benny saw that one was lining up to attack Jock's aircraft. With lightning reactions, Benny called a warning to Jock as he pulled the releases on the Merlins' throttles and slammed them fully open, demanding absolute maximum power. With his engines noisily complaining, Benny hauled his Mossie onto the tail of the Oscar already firing tracer at Jock's port wing. Meanwhile, Ossie was craning his neck to make sure that he kept his eye on the other nearby Oscar, as well as any other threats, keeping Benny informed with short, pithy updates. Totally focused on the Oscar now in his sights, Benny's right forefinger curled around the gun trigger on his stick and he pressed home his attack, closing to within 200yds. 'I managed to get a prolonged cannon and machine gun at one and I believe I damaged it, but we could not get confirmation since I was the last of our six Mosquitos in the attack.' The Mosquitos had been bounced by six Oscars and a Tojo[164] from the north-west at 4,000ft, but only two Oscars came close enough to pose any real threat.

After Benny's successful counterattack, the Japanese pilots seemed to lose their enthusiasm and kept their distance. The six Mosquito pilots sought the relative protection of low-level, whilst they and their navigators kept a keen lookout for any further enemy threats, as they completed their hour-long journey over Japanese-held territory towards the Naga and Lushai Hills.

They all returned safely to base, one still carrying a 'hung up' bomb which hadn't correctly released. Later, during debriefing, even though none of the other crews could independently corroborate the damage to the Oscar, the squadron intelligence officers decided to award the 'damaged' air combat victory to Benny.

Sorties continued through to the end of the month when, on 31 December, 45 and 82 were tasked with their first combined bombing operation on Thedaw airfield. As noted in 82's ORB, 'Much excitement today – our first bombing operation.' Four aircraft from each squadron were tasked to attack in line abreast right across the runway running roughly north and south, together with dispersal areas and aircraft pens down both sides of the strip. All four of 45's aircraft and three of 82's were armed with two 500lb Mk IV bombs with eleven-second delays. The other 82 Squadron aircraft was tasked with strafing 'anything that presented itself on the airfield as a suitable target for his guns.'

All eight aircraft were airborne by 1110hrs and arrived over the target by 1240hrs. However, 82's CO, Freddy Snell, thought they could have executed it better. 'Unfortunately, leadership was not of the highest quality and our aircraft arrived over the landing ground in one formation of six aircraft in rather rough line abreast with Squadron Leader Torrance of 45 Sqn and our CO, Squadron Leader F.W. Snell, DFC, rather crowded out of the picture on their left flank. Squadron Leader Snell to the extent that it was not safe for him to continue over the path of the delayed action bombs already dropped. He accordingly broke off the attack and dropped his two bombs on a corrugated iron roofed building en route for home. The attack was fairly successful, all six remaining bombing aircraft's bombs falling in the target area. As everyone cheerfully remarked, it was a start.'[165]

Having started December with virtually no serviceable Mosquitos, 45 Squadron ended the month with sixteen Mosquitos on charge and 82 Squadron had ten serviceable aircraft. Not only had the wings been 'suitably modified', but the aircraft also had increased capabilities. Many now had the F24 camera fitted in the nose and bomb racks were arriving that doubled their bomb load by enabling them to carry four 500lb bombs instead of the four 250lb bombs. Both squadrons had lost one crew during the month and 82 had posted its CO and his navigator as 'Missing'. With the airframe problems now seemingly resolved, or at least well on the way to being resolved, the tasking for the Mosquitos was ratcheting up!

Squadron	Mosquito Intruder Operations		Aircrew Losses Operations		Aircrew Losses Training/Other	
	Month	Total	Month	Total	Month	Total
No. 45 Sqn	159	303	2	9	0	3
No. 27 Sqn	0	45	0	2	0	0
No. 82 Sqn	27	27	2	2	0	2
Other Units	0	0	0	0	0	9
Total	186	375	4	13	0	14

Chapter 12

Getting Nasty

January 1945

*'It is sweeping over the jungles on the Burmese frontiers,
harrying the Japanese forces wherever they can be spied out in
this difficult land of tropical forests, rivers and streams.'*
The Sphere, *4 March 1944*

The New Year started with a one day stand-down for 45 Squadron's aircrew and 82 Squadron aircrew were delighted to hear that their support personnel were finally to set off from Charra to join them at Kumbhirgram.

On 1 January 1945 a meeting was held at the Ministry of Aircraft Production in London where Major Hereward de Havilland presented a report on the Mosquitos' airframe failures in India stating that 'the accidents were not caused by the deterioration of the glue but by shrinkage of the airframe during the wet monsoon season.'[166] The Ministry accepted these findings, which was probably political expedience to prevent a loss in confidence in Mosquito crews and a propaganda victory for the enemy.

The outcome of this meeting was at odds with the more detailed investigation completed by Geoffrey de Havilland, Chabot and Myers, which identified clear evidence of manufacturing defects. 'This investigation was later confirmed by a team from the Ministry of Aircraft Production, which found faults in six Mosquito marks built at the Hatfield and Leavesden plants. The defects were similar, and none of the aircraft had been exposed to monsoon conditions or termite attack.'[167]

The squadrons in India were not informed of the meeting or its conclusions. They were just focused on receiving as many operational Mosquitos as possible.

The next day, 2 January 1945, engineering received a signal calling for an inspection of the joints around the Mosquito's dinghy stowage hatch. All the aircraft were immediately checked and five of 45 Squadron's aircraft were found to be faulty. Cyril Norridge, an airframe fitter, recalled, 'It was possible to pull off literally yards of ply, and the disintegrated glue would fly up in clouds, almost like French chalk.'[168] The problem aircraft were immediately ferried to Kanchrapara for rectification, leaving the squadron short until replacements were delivered. No. 82 Squadron had only four Mosquitos for operations, so the squadrons worked together.

On 3 January, 45 Squadron managed to field fourteen aircraft and 82 Squadron provided four for Operations Nasty I and Nasty II against two large communication centres at Maymyo, north-east of Mandalay, and Thazi, by the railway line south of Mandalay. Their objective was to force the Japanese from their telephones and make them use their radios more. All aircraft were armed with two 500lb bombs each and were despatched through the day in four waves starting at 0816hrs for Thazi, then 0829hrs for Maymyo, 1335hrs for Thazi and 1400hrs for Maymyo. Unfortunately, in the first wave HR515 suffered engine problems just after take-off and ploughed into the jungle about five miles from the airfield. Warrant Officers John McQueen RNZAF and navigator Bill Edwards were killed. The operations were successful and both communication centres were substantially destroyed.

Poor weather for the next few days made it impossible to fly across the hills to Burma, so everyone stayed at base. 'Living conditions at Kumbhirgram were quite reasonable. Permanent quarters and messes for all ranks constructed from brick, bamboo and rattan. Water was heavily chlorinated and taken with salt tablets as a precaution against dehydration. Some potassium permanganate was also introduced to the washing water as a disinfectant; thus, the term much used – pinki parni.'[169] Benny Walsh recalled that, 'the beds were just wooden frames with ropes bound across on which there was a bedroll, a thin duvet-like cover. The meals were all a variation on the theme of dehydrated potatoes, herbs, corned beef and purple onions, and there was lots of curry! If anyone became ill the nearest hospital was also a basic bamboo structure. Most men had occasional bouts of malaria and while they were unwell they did not fly.'[170] No. 45 Squadron armourer Leading Aircraftman James Gillan recalled that malaria was a real hazard, 'Strict precautions were enforced and Mepacrine tablets were handed out daily at mealtimes. Long trousers and long-sleeved shirts buttoned at the neck were worn from just before dusk. Mosquito nets always had to be used and we were always supposed to dress and undress under them. At dawn a squad would come round and pump DDT, or something similar, into the billet until the place was full of smog. Not pleasant but definitely worthwhile.'[171] Having spent six weeks on a filthy tramp transport rounding the Cape to arrive in north-east India, 82 Squadron aircraft electrician Reginald Barker found himself 'in the jungle fighting mosquitoes and malaria'. Reg said that he 'knew the war was won when the squadron received Mossies – they made the torment of terrible heat, bugs and food seem better after that.'

During these two quiet days, an unofficial aircrew member in 82 Squadron was captured on photograph. Basher, Flight Lieutenant McKenzie's puppy, had started flying on operations with his Australian master and 'their' navigator, Flying Officer Alf Newman. Basher's final operational tally is not documented.

With the weather 'once more perfect and the serviceability after the short respite high', on 8 January, fifteen 45 Squadron aircraft and five 82 Squadron Mosquitos set off in waves to attack the waterfront at Sagaing and 'rhubarb' the Irrawaddy as far as Chauk. The sorties were successful, with relatively little opposition.

The following day 45 Squadron launched ten Mosquitos against a special target at Paleik, followed by a 'rhubarb' towards Chauk. At the start of the day the weather was grim – 10/10ths cloud at 100ft and 500yds visibility in rain. Even so, three of the first wave made it to the target and bombed from between 50ft and 80ft. Opposition was accurate and concentrated. Flying Officers Freddie Fortune and 'Joe' Mears's aircraft, HR526, suffered damage to its undercarriage, wheel and port inner fuel tank. At 1313hrs, when Freddie touched down gingerly at Kumbhirgram, the undercarriage collapsed, leaving him and Joe to a long walk back to the squadron's dispersal. Luckily the damage was pretty light and within a few weeks HR526 was back on the flight line. Later, at 1630hrs, Bob Wilson and Bill Hayward could not lower the undercarriage on HR455 so they were forced to do a belly landing on the kutcha strip. Both walked away. 'The day's operations had cost the squadron two aircraft but fortunately the crews were uninjured.'[172]

On 12 January, four 45 Squadron aircraft were tasked with a dawn bombing raid on Thedaw airfield. Departing two minutes after Arthur Houn, the leader, at 0452hrs, Bob Wilson and Bill Hayward's luck ran out when one of their Merlin engines faltered during take-off. Their Mosquito crashed into the jungle and burst into flames, killing them only one and a half miles from the runway. The other two aircraft took off over their crash site a few minutes later. 'Although so near to the strip it was several hours before the burnt-out wreckage was located by L.A.C. Willoughby who went into the jungle on his own initiative.'[173]

The first of the three remaining aircraft dive-bombed Thedaw at 0617hrs, with its two 500lb bombs exploding in the dispersal and near a road. The bombs on the second Mosquito wouldn't release so the pilot brought them home. The third aircraft bombed at 0635hrs, with its bombs striking on the west side at each end of the runway.

The three Mosquitos patrolled the airfield for thirty minutes before returning to base.

That day, Babe Wambeek and Brian Mooney of 82 Squadron led a Mosquito pair tasked with escorting Dakota STARDUST [most likely carrying either Miss Marie Burke (film star and opera singer) or George Formby (film and concert hall star) and his wife Beryl, on an ENSA tour to entertain the troops]. Departing at 0800hrs, they rendezvoused with the Dakota at Palel and escorted it to Kalemyo where they all landed. At 1235hrs they all took off for Akyab but the other Mossie had to return to Kalemyo with severe fluctuation of the starboard radiator temperatures. Babe escorted the Dakota to Akyab, then flew to Cox's Bazar to refuel. Returning at 1600hrs, he orbited Akyab until the escort duties were taken over by Thunderbolts. Babe overnighted at Chittagong before returning to base.

Finally, both 45 and 82 launched four pairs of Mosquitos 'to attack the Jap stronghold of Monywa.' The four pairs in the morning were also tasked to rhubarb the Chindwin and Irrawaddy to Chauk and back to Mandalay. Two Mosquito pairs from 82 Squadron took off at about 0950hrs and dropped their bombs 'in close concentration south of the jail.' Then the first Mosquito pair hit about sixty sampans during their strafing and the second pair a further twenty. Later that day four more 82 Squadron aircraft repeated the attacks, this time damaging three camouflaged 50ft motor launches on the Mytinge River. Reports from 45 Squadron confirmed that its aircraft dropped bombs on Monywa and that 'uncountable small 20/40ft sampans were strafed by these aircraft and many strikes were seen.'

That same day a flight of Ki-43 Oscars, probably from Meiktila, attacked the forward operating strip at Onbauk, destroying two Dakotas on the ground and shooting down two others. Command reacted immediately to protect the Allied transport aircraft. From 14 January, they would establish a dawn-to-dusk patrol over the Meiktila airfields. Mosquitos from 45 and 82 Squadrons were tasked with keeping the Japanese aircraft on the ground through the morning, with 45 Squadron bombing and then patrolling from dawn until 0800hrs. Then 82 Squadron would relieve them, bomb Meiktila and Thedaw again and patrol until Thunderbolts took over at about 1100hrs.

On 14 January, Benny Walsh and Ossie Orsborn were one of eight 45 Squadron crews tasked. They dive-bombed Thedaw airfield from 9,000ft, releasing their four 500lb bombs at 6,000ft before patrolling both Meiktila and Thedaw at between 6,000ft and 4,000ft for fifty minutes.

Later, eight more crews from 82 Squadron were tasked, operating in four sections, each to provide about an hour patrolling after their initial attacks. Babe Wambeek reported that his bombs hit Thedaw's main runway about 600 yards from its southern end.

The next day, 15 January, the two squadrons were given similar tasking. 'Bad luck again dogged the squadron this morning.'[174] After an early briefing, three 45 Squadron aircraft, piloted by Nick Nicholls, Ron Goodwin and Benny Walsh, took off at about 0500hrs so that they could be over Meiktila and Thedaw at dawn. Unfortunately, less than an hour into the sortie, Benny was forced by technical problems to jettison his bombs and return to base. The two remaining aircraft continued to Meiktila, dive-bombing it at about 0630hrs amid heavy but inaccurate anti-aircraft fire. Nick described what happened. 'We took off in company with Goodwin and Potts, patrolling at Angels 10 over the Jap airfields of Meiktila, Thedaw and Kagaung. The Japs obviously contacted the airfield at Heho as we soon spotted four aircraft boring out of the sun and quickly warned the other crew. To our amazement the other crew took no action, so we literally screamed over the R/T for them to "Break!" The first Oscar hit as Ron Goodwin was slowly turning to port and was acknowledging our warning over the R/T. These words were the last he ever spoke as the remaining fighters bored in on him in succession and the Mossie went straight down and hit the ground in a tremendous explosion. There were no survivors! That left us facing four enemy aircraft, so we dived for the deck and hit 18lbs boost and were doing 550 IAS [sic] and escaped.'[175] Ron and Sammy's Mosquito, HR402, crashed about eight miles north of Thedaw.

Nick managed to get a radio message about the 'bandits' to 82 Squadron, who were on their way to relieve them. Knowing that there were Oscars in the area, Squadron Leader Chris Gotch, leading the pair in HR406, decided to change their attack to low-level. He took the Mosquitos down to deck-level over the Irrawaddy River and at 0818hrs swept east to west over Meiktila at 300mph IAS. Flying Officer Benison's aircraft, following only a couple of seconds behind Chris's, was damaged by Chris's bomb blast and one of the bomb detonators.

'The aircraft were just over the strip when AA opened up. It was intense, accurate and of all calibres – bursts of Bofors being observed all around the aircraft – as well as tracer from other 20mm and other L.M.G. posts. A 20mm shell entered Squadron Leader Gotch's aircraft through the nose and, narrowly missing his left knee, passed through to the rear of the aircraft, filling the cockpit with smoke. Squadron Leader Gotch leaned forward to peer through the smoke and thereby had a narrow escape, for another 20mm shell entered the cockpit, through the Perspex cockpit at his left, almost severing the wires of his Sutton harness, and bruised his shoulder. The shell struck Flight Sergeant Felsenstein in the face, smashing his face below the nose, and passed out through the Perspex blister on the starboard side.'[176] Chris's aircraft was actually hit by six 20mm cannon shells, but he managed to break north-east to make his way to safety and help for his badly wounded navigator, Basil Felsenstein.

Benison's aircraft was also hit many times over the strip. He decided to take avoiding action by flying over Meiktila Lake. It was an unfortunate decision because he was again engaged by heavy and accurate AA fire, sometimes bursting on the lake and throwing columns of water up around his aircraft. Having run the gauntlet, he managed to catch up with HR406 about twenty miles to the north and escorted Chris back to base which, due to poor weather conditions, was the nearest available airfield. Chris's navigator, Basil, remained conscious for much of the flight back to Kumbhirgram, lapsing into a coma shortly before Chris landed at 1000hrs. Basil was rushed to Silchar Hospital where he died a couple of hours later.

A few minutes behind Gotch and Benison, the next 82 Squadron pair attacked Thedaw at low-level and were also met by a hail of accurate AA fire. 'On the way out, Flight Sergeant Armstrong, in taking evasive action, hit a tree, inflicting severe damage on his aircraft, large sections of both leading edges being torn away and the port propellor and spinner were badly battered.'[177] The damaged Mosquito was a challenge to fly, often requiring the strength of both hands on the stick, but Armstrong brought it back to base.

In the third section, just before reaching the target, Warrant Officer McDonald's aircraft started leaking glycol in its starboard engine, so he had to feather it, then dropped his bombs 'fused' and headed for home. His partner, Flight Lieutenant McKenzie, scored a direct hit on the centre of the runway at Kagaung and damaged an Oscar on the ground.

In the final wave, just before Pilot Officer Ted Thynne released his bombs over Meiktila, he felt a shock as his aircraft suffered damage to the port wing and cockpit cover. A piece of stone was removed from his wing when he landed!

All of 82 Squadron's aircraft were accounted for when, after 200 miles of flying on one engine, McDonald completed a tricky single-engine landing safely at Talihal.

That evening, 45 Squadron C.O. Wing Commander Walker wrote letters of condolence. In his letter to Ron Goodwin's parents, he wrote, 'The work that this squadron is doing is more dangerous than most and we have not been without our losses. In fact our losses have been fairly heavy. But I can say without question that the loss of Ron and Sammy has been by far the biggest loss which we have been asked to bear ... This is a terrible war, but never so terrible as when it strikes so closely as this. I am proud to have known Ron, men of his calibre and loyalty are indeed few and far between.'[178]

Group Captain Ernest Whiteley, Khumbhirgram's Station Commander, also wrote to Ron's parents, 'You will hear such details as we know from his squadron commander, but I thought you might like to know that the whole of this station and headquarters (where he previously worked) think that Ron represented the best the nation has to offer. In five years of war I have written several letters to next-of-kin but I've never said that before or anything like it – in his case it seems hopelessly inadequate.'[179]

Five 45 Squadron aircraft were despatched to attack Meiktila again on 16 January, but one had to return with technical trouble. They later rhubarbed from Chauk to Monywa, claiming hits on large bullock convoys. The following day they enjoyed a squadron stand-down, to catch up on engineering and other tasks.

On 18 January, 45 Squadron flew three waves of four aircraft to 'bomb and strafe' a Japanese headquarters at Kokko. The first wave took off at 0900hrs, the second at 0930hrs and the final wave at 1430hrs. Three aircraft in the first wave were damaged by hostile fire and debris. The CO was forced to feather an engine and make an emergency landing at Kalemyo, but the others returned to base. By late-afternoon, after the third wave, Kokko was destroyed, with five fires raging. The intruders also found plentiful targets of sampans and launches during their strafing. It had been a successful day.

No. 47 Squadron, still flying Beaufighters, arrived at Kumbhirgram and started flying operations on 20 January whilst awaiting delivery of their Mosquitos. Both 45 and 82 Squadrons continued to have replacement aircraft priority as their operational load intensified. Bob Willis, one of 47's commissioned pilots, recalled, 'At Kumbhirgram we had comfortable beds, complete with a mosquito net, with cotton sheets washed weekly by the dhobi wallahs with much pounding. We also enjoyed the luxury of an enrolled follower or bearer, a native Indian, usually shared with one or two other aircrew. Our bearer

John looked after us right royally, ensuring that the dhobi wallah also washed and pressed our clothes, even keeping our uniforms in good order with sharp creases in the trousers.'[180]

In the morning, on 26 January, 45 Squadron despatched four Mosquitos, led by Jock Torrance, to bomb a suspected petrol dump in the jail area of Fort Dufferin, at Mandalay. The crews were briefed that the bombs had an eleven-second delay, allowing low-level release. The four aircraft attacked from the east at speeds of between 290mph and 380mph IAS. Benny Walsh was one of the pilots. On his attack, to maximise the accuracy, he dived to just 600ft before releasing his bombs. To his surprise, the bombs exploded immediately, just underneath their Mosquito and rocked it with the blast. The bombs were perfectly on target, resulting in a huge ball of fire from the exploding petrol dump which briefly engulfed their aircraft. As Benny dryly recalled, 'At least, as we flew out of the inferno, we knew that the mission had been a success.'

With Fort Dufferin in flames behind them, Benny carefully checked the aircraft's controls for the signs of any battle damage and was relieved that there didn't seem to be any. Their attacks attracted some anti-aircraft fire, but it was not very accurate. Before returning to base, the four aircraft strafed opportunity targets along the Lashio road towards Nawngkhio, with Ben shooting up three MTs.[181]

After landing back at Kumbhirgram, Benny and Ossie found the tailfin of one of the bombs embedded in the fuselage of their aircraft. It had been another very close shave. Benny was never sure if his aircraft had been fitted with eleven-second delayed bombs or instant fuses.

There had been a growing concern within the aircrew about the variability in the eleven-second delayed bombs. The Operations Record Book noted at the end of the month that 'Low-level bombing operations have had to be curtailed due to the doubtful functioning of the eleven second delay fuses. New ones have recently been received and the squadron will carry out low-level sorties when the target necessitates it.'[182]

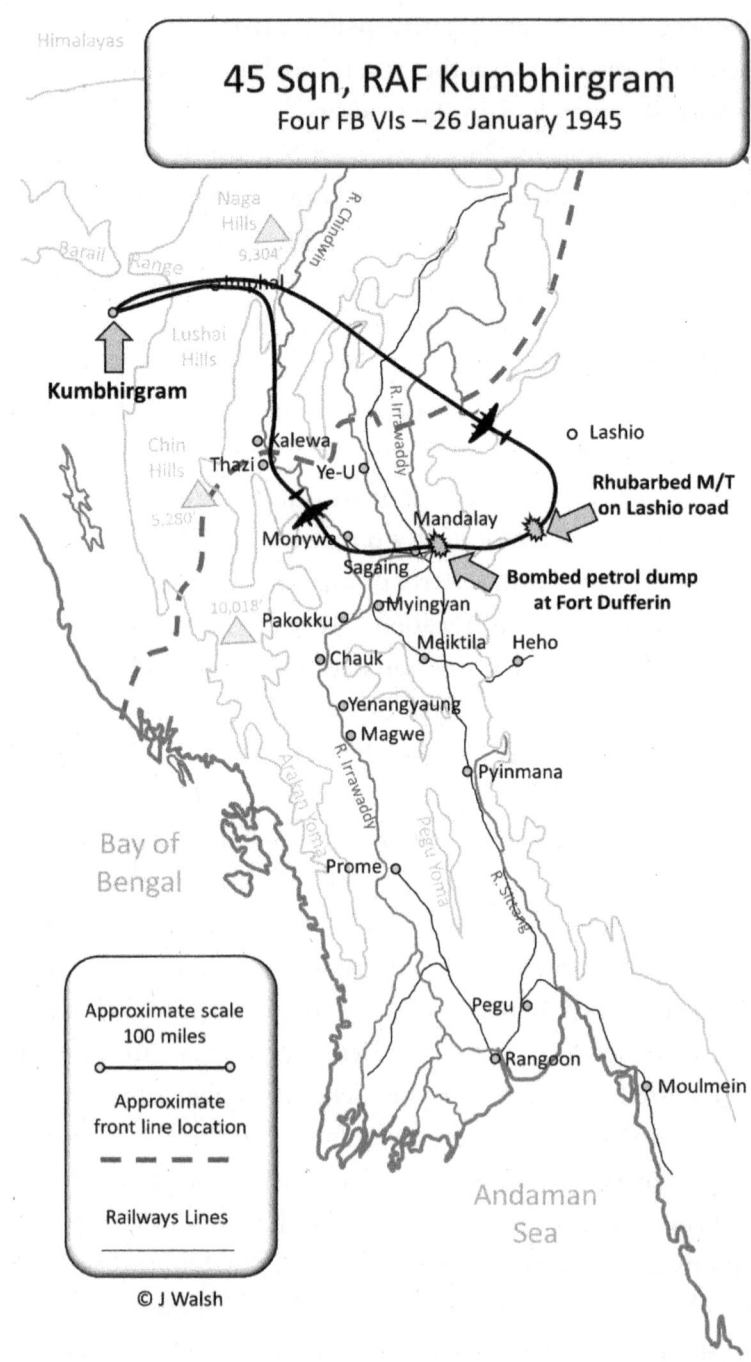

Himalayas

Naga
Hills
5,304'

Barail Range

R. Chindwin

45 Sqn, RAF Kumbhirgram
Four FB VIs – 26 January 1945

Lushai
Hills

Kumbhirgram

Imphal

Chin
Hills

Kalewa

Thazi   Ye-U

5,280'

Monywa

Sagaing

10,018'

Pakokku

Chauk

Yenangyaung

Magwe

R. Irrawaddy

Mandalay

Myingyan

Meiktila   Heho

o Lashio

**Rhubarbed M/T
on Lashio road**

**Bombed petrol dump
at Fort Dufferin**

Pyinmana

R. Irrawaddy

Arakan Yoma

Pegu Yoma

R. Sittang

Bay of
Bengal

Prome

Approximate scale
100 miles

Approximate
front line location

- - - - -

Railways Lines
———————

© J Walsh

Pegu

Rangoon

Moulmein

Andaman
Sea

The tasking for both 45 and 82 Squadrons continually increased. Mosquitos from 45 Squadron hit the oilfields at Yenangyaung and the army installations in Mandalay. Then they completed multiple attacks on the Japanese airfields at Heho, Thedaw, Meiktila and Nawngkio, before supporting the Fourteenth Army bridgehead on the east of the Irrawaddy. Their tasking then changed to bridges and railways, followed by an attack on a Japanese stronghold in the village of Ywabo. Every sortie included rhubarbing, disrupting the Japanese supply lines on roads, railways and rivers.

Meanwhile, 82 Squadron attacked Japanese positions in Mandalay and then paid almost daily visits to Meiktila, Heho and Thedaw airfields, bombing their runways and facilities. On 27 January, they sent twelve aircraft to bomb Japanese gun positions near Singu, again supporting the Army's Irrawaddy bridgehead. This was followed by four more days bombing the Japanese airfields, before an attack on the village of Tonbo which was believed to have a large concentration of Japanese forces.

Having endured a really frustrating period since they arrived at Yelahanka, on 25 January, Wing Commander Arthur 'Soapy' Saunders, the CO of 110 Squadron, received the signal he and his squadron had been awaiting. 'Signal 956 dated 24 January 1945 from B.A.F., S.E.A., orders the allotment of six Mosquito Aircraft from CMU to 110 Squadron.' Soapy immediately contacted 225 Group to arrange their collection. He and his aircrew delivered the first four to Yelahanka on 28 January. At long last, they could start their conversion. Soapy was optimistic, 'The morale of the squadron is at a high level. During the last few days of the month the Mosquito aircraft commenced to arrive, thus giving everyone a job of work to do. I feel sure morale will be higher still when we really get "cracking" with our Mosquitos.'[183]

During January, 45 and 82 Squadrons completed 217 and 198 operations respectively for the loss of seven aircrew. Throughout the month, their COs liaised with the R.S.U. about on-going concerns of structural weaknesses with their Mosquitos. It was clear that the modifications hadn't resolved the underlying problems. They were just ensuring that the aircraft could fly operations for as long as possible. There wasn't the time or resources to replace the Mosquitos and their strike capability was essential in the offensive against the Japanese.

Johnny Walker was outspoken in his private remarks in 45 Squadron's Operation Record at the end of the month: 'Seeing that the squadron has been grounded three times since October with suspected structural weaknesses, it is amazing to find that no crews have any question about possible weaknesses today. It is therefore most alarming to hear that all Mosquitos are to be painted white as a final safety measure, which will reduce the internal heat in the wings. I should be impressed if any Mosquito designer can convince me and my crews that a white Mosquito is safe to fly and a camouflaged one is not. From an operational standpoint the proposal is too stupid to warrant comment. To date this development has not been passed on to crews. No. 124 R.S.U. are painting one wing of a Mosquito white and will take internal wing temperatures of both wings at hourly intervals in the hope of proving that the differences, if any, are so slight that it will not be worthwhile putting in to effect.'[184]

Squadron	Mosquito Intruder Operations		Aircrew Losses Operations		Aircrew Losses Training/Other	
	Month	Total	Month	Total	Month	Total
No. 45 Sqn	217	520	6	14	0	2
No. 82 Sqn	198	225	1	3	0	2
No. 27 Sqn	0	45	0	2	0	0
Other Units	0	0	0	0	0	9
Total	415	790	7	19	0	13

Chapter 13

Consolidation

February 1945

'Against the sampans which the Japanese are using on the Burmese rivers the Mosquito has been particularly deadly. The sampans mortality rate, already high, has been stepped up still further by this swift twin-engined monoplane.'
Associated Press, *February 1944*

Kumbhirgram now had an establishment of over sixty intruders, Mosquitos and Beaufighters, flying day and night. It also had a number of non-combat 'squadron hacks', like Harvards and Beechcraft, which were used to fetch and carry. The airfield had only one runway and was operating at maximum capacity. Throughout the day convoys of trucks delivered fuel, bombs, ammunition and spare parts, as well as the food and drink required to sustain over four hundred front-line RAF personnel and their local support. Minor repairs were completed, engines were tested, aircraft were serviced, refuelled and re-armed, and training flights were completed. It was certainly not a quiet jungle base and the continual activity, heat and humidity, together with the open-sided bashas, made sleep challenging, day or night. The intensity of operations continued for the two Mosquito squadrons.

On 1 February, Flight Lieutenant G.F. Mahoney and Warrant Officer Roy Trew of 82 Squadron were on a night raid on Heho airfield when they were hit by flak. Mahoney recalled, 'The weather had become very bad and we diverted to Kalemyo, but Kalemyo had been caught before by intruders and declined to put up a flarepath. We now had been airborne for six hours and could not wait for first light. With about ten minutes fuel remaining we headed a little way towards the Chindwin, feathered the starboard 'prop' and abandoned. I may have discovered a new experience by hitting the back of my neck on the tailplane as I left through the side exit.

'Eventually, I joined up with habitation and I sought to know where my navigator was. Some difficulty, but a lot of beating of drums seemed to be going on and eventually the penny dropped that this was broadcast signalling, and distant replies could be heard. I believed I understood that Roy was safe some twenty miles down the Chindwin. We took a dugout and paddles, and lo and behold, there he was – beside the Chindwin, expecting us! His parachute [had] sustained a tear and kept twisting and untwisting on the way down. We were at Mawleik, on the Upper Chindwin, a remote supply-drop strip. They had a radio and it took days to get through to Kalemyo (drums did it much quicker). The supply drop strip was made good enough to tempt a Stinson Sentinel to arrive and we were lifted out, one by one.'[185]

On his return to base, Mahoney was checked by Flight Lieutenant Dawes, the medical officer, who reported that he seemed 'quite unaffected by what must be considered as one of the worst hazards of aerial warfare in this part of the world. In fact, he gave the impression that he had more confidence as a result of the incident.'[186]

No. 45 Squadron started the month with a daylight attack on the 'oil village of Lanywa, on the Irrawaddy, where the Japs are believed to be constructing defence works.'[187] They dive-bombed from 6,000ft to 2,000ft, before rhubarbing sampans along the river, striking 'approximately 100 20/30ft sampans.' That night, 82 Squadron also bombed Lanywa, and then visited it daily for three days, intent on degrading its facilities. Their rhubarbs proved fruitful, including a three-tonner left as 'a flamer', 'thirteen lighted MT', a large basha which 'burst into vivid red flame and gutted immediately, together with several adjoining,' and sampans hit. That night 45 Squadron attacked Myitnge bridge, bombing from low and medium levels. The following night they visited the Japanese airfield at Annisakan, glide bombing using eleven-second delayed bombs, four of which hit the main runway. Aungban, Heho and Kunlon airfields were next to receive unwanted visits from 45's Mosquitos, with sixteen 500lb bombs being dropped from 10,000ft to 6,000ft and four more dropped from 'zero feet.'

The new batch of delayed-action fuses for the bombs did not remove the concern about their use. Sometimes a crew felt that they hadn't been fitted because the detonation was virtually instantaneous. A different problem occurred when releasing them from low-level, because the bomb sometimes skipped, as Doug Goodrich explained, 'On many occasions bombs were seen to bounce off the ground to a greater height than that of the aircraft which had dropped them.'[188] If the time-delay was not sufficient, these bouncers could be close to the Mosquito that had dropped them when they airburst. The delayed fuses and bomb hang-ups were sources of gripes from the crews when they returned from ops.

On 4 February Pete Ewing and Pinkie Pinkerton were tasked with a dawn raid on Heho airfield. During their bomb run in HR404, they saw a Ki 21 taking off. 'Switching to guns, the enemy aircraft was attacked at 500ft, fire being opened at 1,000 yards closing to 200 yards and the enemy aircraft burst into flames and is claimed totally destroyed.'[189] It was unusual for intruders to record an air combat victory.

Both squadrons concentrated through the month on improving bombing accuracy, so most crews had three or four sessions, covering dive bombing, glide bombing and quarter attacks, on the local bombing range at Pispur. On 5 February, Pete and Pinkie acted as the ground party on the bombing range. They were also accompanied by Flight Sergeant Norman Smith, a navigator who had joined the squadron in December. On their way back to base at the end of flying, their Jeep skidded on loose gravel and fell fifteen feet into a culvert. All three were hospitalised. A surgical team was flown from Imphal to attend to Norman Smith, but he died the following day.

Meanwhile, 82 Squadron had spent several days carrying out multiple night attacks on Meiktila, Heho and Kunlon airfields, usually with 500lb bombs. The main runway at Meiktila was hit several times. The aircrew and engineers were pleased when 7 February was declared a stand-down.

Both Mosquito squadrons took part in an 'Earthquake' on 8 February – a forty-eight-hour aerial onslaught on a key target. As well as twelve Mosquitos from each squadron, Mitchells and Thunderbolts also played their parts. The objective for this 'Earthquake' was to neutralise the Japanese heavy artillery which was trying to dislodge 19th Division's Irrawaddy bridgehead at Singu. Station Commander Group Captain Whiteley led the twenty-four Mosquitos, each carrying their maximum 2,000lb bombload, as they bombed and strafed the Japanese gun positions, causing extensive damage. He remained in the target area throughout their action to observe the results.

On 10 February, the intruders played a key role in supporting the Army's advance on Rangoon. The army's next strategic objective, led by IV Corps, was to cross the Irrawaddy River. For some time, IV Corps had been feeding misinformation to locals suspected of being Japanese agents or informers, so that the Japanese intelligence analysts would infer that their operation was only a Chindit-scale attack of a limited duration. Lieutenant General Slim's 'Extended Capital' plan was for IV Corps to move undetected down the Myittha Valley, cross the Irrawaddy and push directly to capture Meiktila, the key strategic supply and administration centre. He had created an elaborate deception plan, Operation Cloak, to make the Japanese believe that the Fourteenth Army's main objective was Mandalay, Burma's second largest city.[190] IV Corps had, in fact, been tasked with leading the Allied forces across the Irrawaddy near Nyaunga and Pakokku. The crossing points were close to the confluence of the Chindwin and Irrawaddy rivers, about 100 miles south-west of Mandalay.[191] However, to minimise opposition, the army wanted to create the deception that the crossing would be substantially to the south of the actual crossing point.

That day, eight Mosquitos were tasked with a 'special mission' as part of Operation Cloak to create the impression that the Allied Forces were crossing the Irrawaddy River at this southern point. Four 45 Squadron aircraft were flown by Wal McLellan and Jim Vernon, Ron Wilcock and Andy Andrews, Nick Nicholls and Bob Barclay, and Benny Walsh and Ossie Orsborn. Four Mosquitos from 82 Squadron were crewed by Squadron Leader Albert Tooth and Arthur Maude, Pilot Officer Ian Pease and Warrant Officer Bill Storey, Babe Wambeek and Brian Mooney, and Ted Thynne and Warrant Officer Bill Flatt.

Under cover of darkness, each Mosquito would each drop two pieces of special time-delayed ordnance on the east bank of the Irrawaddy between Chauk and Yenangyaung, where IV Corps wanted the Japanese to believe that the crossing was taking place. Each ordnance was a 'battle in a canister', a 'Parafex'. Due to the time-delays on the Parafexes, there would be no explosions when they were covertly dropped. Supporting the deception, the Mosquitos were to continue onwards and strafe Japanese lines of communication before they headed home. Depending on the time-delays, one or two hours later, the Parafex cannisters would activate, creating decoy 'attacks' by imitating the sound of rifle-fire punctuated with the sounds of hand grenades exploding.[192] The deception was executed just a few days before IV Corps and the main Allied forces reached the Irrawaddy's west bank to begin their actual crossing at Pakokku.

The eight aircraft took off in two waves between 1705hrs and 1730hrs, just before dusk. Ted and Bill suffered engine problems immediately after take-off, so they dropped their Parafex and returned to base. Benny and Ossie, in F-Fox HR567, took off at 1705hrs. 'We were sent out ... over the 8,000 to 10,000ft mountain range for army support, to drop Parafex containers (these were six feet long containing explosives which simulated hand grenades, mortar shells, machine gun and rifle fire) in a pre-determined spot on the Irrawaddy River, to assist in an army crossing.' All the Mossies routed separately at low-level through the darkness to their slightly different target locations. As Benny and Ossie approached their target location and popped up to 2,500ft to drop their Parafex, 'we experienced a total electrics failure.' After releasing the Parafex cannisters, without their radio, electrical instruments, or even the navigator's map light, Benny decided against strafing. With no electrics, darkness and deteriorating weather, they headed north for their base. 'Believing we had dropped the Parafex on target, we endeavoured to make our way back to base without radio. Needless to say, with no moon, flooding and swollen rivers and increasingly high cumulus, especially over the mountains, we got hopelessly lost and were very low on fuel.'

The weather conditions continued to deteriorate but the six other aircraft made it back to Kumbhirgram by 2100hrs. An hour earlier, Chris Gotch, 82's 'A' Flight Commander, set off on an op after being briefed that the weather was not good and on no account was it safe to enter cloud. 'I decided to make height over base to at least 10,000ft. It was a dark night with no moon, but seeing some broken patches above, I tried to find a gap through which to climb. At 8,000ft, while heading for a gap, I found myself in cloud without warning. The bumpy conditions were so severe that I had no apparent control of the aircraft. Relying solely upon instruments, I saw that the artificial horizon was showing that the aircraft was upside down. I carried out the normal correction as best I could. The aircraft then stalled, the

ASI showing 80mph and the rate of dive 4,000ft per minute. What happened next is extremely confused but, after being in cloud for not more than two minutes, I found myself in a gap at 13,000ft, the cloud top continuous above to at least 16,000ft. Seeing the airfield lights below, I dived immediately and landed straight away.'[193]

Benny and Ossie assessed their situation. It was night, there was no moon, thick cloud and the rivers were swollen, making navigation challenging. With no radio, they couldn't speak to anyone or get a homing fix to one of the airfields near their route. They were still near or over Japanese-held territory, so baling out was very definitely their last resort.

'We were almost at the point of baling out when, by a sheer stroke of luck, we spotted the lights of a very small landing strip,' but the visibility was not good. 'We made an emergency landing (downwind as it happens) on a short strip. The plane overshot the lights and ploughed through a burnt-out DC3.'

'This forward landing strip was Onbauk, near Mandalay, and the Jap forces were all around it, often attacking it at night with mortar and machine-gun fire.' US and Indian forces, part of XXXIII Corps, were forcing the Japanese retreat in eastern Burma, working in concert with the British IV Corps to their west. Onbauk had been recaptured in mid-January, but Japanese forces remained in the area. The airfield was defended by two RAF Regiment Field Squadrons, 2945 and 2968. It was being used by 'Hurribombers' from 34 and 42 Squadron, but they closed down their operation at night due to the proximity of the Japanese forces.

Once they were out of their Mosquito, Benny and Ossie realised that it 'was badly damaged and because of the electrics failure we found the Parafex still on board!' They felt extremely lucky that the cannisters hadn't gone off on landing or when they hit the DC3. As soon as they were out of the aircraft, some Americans drove up in an unlit Jeep and shouted at Benny and Ossie to get in. As they climbed into the Jeep, the Japanese started shooting! 'The Yanks gave us a lift back in their Jeep, and that was more frightening than any flight. The way they drove!' No. 2945 Field Squadron of the RAF Regiment mounted a crash guard on their Mosquito, to prevent the Japanese getting too close.[194]

Although Benny felt it was badly damaged from hitting the DC3, the next morning he had the aircraft fuelled and, together with one of the groundcrew, flew it on a short air test to see if they could ferry it back to base. He was not happy with it and decided to leave it for the recovery specialists. Benny and Ossie hitched a lift to the airfield at Shwebo. 'We got transport to Imphal and then back to base.'[195]

The next night, as planned, eight more Parafexes were dropped. Having dropped their battle cannisters, Rex Garnham and Nank Nankervis started strafing roads and railways, taking in the airfields of Allanmyo and Magwe. However, the AA fire was accurate at Magwe and their aircraft was sufficiently damaged for them to complete a precautionary landing at Kalemyo.

The final Parafexes were dropped by 82 on 14 February. The deception worked.[196] When the real crossing at Pagan was launched a day or so later the Japanese forces, believing that they were faced with no more than a column of somewhat active commando troops, had been drawn to the noises further south.[197] The Allied forces successfully crossed the Irrawaddy River, even though the Japanese defences were 'fanatical'.[198]

After the op, General Messervy, GOC IV Corps, sent a 'strawberry', a message of thanks, to 221 Group. 'I would like to thank you very much indeed for your help with the Cloak scheme. I attach the greatest importance to it and am quite sure that it will have had a considerable effect on the Jap and will prove to be instrumental in saving us a lot of time and a lot of casualties in securing our main objectives.'[199] Strawberries were always appreciated, fostering close co-operation between the armies and air forces.[200]

The rout of the Japanese Fifteenth Army had started. The Fourteenth Army was consolidating its position and effectively controlled the western bank of the Irrawaddy to thirty miles south of the confluence with the Chindwin. The Mosquitos would be tasked with providing ground support further south and as far to the east as the Sittang River.

Until the aircraft could be moved south, 908 Wing commissioned an Advanced Landing Ground at Thazi, to the east of the Chin Hills, near Kaleymo. Army engineers had levelled the 6,900ft runway and given it a light tarmacadam covering. The Mosquitos would use it both day and night, even though its runway lighting was 'minimal'– just a lorry-mounted Chance floodlight and a few goose-neck paraffin flares to indicate the line of the runway.

From 14 February Thazi would act as an intermediate refuelling point for crews to top-up on their return, should they run short. Alternatively, aircraft could transit to Thazi and then refuel before an op. Either option would allow them to continue to carry four 500lb bombs.

Additionally, there would be greater call for even longer-range rhubarbs and strafing, restricting the bomb load to two 500lb bombs in the bomb bay and using external 'slipper' fuel tanks fitted under the wing leading edge.

Unlike in other theatres, being based in the jungle meant that there were very few opportunities for the pilots and navigators to dissociate from their jobs, properly relax and recharge their batteries. Stand-down days were spent on the base. Forty-eight-hour passes were virtually unheard of. There were no local girls with whom they could socialise, no welcoming pubs or bars to visit and the messes were extremely restricted in the alcohol that they served.

The strain of intruder flying – hours of intense concentration, inherent danger and proximity with death – showed in different ways. If they were both officers or both NCOs, then the two-man crew would work and socialise together, often becoming inseparable. If the crew consisted of an officer and an NCO, although still close, they went to separate messes when work finished. Alf Pridmore knew that he didn't quite have the same relationship as some others, such as Benny and Ossie. He had been teamed up with Don 'Blink' Blenkhorne. 'Unfortunately, both my pilots were in the Officers' Mess and I was in the Sergeants' Mess, so we were not able to spend much time together socially, but we were good friends.'[201] Some crews did not want to form new friendships. It was not that they were standoffish, they just wanted to insulate themselves from the pain when another crew was killed.

Some aircrew suffered from nightmares. Nervous afflictions, often known as 'the twitch', were relatively common. The squadron medical officers continually monitored the crews for signs of excessive strain and, even though the operational tasking continued to increase, the senior commanders ensured that the aircrew did get their annual leave. Freddy Snell and Arthur Maude grabbed a week's leave this month. Duke Duclos and McFadzean had fourteen days leave starting 2 February and then Benny and Ossie went to Calcutta for leave towards the end of February, as they had done in February 1944. Like most aircrew, Benny and Ossie hitched a lift to RAF Baigachi, near Calcutta, in the squadron's Beechcraft, saving themselves up to three days travel each way.

Also, having completed three-year tours, some of the aircrew returned home. Flying Officers Neill and Hallett of 45 Squadron were repatriated to Australia on 2 February and Joe Cartlege left for Australia on 11 February. Replacements arrived from the UK for both squadrons, most of them being experienced Mosquito crews.

Additionally, a large number of married groundcrew from 82 Squadron and the servicing echelon were repatriated to the UK on expiry of their tour. They had joined 82 Squadron in March 1942. 'About fifty airmen of all trades were involved, and it was very obvious that the joy of returning to "Blighty" was tempered with regret at leaving the squadron to whose traditions and achievements they had contributed in no small measure. A farewell party was given for them and it is a recorded fact that even the ex-squadron warrant officer, Mr Wood, failed to notice that several airmen passed over the borderline between sobriety and drunkenness.'[202]

Pete Ewing had still not fully recovered after the Jeep crash on 5 February, but Pinkie Pinkerton was fit to fly so he was temporarily teamed up with Flight Sergeant Gordon Ashworth. On 17 February they were one of six crews tasked with bombing Japanese airfields in central Burma. The six aircraft all took off just before 0400hrs. Gordon and Pinkie were allocated Heho airfield and carried two 500lb bombs. Whilst the others returned safely from their sorties, 'No information has been received of this aircraft since it left base.'

The next day Johnny Walker despatched Wal McLellan and Jim Vernon to search for any signs of Gordon and Pinkie, but they found no trace.[203] In due course, they were posted 'Missing believed killed.'

One of 82 Squadron's replacement crews were pilot Flight Lieutenant Vic Hewes and navigator Sergeant Gordon Thewlis. They flew their first Mosquito intruder op on 24 February. A particularly unforgettable op followed soon after, as Gordon recalled.

'Quite a lot of our intelligence for targets was obtained via Force 136. These were small groups of men, usually four in number, with a wireless operator in the team, working in the jungle behind Japanese lines, sending information back on targets to attack. On this occasion the Japanese were trying to hoodwink us, as they were always vulnerable to air attack if keeping to jungle roads during daylight hours. Medical supplies were urgently needed for the Japanese troops of 33rd Division. They utilised local bullock carts, disguised with a hay top covering. Force 136 discovered this ruse as they monitored a convoy of 8-10 carts making their way north towards the front line. The Japanese 33rd Division was retreating down the Chindwin valley to the south and west of Mandalay. Taking off from Thazi, a forward landing strip to the east of the Chin Hills, as dawn was breaking, we set course in a south-easterly direction.

'The target given to us was Ywadon, but the bullock cart convoy had moved on a little by the time we arrived there. After a few moments searching in the general direction they were heading we spotted them in line astern, about eight of them in total, edging along a narrow track banking alongside rice paddy fields. Making a broadside approach we hit the first two, made a steep turn to port and made a similar attack on the rear three, finishing off the trapped middle three with a third strafing.'

Like many others, Gordon took no pleasure in these attacks, 'Our ammunition belts on both the .303 Browning machine guns and the 20mm Hispano cannon had been loaded with extra incendiary bullets and shells to cause the most effective damage. Flame and smoke damaged medical supplies would be of little use. The horrifying part was seeing the bullocks in the shafts falling to the ground, having been hit with either stray bullets or shells. It was also unfortunate for the Burmese Teamsters who were caught up in the attacks. They had probably been drafted into this job under duress by their Japanese conquerors.

'My conscience didn't play any part at this point. We were a highly trained crew. We had to do a job, which we did to the best of our ability. But we did come to realise that this was the horror of war at close hand! With our complete domination of the air, Japanese motor transport was usually kept well hidden in the jungle in daylight hours. Carts drawn by bullocks would generally be less vulnerable to attack. Hence our reliance on Force 136. On this occasion we were to continue our sortie to Ywathit where we strafed a lone truck heading north and then more "business" as we spotted four more covered trucks heading north, which we duly strafed and certainly caused considerable damage. We were by this time south and west of Mandalay near Monywa on the Chindwin. It was time for home.

'On all these low-level sorties the cockpit became hot with sweat stinging the eyes and the body saturated with perspiration. The sticky acrid smell of cordite fumes, all added up to make a sortie a very unpleasant and unforgettable experience.'[204] The noise of a pair of Merlins bellowing away beside the cockpit and the continuous turbulence of flying over dense jungle and mountainous terrain ensured that these sorties were exhausting. With the constant danger of enemy action, mechanical failure, and extreme low-level flying, they were also very stressful.

'On the return flight we were obliged to land at Thazi, one hour short of our home base at Kumbhirgram, due to a dangerous build-up of cumulus over the Manipur Mountain range. Our operational flight time was a gruelling three hours and forty minutes, arriving knackered at Thazi to the point of collapse. Had the weather been clear, I doubt if we could have made it to our home base. Perhaps God was on our side clamping down the weather. As it was, we were diverted again from Thazi to Imphal because of bad weather, taking off later for base at Kumbhirgram. All in all, this operation had taken nearly two days to complete. It was then debriefing and bed to recover. In many ways, it was a sortie which left little sense of satisfaction, as it was difficult to see if the end, with native Burmese and bullocks killed, justified the means.'[205]

At Yelahanka, 110's conversion to the Mosquito continued at pace, but sadly claimed its first casualties. Flying Officer Tullett and Warrant Officer Quinn took off in HR618 at 0935hrs for practice on the Kolar bombing range. When they became overdue, the squadron contacted Kolar. 'They could tell us nothing.' The CO and his navigator, James Stephen, took off at 1200hrs and carried out an extensive search but could find no trace. 'Later, wreckage was found near the bombing range strewn over hundreds of yards. The bodies were moved to Kolar. The reason for this accident is unknown – we have lost a valuable and highly respected crew.'

Four 82 Squadron crews were tasked with dawn rhubarbs on 19 February. First to be despatched was Ted Thynne, with Bill Flatt navigating. Taking off at 0458hrs, something almost immediately went tragically wrong. They crashed into the trees just 1,500yds from the end of the runway and the aircraft immediately burst into flames. Ted and Bill were really popular and the crash was so shocking that the operation was postponed.

Finally, in mid-February, 47 Squadron started taking delivery of their Mosquitos, with 'A' Flight converting first. They were not camouflaged, nor were they white, but they were painted silver. Pilot Officer Bob Willis, with his navigator, Pilot Officer Tommy Thompson, quickly completed their conversion to the Mosquito. 'We air tested our new Mosquito Mk VI fighter bombers in February 1945. Tommy and I were allocated Mosquito HR518, "D for Dog", which was to prove an exceptionally reliable aircraft. The aircraft in their new reflective silver paint, instead of European style camouflage, and with inspection panels installed gave us total confidence that we had a first-class aircraft to fly.'[206]

Bob and Tommy flew 47 Squadron's first Mosquito op on 23 February 1945. They were paired for a daylight rhubarb with Flight Lieutenant Bill Bailey and Warrant Officer F.W. Poree. Due to a shortage of 50- and 100-gallon drop tanks for the Mosquitos[207], their aircraft were equipped with a long range 63-gallon fuel tank in the bomb bay. 'We flew from Kumbhirgram over the Chin Hills at 10,000ft, skirting the mountains to the east of Mandalay at Maymyo, then south-west to Kyaukse on the main railway line thirty miles south of Mandalay. Continuing south we had reasonable success on this four hour and twenty-minute sortie, catching and strafing a locomotive in sheds at Pyananggazu, thirty miles east of Meiktila.'[208]

It was going to be a further six weeks before 47 Squadron had received its complete establishment of Mosquitos.

Also new to 82 Squadron was Australian navigator Flight Sergeant Charles Carruthers. His pilot was Warrant Officer R.W. Murkin. Having completed his navigator training in Australia, Canada and the UK, Charles had arrived at Kumbhirgram on 10 February 1945. He had flown out from the UK in a Sunderland flying boat bound for Karachi via Gibraltar, North Africa, Cairo, Lake Habbaniya and Bahrain. One of his fellow passengers was George Formby, the famous entertainer.

On 19 February, they were tasked as part of a Mosquito pair to rhubarb the road and railway from Mandalay to Lashio. Flying Officer 'Mac' McKenzie and Flight Lieutenant R.K. Pears were leading the op.

Charles recalled arriving at Sadaung: 'We proceeded to detour around Mandalay as there are very strong ack-ack positions there. Turning south we finally located the road and railway and proceeded to follow it. Everything was going quite well and I was keeping a wary eye on our tail for Oscars – those nasty little Jap fighters. After a quarter of an hour or so we spotted a loco in a bamboo hut (the Japs' poor attempt at camouflage). This we strafed and saw dust and possible steam rising from it.

'Proceeding happily up the railway line, weaving from side to side, suddenly the sky was filled with little black puffs of smoke. They looked quite harmless but knowing what Bofors can do caused us no little anxiety. Our nose went down immediately – throttles open – and we left at great speed. Having thought we were out of range, I glanced behind and was shaken to see those little black puffs following closely on our tail. Luckily however we got away with it. Mac thought he got hit as he told us over the R/T, so we turned for home. But apparently his aircraft was functioning OK so we carried on after a couple of minutes. There is no doubt that they had been waiting for us, as their fire was so accurate. I think it was because of the fact that we unconsciously flew right over their position without seeing them that it might have surprised them a little. Anyway, that was that and eventually we located the road leading south and started to patrol it.

'Then like a bolt from the blue, we heard Mac yell, "Bandits – for God's sake open her out!" So once again down went the nose and throttles through the gate this time and we hurtled along at a steady 350mph right on the deck. It didn't take us long to outrun them – possibly they didn't see us but there is nothing like "safety first". They were probably sent up to intercept us as they were heading north along the road and we were coming south. However, once more we managed to avoid danger.'

Suspecting that other fighters might be in the area, the two crews headed west, hoping that the danger was now behind them. Charles continued: 'Then a further Oscar was sighted which caused us great alarm as he appeared to be turning in to attack us. This time it was not so easy as we were flying at about 50ft, right in front of us was a range of mountains. Somehow we managed to top the rise and screamed down the other side approaching the 400mph mark. The old Merlins were dragging at their anchors and the whole kite was shuddering. This was the least of our worries and we finally reached our lines and set course for base. We landed OK after four hours of very exciting and nerve-wracking experiences.

'Taxing back to dispersal the groundcrew seemed to be taking undue interest in us. Imagine our surprise when we got out and saw part of the starboard wheel cover torn and bent by shrapnel. Peculiarly enough, Mac thought he had been hit and hadn't. We didn't notice a thing at the time we were shot at and yet a stray bit of shrapnel had damaged us. Ignorance is bliss!'[209]

On 24 February the Accident Investigation Branch issued a further report, classified as Secret, into Mosquito structural failures. Whilst they might not have had the responsibility for investigating failures outside the UK, previous reports had mentioned failures in India, Australia and Canada. This report started with:

> *'During the period under review October – December 1944 only four cases of structural failure were reported, all of which were investigated by this Branch.'*

Later the report states:

> *'In the case of NS.882 it was noted by the pilot that the first part to break up was the starboard wing. Modification 638 was not embodied so there was reason to believe that the wings failed to develop their full strength.'*

Later the report adds:

> *'At the time of the issue of Service Accident Report No. Misc. 23G for the period July to September 1944, the total flying hours were not available. These now show a structural failure rate of 1 in 7,800 flying hours which is slightly worse than previous figures. The rate for the quarter under review is 1 in 22,000 flying hours, which is a marked improvement on any previous rate. It indicates the modifications and other preventative actions are having beneficial results.'*[210]

Whilst the report did note poor manufacturing of butt joints on the leading edges and aileron shrouds on a batch of aircraft at RAF Coltishall, no mention was made of the major investigation in India, the issue of poor manufacturing nor of the meeting with the Ministry of Aircraft Production on 1 January 1945.

On 25 February, 82's Squadron Leader Albert Tooth, with his navigator Warrant Officer Tippett, 'were jumped by an Oscar which shot away their elevator cables', so he was forced to return to base controlling HR406's elevator with the trim tab. He eventually brought the aircraft in to land at Kumbhirgram, wheels up, at 200mph! The medical officer, Flight Lieutenant Dawes, described it as 'a spectacular but terrifying exhibition. Squadron Leader Tooth completely unmoved by the event. This officer is one of the most fearless – and ruthless – men I have ever met and is a very great asset to the squadron.'[211]

On the last day of the month, Bob Willis and Tommy in 47 Squadron were tasked as part of a two-ship night rhubarb, led by Flight Lieutenant Al Scott, a popular Canadian and the new 'A' Flight Commander. 'We left together in daylight but, as darkness fell on clearing the Chin Hills, we went our separate ways. My route was down to Tatkon and Pyinmana covering the main railway line and roads running south from Meiktila to Rangoon, over four hundred miles from base. It was a clear moonlit night as we spotted a locomotive which was duly strafed at Kume Road Railway Station south of Tatkon. Light ack-ack came up from the railway station but we escaped any hits on our aircraft. Then back to Thazi.'

'Landing at Thazi at night was far from easy with the strip sloping away as you touched down. We approached the runway in a long and steady descent not daring to overshoot, touching down as close as possible to the Chance light situated to the right at the near end of the strip. The landing lights in the wings were full on. As soon as the pilot could see the ground from the illumination of his landing lights, then it was time to level off and effect a landing.'

All the pilots used their landing lights to supplement Thazi's meagre lighting. On arrival, they arranged refuelling and bedded down for the night. 'If staying overnight it was in tented accommodation, hoping to find a spare camp bed on which to snatch a few hours' sleep, still in full flying clothing. Breakfast would be lots of tea and probably fried Spam before taking off for base and debriefing.'[212]

Sadly, two of 45's new replacement aircrew did not see the month out. That same day, Flight Lieutenant Brian Draper DFC and Warrant Officer Peter James were killed. Two sections of four aircraft were tasked with a bombing attack on a concentration of Japanese troops and armour near Sedaw. The weather was good but with some ground haze. Draper and James were killed when HR457 broke up at about 4,000ft in a dive. Wal McLellan was flying the following aircraft and saw what happened. 'We were doing some shallow dive-bombing attacks on Jap positions when the aircraft preceding us broke up in a shower of confetti. That may have happened with other crews and never been witnessed.'[213] It was clear to the crews that the Mosquito's airframe problems were by no means fully resolved.

Tiff O'Connor had his own problems on this operation. He and Warrant Officer McKie were flying HR462 and one of the bombs didn't release. 'We had several cases on Mosquitos, fortunately always with wing bombs which tended to fall off on the final approach after all previous efforts to dislodge them had failed. Thus we discovered that they fell off when the flaps were lowered – a jettison procedure! All the armourers insisted that "open hook" hang-up was impossible. My port wing bomb hung-up but fortunately it fell in a ravine on the approach to Kumbhirgram, so we escaped the major part of the blast.'[214] The bomb actually exploded just 500 yards from the north-east end of the runway.

Finally, after months of delays, a third squadron had started flying Mosquito intruder operations. The number of operations delivered during the month fell slightly from January, although the number of aircrew lives lost increased. However, 45 Squadron passed a key milestone, having now effectively lost half of its aircrew establishment since starting conversion to the Mosquito. It was also clear that the problems with the Mosquito airframe were not fully resolved. Even so, the crews loved the aircraft.

Squadron	Mosquito Intruder Operations		Aircrew Losses Operations		Aircrew Losses Training/Other	
	Month	Total	Month	Total	Month	Total
No. 45 Sqn	171	691	4	18	1	3
No. 82 Sqn	182	407	2	5	0	2
No. 27 Sqn	0	45	0	2	0	0
No. 47 Sqn	14	14	0	0	0	0
No. 110 Sqn	0	0	0	0	2	2
Other Units	0	0	0	0	0	9
Total	**367**	**1,157**	**6**	**25**	**3**	**16**

Chapter 14

Total Commitment

March 1945

'Stiff Burma Fight Rages at Meiktila;
Japanese tanks bid to regain airfield is frustrated –
Bitter fighting at Kaukse.'
New York Times, *29 March 1945*

With the monsoon season approaching, the weather was becoming hotter and visibility was decreasing due to the haze. As Warrant Officer 'Bill' Storey, a navigator with 82 Squadron, said, 'The weather, the communication, all served to make low-level flying operations particularly hazardous, quite apart from the attentions of the Japanese.'[215] The demands on the Mosquito intruders continued to increase, with often more than twenty operational sorties rostered each day.

March started disastrously for 82 Squadron! The weather was bad at Kumbhirgram, so the aircraft tasked on 1 March operated from Thazi. Their tasking was to bomb the airfields at Pyinmana and Toungoo, then carry out night rhubarbs. At 2115hrs, detailed with attacking Pyinmana, Pilot Officer Kinnell received a green light from the watch tower and started his take–off run in HR458. He had barely completed 100 yards when the Mosquito inexplicably swung off the runway. The aircraft ran into some cattle, turned over and immediately burst into flames. Both Kinnell and his navigator Warrant Officer Lambert were killed. On investigation, it was found that a tyre burst had caused the crash.

Just three hours later, at 0015hrs the following morning, Flight Sergeant Robert Best and his navigator, Sergeant Andrew Lorimer, took off in HR439 to attack Toungoo. 'This crew has failed to return and nothing has since been heard of them.'[216] It was later discovered that they had crashed near Rangoon.

For the next few days, most of the operations continued to use Thazi as their start point. On 4 March eight of 45's crews were detached there in late afternoon. After a few hours rest, just after midnight they prepared for their op. At 0140hrs on 5 March, Tiff O'Connor started accelerating HR404 for take-off when a water buffalo ran across the runway. His Mosquito was destroyed and the buffalo killed, but luckily Tiff and McKie were able to walk away from the crash. Thazi was temporarily closed by the wreckage. There were some rumours that Japanese sympathisers were stampeding the animals on to the runway to hinder operations.

An advance force of the 17th Indian Division with 255 Tank Brigade had crossed the Irrawaddy in late February where Japanese forces fought a savage and tenacious rearguard action. The British Fourteenth Army continued to push forward the eighty miles towards the strategically important town of Meiktila. After days of heavy fighting, they managed to take it on 4 March, but the Japanese quickly closed in behind them. All reinforcements and supplies, including petrol and ammunition, had to be ferried in by air. The Japanese counter-attacks were frequent and vicious, but they were consistently driven back. Japanese patrols were even infiltrating during the night to mine the airfield, so every morning the airfield had to be cleared of both Japanese and mines before aircraft movements could start. For days the Allied grip on the town and airfield remained on a knife edge, with aircraft often operating during mortar attacks.

The Mosquito tasking had moved up a gear, requiring everyone to work to their limit. Having tried to rest through the evening of 7 March, Benny Walsh reported to the flight hut after midnight to prepare for his next op, scheduled to use the cover of darkness in the early hours of 8 March. Ten aircraft from 45 Squadron were tasked with attacking four Japanese airfields – Heho, Tougoo, Pyinmana and Tennant. Benny and Ossie were one of three crews tasked with glide-bombing Pyinmana airfield, about 100 miles south of Mandalay, with two 500lb instant-fused bombs. The three aircraft took off at intervals of ninety-minutes or more, flying as singletons to ensuring the airfield attacks were well separated. The weather wasn't great, requiring over an hour of flying on instruments. However, Benny and Ossie found their target before dawn, completed their attack and noted that a 'skeleton flarepath was lit'. They then patrolled the airfield for a while but did not see any activity. They landed at Kumbhirgram at 0645hrs, drained from the concentration required during the four-and-a-half-hour long night sortie.

Thinking of breakfast, sleep and the afternoon off, Benny and Ossie went straight into debriefing. They were told that, since the Japanese were attempting to lay siege to Meiktila and recapture it, the squadron's tasking was switched for the next few days and nights to destroying strategic rail bridges to break their supply lines.[217] Then, to their surprise, they were told to get a few hours rest, because they were detailed to report back to the flight hut at midday. They had been rostered to fly again that afternoon!

Earlier that morning, six 82 Squadron aircraft were tasked with bombing the Pyinmana railway bypass bridge over the Sittang River, denying use of the railway to Japanese reinforcements. The op was led by 82's CO, Freddy Snell, with Arthur as his navigator, in HR497 'A'. Two of the other crews were Flight Lieutenants Dick 'Scotty' McKenzie and Ray Pears in HR545 'S', and Babe Wambeek and Brian Mooney in HR311 'P'.

The aircraft took off from Kumbhirgram at 0730hrs in fine but slightly hazy weather. The sortie report noted that: 'All aircraft dropped bombs close to the target without actually hitting the bridge – bursts were seen close to the west and east of the bridge at the north and south – two bursts were seen on the southern approaches and two bursts were seen close to the centre of the bridge on the east side – all bombs were near misses and the bridge may have been damaged by blast but crews do not report any visible damage.' But that only told part of the story!

Freddy Snell made a low-level bombing run, but as he pressed the bomb release button a very heavy explosion occurred beneath their aircraft, with debris flung violently against the aircraft, injuring his navigator, Arthur Maude. Flight Lieutenant Dawes, 82 Squadron's medical officer, reported, 'The aircraft was making a low-level attack flying at about 50ft when a landmine exploded directly below it. A stone thrown upwards by the force of the explosion, penetrated the undersurface of the aircraft, pierced the navigator's seat and hit his right testicle. Shock and pain were severe. Wing Commander Snell very wisely administered a tubunic ampoule of morphia which relieved symptoms and resulted in the navigator falling asleep.'[218] The aircraft was inspected on returning to base which 'showed that the fuselage from nose to tail was riddled with holes and mainplanes and tailplanes were likewise riddled with holes – a huge gaping hole had been torn in the Browning machine-gun stowage in the nose. On further examination of the interior of the fuselage, several medium-sized pieces of flinty stone weighing from ½ to 3 ounces were discovered and examination of the damage to the whole aircraft seems to indicate blunt objects rather than shrapnel caused the majority of the damage.'[219] Arthur's injuries kept him out of action for six weeks.

Having completed their bombing runs on the bridge, Scotty and Babe then swept low over the nearby Lew II airstrip in the hope of catching some Japanese fighters on the ground. Babe, flying as No. 2 to Scotty, explained, 'Having alerted the whole area, it was hardly surprising that we picked up some flak there. My port engine was struck and streamed glycol; intercom with my navigator, Brian Mooney, ceased, and it became apparent that our hydraulics were damaged. With the port propeller feathered I set course for Sadaung, approximately 200 miles to the north, and some twenty-five miles north of the Irrawaddy River, the most advanced airfield at which repairs could be carried out before crossing the mountains to our base in Assam.'

Ray Pears, Scotty's navigator, felt some responsibility, 'He was shot up because we failed to avoid a small landing strip called Lew II, which was defended. It was my fault as leading navigator and was due to a slap-happy feeling that we had got the Japs on the run.'[220]

Scotty and Ray stayed with Babe and Brian, recognising their plight. Prior to the op, they had been briefed that, in an emergency, they could use Meiktila. Babe continued, 'In retrospect it was surprising that we had been briefed that we could use the strip in an emergency. The instructions must have been intended for the single engine fighter-bombers that were giving close support to our ground forces. Now, with one engine feathered and the radiator temperature off the clock, our chances of reaching our own lines were slender.

'Approaching at 2,000ft, I could make out a hive of activity in the circuit, but on descent we entered a thick haze with poor slant visibility at about 1,000ft. Not being able to contact the controller on any of my eight VHF frequencies, but being in a good position to start my approach, I selected "Wheels down" to indicate my intention, in the hope that seeing our plight he would give us a "Green". At that moment a Dakota on take-off threw up a thick cloud of dust, completely obliterating my view of the strip. Seconds later, on checking, I found that my starboard wheel was hanging down but not locked, and my port wheel remained locked up.'

Babe needed to make a decision quickly, whilst he still had sufficient height and airspeed from his one remaining engine. 'With poor visibility and lack of contact with the ground, the risk of collision was high. In addition, without hydraulics, we were now committed to a crash-landing, which could put the strip out of action for the rest of the day. I decided to make for the small satellite strip about seven miles to the south-east, although it was not in our hands at the time. Uneven ground, trees and large boulders precluded a crash-landing elsewhere, and it was better to take the gamble of evading the Japs than risk certain death on that terrain.

'At about 700ft I opened the starboard throttle and, with the undercarriage selected up (but to no avail), turned south-east towards the satellite strip. It appeared out of the haze sooner than expected, and I throttled back and shoved the nose down, but with no flaps my speed built up rapidly. Before belly landing the port airscrew had to be unfeathered to prevent it breaking off at the shaft and cutting into the wing tanks, or into the side of the cockpit and trapping me. The (un)feathering buttons on the Mk VI were on the starboard side of the cockpit, and I was unable to reach them with my harness tight. With no spare hands to loosen my shoulder straps, and no intercom with Brian, I pulled the quick release pin out of my Sutton harness and reached for the button. There was no time to refasten it.

'The ASI was indicating 160 knots [185mph] as we crossed the boundary, with the rough grass strip only 700–800 yards, and a steam roller two thirds of the way down, to the left of centre. Without flaps we would have floated a mile. I cut the remaining fuel cock and ignition switches, threw my left arm across the gunsight, slid forward on the seat placing my face on my arm, and with my forehead pressed against the bullet-proof windscreen, and feet braced against the rudder pedals, eased the stick forward until we struck the ground. The initial deceleration was alarming and would have been of the order of 12G. I was forced rigidly against the windscreen and rudder pedals, and we careered straight for the steamroller. At the last moment the aircraft slewed round to the right and the fuselage broke in half just behind the wing roots.'

Brian had tightened his four-point Sutton harness before impact and, due to taking his crash position, Babe was also unharmed. Babe continued, 'Even before we had ground to a halt, [Scotty] from the leading aircraft was yelling over the R/T "Get out of that aircraft bloody quick." We were out of the top hatch in a flash, and into the scrub and undergrowth nearby, hoping he would get a message to the army. A sickly stench of rotting flesh pervaded the whole area. We heard later that an estimated 4,000 Japs had been killed in the fighting.

'We were reluctant to move until dark in the hope of rescue and about two hours later an army patrol on two Jeeps, each with a Lewis gun mounted on the bonnet, drove cautiously down the side of the strip. When we were certain they were "ours" we came out into the open. They took us on board, standing room only, with the bare hood superstructure to hang on to. The drivers proceeded slowly, and we had to run the gauntlet of snipers in the attics while driving through Meiktila. Before reaching town, we passed along the shore of Meiktila Lake, with numerous bodies floating high in the water in the shimmering heat of the tropical afternoon, all with huge grotesque gas-inflated bellies. The effect was weird and unreal.

'Later, in the safety of the box, after we had thanked our rescuers, we were thanked by the RAF Liaison Officer for not obstructing his airfield. While waiting our turn to be evacuated with the wounded, the army gave us cups of hot sweet tea. As I sipped mine, a ghastly thought occurred to me, "Where had the water come from?" Meiktila Lake, we were told.'[221]

The failure to destroy the strategically important Pyinmana bridges earlier that day was the reason for Benny's and Ossie's additional op. Just four hours after debriefing from their night op, Benny and Ossie were back at the flight hut to be briefed on attacking Pyinmana bridge as part of a Mossie pair, accompanying the CO, Johnny Walker, and his nav, Flying Officer Frank Harper. At the briefing they were also told that Jock, their flight commander, was being posted and promoted with immediate effect. He would leave within the next couple of days. Their new flight commander would be Squadron Leader D.A. Braithwaite DFC*, who would soon arrive at 45 from HQ RAF Burma but needed to work up to operational status on the Mosquito.

Having checked their aircraft, at 1345hrs the Mosquito pair took off, tasked with bombing the Pyinmana railway bridges to the south of the Meiktila junction. After nearly two hours flying low-level through the heat of the afternoon, they arrived at their primary target to find that one span on the main bridge was already down. However, throughout the war, the Japanese had reinforced the vital railway system by building 'bypass' bridges alongside strategically important bridges. Pyinmana was one such bridge and both the main and bypass bridges had to be destroyed to cut the railway line. The CO immediately focused on bombing its bypass bridge. He completed his glide attack at 320mph IAS and his bombs landed just to the east of the bridge. A large blue flash was seen about a quarter of a mile from the south-west end of the Pyinmana main bridge and the blast rocked the CO's Mossie, causing temporary failure of his elevator control. Johnny thought it could have been a land mine – just what had happened to Freddy Snell earlier in the day, near the same bridge. Clearly, the Japanese were using a new tactic against the low-flying Mosquitos.

The two aircraft then followed the railway to the north towards another of the secondary targets. As soon as he and Ossie identified Sinthe rail bridge, Benny started his attack run. He decided to use a slightly slower approach to increase his accuracy, putting his Mosquito into a shallow glide attack at 275mph IAS. Benny released his four 500lb bombs from 400ft onto the bridge, tearing up the railway line. Both crews then looked for opportunity targets as they rhubarbed towards the north, with Benny claiming a train damaged. They landed safely back at base at 1748hrs, as dusk fell, with Benny and Ossie now truly exhausted. After debriefing and a meal, they retired to their bashas.

It wasn't just Meiktila under frequent attacks by the Japanese. The forward airfield at Onbauk, north-east of Mandalay, was also under constant threat so 2945 Field Regiment had mounted a continuous patrol to protect the airfield. In the early hours of 8 March 1945, Japanese Captain Inane and his Butai, disguised as Burmese peasants, reached the outskirts of the airfield. They were surprised by a 2945 Squadron patrol, led by Flight Lieutenant Hollingdale, which resulted in a short, intense fire fight. The Japanese intruders left an officer's pack and sword, radios, arms, ammunition, and demolition charges on the bloodstained ground as they fled, taking their dead and wounded with them. One Japanese soldier was taken prisoner, but when he attempted to escape, he was shot and killed. RAF Regiment casualties were one airman killed and three wounded.[222]

That same day, Bohmu Ba Htoo, the communist commander of the Burma National Army's (BNA's) command unit based in Mandalay, started a local rebellion against the Japanese, diverting attention from the BNA's national leader, Aung San.[223] The Japanese rout was becoming irreversible.

Having completed 'Exercise Beat-Up', a twelve-aircraft dummy attack on Cochin, a few days earlier as the final preparation before operations, on 11 March, thirteen Mosquitos and crews from 110 Squadron flew from RAF Yelahanka direct to RAF Joari, near Cox's Bazar. However, the armourers and ground support had to make their way by train and truck, which would take many days.

That same day, at Kumbhirgram, the CO of 47 Squadron flew his first op in a Mosquito. Until then, Wing Commander Billy Filson-Young had continued to fly operations in the Beaufighter. Their Mosquitos were fitted with RP rails so that they could continue to specialise in using rockets for ground attack. At 1019hrs Billy took off, together with Bob Willis, to rhubarb the roads along the Irrawaddy. Both aircraft scored hits on three open trucks, but both were also hit by Japanese flak during their four-hour operation.

The intruder ops were getting longer as well as more frequent as they tried to hinder the Japanese retreat. On 13 March 1945, Charles Carruthers took part in one of three 82 Squadron ops totalling eleven Mosquitos. Charles was navigating one of the five aircraft tasked with bombing Toungoo, a town on the main railway line midway between Mandalay and Rangoon. 'We took off at 0730hrs … reforming over Tuxedo Junction we continued on to Toungoo and eventually bombed our objective, a telephone exchange being used by the Japs. We also made a strafing attack but nothing caught fire. Turning for home, we eventually landed after four hours forty minutes flying – our longest trip to date.'[224]

On 15 March, 45 and 82 Squadrons collaborated on a joint operation in which each despatched twelve Mossies to attack the oil installations at Yenangyaung. In the attack co-ordinated for 1300hrs, 82 Squadron would deliver their bombs in a shallow–dive attack from 12,000ft, whilst 45 Squadron approached from the east at low-level in line abreast with eleven-second delays on their bombs.

As 45 Squadron flew in at about 300mph at 50ft, some of the aircraft started to draw ahead of the others. The Japanese guns opened up, but flak was just one of the concerns for the crews who had fallen a little behind the others, like Wal McLellan and Jim Vernon in HR451. They also had to contend with their colleagues' bombs, since the time-delays did not seem to work.

Wal recalled, 'Over the target the whole ground came up to meet us as thirty-two 500lb bombs dropped by the preceding aircraft exploded together. We seemed to be flying through solid earth mixed with all sorts of junk from trees to 40-gallon drums. The noise was mind bending and holes, large and small, appeared everywhere in the aircraft. A black log, about six feet long, hung suspended perpendicularly in the air in front of me but there was nothing I could do to avoid it. We hit it with a terrific jar which yawed the aircraft. The log jammed in the leading edge of the wing between me and the port motor and stayed there against the main spar. This was not a good thing as the leading edge also contained the oil radiator for that engine and oil was pouring out. At the same time, every Jap gun was concentrating on us and we could feel the thuds of hits and hear the explosions. I had accepted that this was the end but felt quite calm.'[225]

Wal continued, '... we were really shot up by 40mm flak; I had six feet of teak log jammed in my port oil radiator and the engine consequently seized. In addition, I had a 500lb fused bomb hanging on an open hook in the bomb bay. The starboard engine was overheating, and I could not get above 1,000ft with 500 miles to go to the nearest advanced fighter strip. I was waiting for the glycol in the starboard engine to blow off so I told Jim, my nav, to bale out and I would follow. He refused to go because he was of the opinion that I was quite competent to make a dead stick belly flop in the river or a clearing when the remaining engine quit. Flattering but not too practical! I pointed out that we had a 500lb bomb hung up which would send us sky-high, but he was still unmoved.'

Wal and Jim set course for the airstrip at Kalewa but still had about 100 miles to go when, quite by chance, they found the newly opened Thunderbolt strip at Sinthe.

'We were still arguing amicably when the fighter strip came into view and I landed from a right-hand circuit cursing a Dak which was in its landing circuit ahead of us. With the aid of the handpump we had enough hydraulic pressure to lock the undercart as we touched down but did not have enough pressure to put down the flaps. The coolant blew off in the starboard engine during our approach. Without flaps we were doing 100mph without brakes when we came to the end of the strip on rough ground.' The Mosquito careered through various storage areas and, once the undercarriage collapsed, it slid to a halt on its belly. Happily, the hung-up bomb in the bomb bay did not explode.

'However, the good old Mossie did bring us home, or nearly home, every operation. The aircraft did not get us back to base but we were down in friendly territory.'[226]

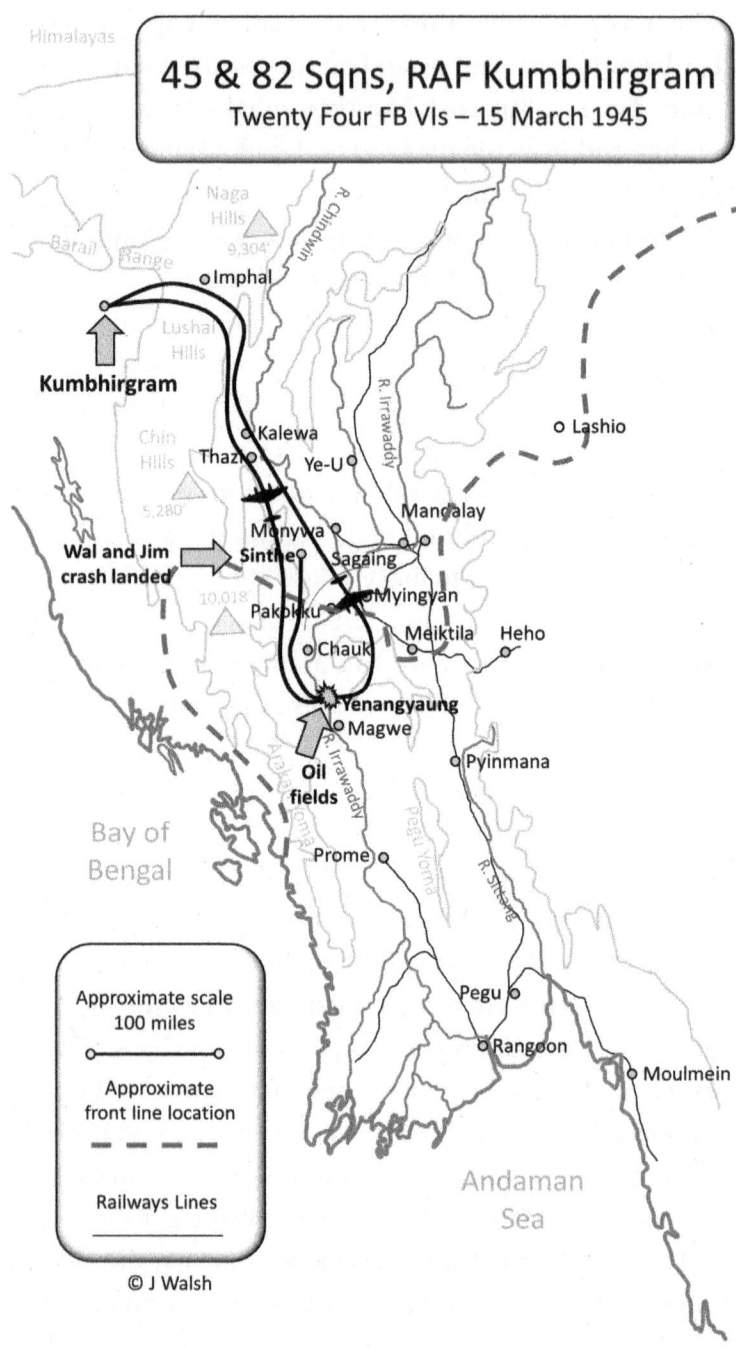

45 & 82 Sqns, RAF Kumbhirgram
Twenty Four FB VIs – 15 March 1945

Himalayas

Naga
Hills
9,304'

Barail Range

R. Chindwin

oImphal

Lushai
Hills

Kumbhirgram

Chin
Hills
5,280'

oKalewa

Thazi o

Ye-U o

R. Irrawaddy

o Lashio

Mandalay

Monywa o

Sinthe o

Sagaing

Wal and Jim
crash landed

10,018'

Pakokku o

Myingyan

Meiktila

Heho

o Chauk

Yenangyaung
o Magwe

Oil
fields

R. Irrawaddy

o Pyinmana

Bay of
Bengal

R. Sittang

Pegu Yoma

Prome o

Approximate scale
100 miles

o————————o

Approximate
front line location

– – – – –

Railways Lines

————————

© J Walsh

Pegu o

o Rangoon

o Moulmein

Andaman
Sea

On 16 March, the convoy of groundcrew and equipment for 110 Squadron finally departed on its way to Joari. However, it would take eleven days to reach them, delaying the start of their operations again. Their CO, Soapy Saunders, was not impressed at all. 'It would appear that little or no organisation was made for the transfer of the squadron equipment onwards to Joari from Calcutta. This is being referred to higher authority.'[227]

The tasking for the intruders now focussed on cutting off supply lines and the Japanese retreat. They attacked bridges and by-pass bridges, servicing and re-arming the aircraft as quickly as possible. The strain on the aircrew, groundcrew, armourers and maintenance staff was intense but they remained focussed, determined not to let their colleagues or the Army down. They were now delivering over twenty-five sorties each day. On 20 March the flag of the Fourteenth Army was raised above the high red walls and the wide moat of Mandalay's Fort Dufferin. Lieutenant General Slim declared, in his Order of the Day, that 'there could have been no victory without the constant support of the Allied air forces .... it is their victory as much as ours.'[228]

On 25 March 1945, 45 Squadron's CO, 'Johnny' Walker, flew another sortie in HR627 with his navigator, Frank Harper. They took off at 0655hrs to attack an important bridge over the Sittang River at Toungoo. The bridge was well defended and Johnny made several runs over the target before releasing his bombs. He then returned over the target to secure a photograph of the results. His aircraft was hit, smashing the bullet-proof windscreen in front of him. Johnny was cut about the eyes, temporarily blinded and lost consciousness. Frank immediately unbuckled from his seat, leaned over Johnny and took over the controls of the aircraft, flying clear of the target. When the CO came round, Frank gave him first aid and staunched the flow of blood. Meiktila refused them permission to land. However, with shepherding from wing-man George Dyke and 'Joe' Zussen, Frank and his badly injured pilot managed to fly their damaged aircraft to Monywa. After two aborted landing attempts, Frank and Johnny touched down successfully at 1030hrs. Johnny was transferred to hospital in Comilla where the surgeons were able to save the sight of both of his eyes, although one had permanently impaired vision. Having completed fifty-three Mosquito intruder ops, Johnny Walker was repatriated to the UK, starting his journey home on 21 April 1945. He was later awarded the DSO. Duke Duclos was immediately appointed as the new CO, replacing Johnny.

The next day, two 45 Squadron Mosquitos departed at 0415hrs to patrol the Toungoo-Pyinmana area, arriving at 0615hrs. Warrant Officer Alan Holmes, flying HR527, sighted two vehicles near Toungoo, attacked and scored hits on one of the vehicles. Unfortunately, he failed to pull out of the dive and the aircraft crashed, bursting into flames. Both Alan and his navigator, Flight Sergeant Bill Austin, were recorded as 'Missing believed killed'.

On 27 March, reflecting the way that the war was going, the BNA openly declared war on the Japanese. Aung San successfully led the BNA in a national uprising against the Japanese in collaboration with the Allied Forces. BNA units near the British frontlines on or near the Irrawaddy River requested arms and supplies from Allied units operating in this area. They also seized control of the civil institutions in most of the main towns.

The Mosquito crews continued delivering maximum effort. On 29 March, 82 Squadron recorded the loss of another aircraft, HR489. 'Once again tragedy marred a good day. Just south of Allagappa, Flying Officer Hayes was heard over the V.H.F. warning his section leader that his aircraft was on fire. He was ordered to abandon his machine but was not seen to have obeyed. The aircraft crashed in flames and although other aircraft flew around the blazing machine for some considerable time no sign of the crew could be seen. It would appear that the pilot Flying Officer G.G. Hayes and his navigator, Sergeant R.E. Black, were both killed but in the absence of definitive proof are posted as "Missing believed killed."'[229]

Operational tasking for 45 Squadron reached a crescendo at the end of the month. Alf Pridmore recalled the ops that he and his pilot, Don Blenkhorne, flew. 'On the 30th, the first sortie was flown at 0655 in Mosquito HR368 [to Loikaw road bridge], and it lasted four hours. After a brief rest the second sortie [to a road bridge SW of Ywashhit] began at 1400 and ended almost four hours later! With a little rest, the next sortie was flown [to Loikaw road bridge again] at 0720 the next morning. On all of these sorties the targets were damaged.'[230]

On 31 March, ten 45 Squadron Mosquitos were tasked with an early morning attack on road and rail bridges. Benny and Ossie's target was a road bridge to the east of Toungoo, over 120 miles south of Meiktila. Setting off just after 0700hrs, immediately Benny realised they had a problem with their wing-mounted bombs, so he jettisoned them on take-off. Since they still had two 500lb eleven-second delay bombs in their bomb bay, they continued with the raid. They bombed the bridge from low-level, with both bombs on target. However, the bridge was not destroyed. Benny then dropped the Mosquito to treetop height to rhubarb any traffic on the roads and railway north towards Yamethin. On their journey north, they checked the state of the Sinthe bridge that they had bombed the previous day, as well as the Sinthe bypass rail bridge. They didn't find any opportunity targets to strafe and returned safely to Kumbhirgram after another gruelling four-hour twenty-minute sortie. Benny and Ossie handed their aircraft back to groundcrew, who immediately started to service, refuel and rearm it. The squadron was now very short of serviceable aircraft and eight of the ten aircraft from the morning op were being used again for another op that afternoon.

At Joari, determined to start operations during March, Soapy Saunders arranged for two crews to fly ops on the last day of the month. Finally, 110 Squadron's Mosquitos were operational.

For the crews, the month had been exhausting. As Benny Walsh recalled, 'Between 5 and 31 March the squadron kept up a relentless and intense bombing and strafing campaign against the Japs. Road and rail transport were shot up at every opportunity and bridges were bombed. My bridge bombing efforts included Thamkin (missed), Thwatty (badly damaged), Sinthe (damaged) and Toungoo. By the end of the month we had notched up sixty-four hours day and fourteen hours thirty minutes night operational flying. One of the best results was obtained on 26 and 27 when Salin was bombed at first light. Four 500lb bombs were dropped accurately on a Jap camp. The following day a rhubarb was carried out on the railway and road between Kyaukpadaung and Pyinmana, two locos were shot up and a three-ton MT was set alight before ammunition ran out.'[231]

During the month, the Mosquito intruder squadrons delivered an impressive 749 operational sorties, with 45 Squadron alone flying 1,092 daytime operational hours and 256 night-time operational hours in 352 operations. In just one month it had dropped 556,500lb of bombs, more than during its entire sixteen months flying Vultee Vengeances! Serviceability had been high, at eighty-seven per cent, but this had come at a cost. Spare parts and replacement aircraft had dried up towards the end of the month, with parts being scavenged from crashed aircraft. Unfortunately, most of the serviceable aircraft required major inspections in fewer than forty flying hours. The engineers had already started scrapping Mosquitos during the month.

No. 45 Squadron now had a new CO, one new flight commander and one vacant flight commander position, since Squadron Leader Braithwaite was posted out at the end of the month. With only thirteen serviceable Mosquitos, Duke Duclos reported that, 'unless the supply position improves, we shall be very short indeed.'[232] He also raised two concerns, starting with the eleven-second delay fuses, 'The uncertainty of delay which has been stated to range from four to twenty seconds on the supposed eleven seconds has prevented more than two aircraft bombing line-astern – and that fairly close – because of the real danger of being damaged by our own bombs.

Secondly, the increasing number of silver-doped Mosquitos is being met with increasing disapproval of the air crews. Whatever the technical advantage of this scheme may be, and it is considered to be very limited, the operational disadvantages incurred are considerable.'[233]

Freddy Snell, 82's CO, echoed the concerns about aircraft. 'The large number of hours flown this month, although excellent in its way, has put a great strain on the replacement situation, in the rear areas, with a consequent drop in serviceability which may be felt for some time.'[234]

Eight aircrew had been killed in operations during the month, six from 82 Squadron and two from 45 Squadron.

Squadron	Mosquito Intruder Operations		Aircrew Losses Operations		Aircrew Losses Training	
	Month	Total	Month	Total	Month	Total
No. 45 Sqn	352	1,043	2	20	0	3
No. 82 Sqn	269	776	6	11	0	2
No. 47 Sqn	126	140	0	0	0	0
No. 27 Sqn	0	45	0	2	0	0
No. 110 Sqn	2	2	0	0	0	2
Other Units	0	0	0	0	0	9
Total	749	2,006	8	35	0	16

Chapter 15

Early Monsoon

April 1945

'Death Of A Thousand Cuts Imposed On Japs By RAF. Air Power Has Been The Decisive Factor In Defeat Of Enemy In Burma – Hamstrings Foe And Helps Our Own Army.'
Toronto Telegram, *7 April 1945*

L ieutenant General Slim feared that the Japanese would defend Rangoon to the last man through the monsoon, which would put the 14th Army in a disastrous supply situation. In late March, he therefore asked for Operation Dracula, the capture of Rangoon, to be reinstated at short notice. The push forward had to continue.

March had been a punishing month for both the aircrew and aircraft, especially in 45 Squadron with seven of their crews having flown eighteen or more ops during the month. After normal operations with four aircraft bombing a fuel dump on 1 April, new CO Duke Duclos arranged a much needed forty-eight-hour stand-down. The aircrews caught up on some rest and the engineers returned a couple more aircraft back into service.

Operations resumed on the morning of the 4 April 1945 with six aircraft flying on operations in the morning. Benny and Ossie were one of the four 45 Squadron crews tasked that afternoon with attacking Zinga village, well into Japanese-held territory. Their mission was to use incendiary bombs to destroy the village, which the Japanese were using as a military base.

Benny and Ossie would be the final aircraft in the attack and had been allocated F-Fox (HR567). They knew this aircraft well, having last flown it on 10 February when they had crashed it into a burnt out DC3 during a night-time emergency landing at Onbauk. It was early afternoon, hot and humid, when they walked out to their aircraft, now repainted with the silver dope. Although for night ops this colour scheme could make the aircraft more vulnerable, Benny wasn't particularly concerned. The silver could be useful with their task that day, since they would be attacking from the west as the sun set. Benny and Ossie walked around the outside of their aircraft carefully completing the external checks, since it had just been returned to the squadron. Finally, a check in the bomb bay and under the wings that the armourers had armed her with two 500lb HE bombs and two 500lb incendiaries.[235] All was good.

Even with the cockpit windows open, the cockpit was stiflingly hot inside. As soon as they were settled, they ran their pre-start checks. Benny fired up the two Merlins in turn, checked temperatures and pressures and, with a green light from the watch tower, immediately taxied to the runway holding point for take-off. The first leg of their sortie was the familiar transit over the Manipur Range, through the pass between the Naga and Lushai Hills, and then south along the Chin Hills to their forward landing strip at Thazi. They had done it many times before and it required no real planning. Since Thazi was now well behind the Allied 'bomb line', it was a relatively relaxed one-hour flight to the jungle strip. Once parked up, they handed their aircraft to the groundcrew, who set about refuelling the Mosquitos ready for the main part of the op itself. In shade from the afternoon sun, all four crews involved in the operation finalised tactics.

Zinga was a further 200 miles south along the Sittang River valley. However, to ensure surprise, the Mosquitos would separate into pairs and aim to arrive at dusk for a co-ordinated attack on the village. Benny and Ossie's route would take about 100 minutes to fly. They would fly low-level behind the Pegu Yoma range of hills, on the eastern side of the Irrawaddy River valley. Benny and Ossie watched as the first pair departed down the strip from Thazi, then they fired up F-Fox and taxied to the holding point, accompanied by HR332 flown by Flying Officer Freddie Fortune, with Joe Mears as navigator. It was time!

The Mosquito pair headed south-west, initially following the Chindwin River. South of Monywa, they changed course towards Meiktila, which they used as a way point south towards the Pegu Yoma and Japanese-held territory. Hugging the western side of the hills, they were now on maximum alert, scanning for fighters from the still active Japanese airfields at Magwe, Pyinmana and Toungou. They continued at low-level throughout, even though it consumed more fuel. The leg was uneventful, not even any small arms fire. Ossie located the ground feature that he was using to start their attack run on Zinga. He gave Benny their easterly heading and, with the setting sun behind them obscuring their arrival, they set off over the Pegu Yoma hills and across the Sittang River floodplain. With Freddie leading towards the village, fires were evident from the first attacks. Benny positioned his Mossie for their attack run, dropping the incendiaries and high explosives, strafing the village with cannon and machine gun. Fifty years later Benny recalled the attack in a quite detached way, 'As the evening light began to fade we ran in to bomb Zinga village and, as we left the target, it appeared that it had been accurately hit.'[236] Their mission was accomplished and the village was left burning.

With darkness falling, the four Mosquitos started their journeys back to Kumbhirgram. Having cleared the mountains to the east of the Sittang River valley, they headed north. Even though it was more tiring for the crew, they remained in their pairs at low-level, reducing the chance of hostile attacks.

Usually, they maintained radio silence during ops, however Freddie called through to Benny because their Mosquito's air speed indicator had failed, making navigation at night extremely difficult and landing hazardous. Benny immediately adopted the role of 'shepherd', with Freddie in loose formation on him. The return trip in the dark would take longer because Benny and Ossie couldn't risk losing Freddie and Joe.

As they headed back towards base, Ossie became increasingly concerned with F-Fox's unusually high fuel consumption. Climbing to a higher altitude and reducing their speed would improve their consumption but make them an easier target. With fuel becoming more critical, Benny and Ossie reviewed their alternatives, recognising that Freddie and Joe were relying on them. Even though they were still over Japanese-held territory, Benny suggested to Ossie that he could climb for height and they could bale out over the jungle. Ossie was totally against this proposal. 'You have to be kidding! I packed this parachute myself and there is definitely no way I am going to rely on it.'[237] They concluded that their best and possibly only option was to try to make it to Monywa, which could light up a flarepath for them. Benny climbed the Mosquito to 5,000ft, with Freddie shadowing him, and then set it up for maximum endurance. They called for a QDM, an emergency homing, to Monywa, advising them that they would need an 'immediate landing'.

Descending from 5,000ft, they could see Monywa as soon as the flarepath was lit. Benny had very little fuel left so he flew directly towards the airfield, with Freddie following relatively closely behind and relying on Benny to keep the right airspeed. Having positioned his Mosquito to land, Benny ran his landing checks, selected flaps, lowered the undercarriage and switched on the landing lights. As he continued his final approach to the runway threshold, his aircraft's lights revealed the runway already below them. To his horror, Benny realised that Monywa had only lit a flarepath long enough for the Hurricane fighters based there. Even worse, the flarepath was at the far end of the runway! They had no fuel and Freddie's Mossie was just a few seconds behind them. They didn't have any options other than to land.

'Brace, Ossie. Brace,' Benny shouted.

Benny touched the Mosquito down at just over 120mph at the start of the flarepath, switched off the fuel, throttled back the engines and started applying the brakes. He and Ossie prepared themselves for the inevitable crash, as well as a possible impact from the following Mosquito. They went off the end of the runway and continued into the darkness. Barbed wire at the airfield perimeter tangled with the turning propellers and flailed the nose and cockpit of their aircraft. Then they hit a defensive gun position which ripped off the Mosquito's undercarriage. Freddie's Mosquito couldn't avoid hitting them, ripping off its undercarriage during the impact.[238] After the cacophony of noise from the crash, there was near silence, apart from the ticking of the hot engines. Released from their seats and their parachute harnesses, Benny and Ossie scrambled to get out of their Mosquito. They quickly realised that their cockpit hatch was blocked by barbed wire and popped the emergency exit panel in the cockpit canopy, climbed out onto the wing root and clambered down to the ground. There was no fire but there was no time to hang around with hot engines, fuel and a damaged aircraft made of wood. As they jogged away from their aircraft, they checked with Freddie and Joe. Incredibly, no one had been hurt, even in the gun position. Both HR567 and HR332 were total write–offs.[239] It was Benny and Ossie's final Mosquito op.

In Joari, 110 Squadron had quickly settled into the rhythm of operational flying, with two Mosquito pairs tasked on both 1 and 2 April, increasing to three pairs on each of the next three days. On 6 April, again three pairs were tasked but, sadly, Flight Lieutenant Bernard Findlay and Flying Officer Lawrence Hurst failed to return from their road and rail recce from Pegu to Martaban. They were 110 Squadron's first operational losses with the Mosquito.

The tasking for the intruder Mosquito squadrons was changing, now involving destroying enemy fuel and supply dumps, as well as troop concentrations and railways. The railway station at Hngettheik was 45 Squadron's target on both 5 and 6 April, then six aircraft took out an ammunition and supply dump at Pasawng. However, after the total commitment in March, they rarely managed to exceed eight sorties a day. Supply of replacement aircraft had reduced to a trickle and most needed some form of 'Minor' service, delaying operational use. Additionally, a Special Technical Instruction required that all Merlin engines needed their valve covers removed, but incredibly, no replacement gaskets were available. The fitters resorted to cutting up maps from the map store and making gaskets out of compressed map paper!

The conversion from Beaufighters to Mosquitos continued for 47 Squadron, increasing the number of daily Mosquito sorties from two and four towards six and eight. Again, fuel dumps, bridges and troop concentrations were their targets.

On 12 April, 47's CO, Billy Filson-Young, led three other Mosquitos to attack a reported troop build-up near Allanmyo. They searched thoroughly but could only see a few seemingly deserted bashas. After strafing them, they searched for other opportunity targets. First, they attacked the oil pipeline at Malun, without noticeable success, before strafing three camouflaged oil tanks at Minbu. One gave off a 'belch of flame' and the camouflage netting caught fire on them all. They concluded that the tanks must have been empty apart from residual gases.

A couple of days later, a pair of 47's Mosquitos were tasked with attacking a fuel dump at Toungoo, close to a reported Japanese rest camp. The attack was very successful, with three bashas on fire and black smoke rising to 1,500ft. During the attack, the port engine of the Mosquito piloted by Canadian Flight Lieutenant Alward Scott caught fire after being hit by 20mm flak. Both Scott and his navigator, Flying Officer Fisher, baled out. The other Mosquito crew watched Fisher land in a clearing but last saw Scott suspended in a tree, struggling. Their crashed aircraft was burning furiously about 200 yards away. Alward Scott had been seriously wounded in the arm by the flak and died from loss of blood. He was twenty-three years old, the only son of Annie and Elmer Scott from New Brunswick in Canada. Fisher returned to the squadron after about two weeks, evading capture with help from friendly Burmese.

Three days later, 47 Squadron carried bombs for the first time on their Mosquitos. Information had been received the previous evening that a Japanese division on the move in the Mawchi area was bottled up by a bridge destroyed by British forward troops. Three Mosquitos from 47 Squadron joined with seven from 82 and two from 45. All were armed with 500lb eleven-second delay bombs. Unfortunately, Flight Lieutenant Butler and Flight Sergeant Robson from 47 Squadron crashed just after take-off from Kumbhirgram, their bombs exploded and their aircraft caught fire. Both pilot and navigator were killed. On investigation, there seemed no indication of mechanical failure. The remaining aircraft reported successfully bombing the troop concentration at Mawchi, with 82 Squadron's Albert Tooth reporting direct hits on both a powerhouse and store houses.

At Joari, after a stand-down on 9 April, 110 Squadron continued to be tasked with roads, waterways, railways and bridges between Toungoo, Pegu and Moulmein, extending as far as the Burma-Thailand railway. Mostly they operated in pairs, with occasionally three Mosquitos being tasked. CO Soapy Saunders encouraged relaxation, such as being entertained on 15 April by the RAF Road Show at the Paddibird Theatre. On 17 April, a stand-down, he organised a bombing range for the aircrew to practice. Those not involved had the opportunity for some sea bathing at Cox's Bazar.

On 18 April two crews were tasked with searching the Twante Canal south from Kawetkin for reported heavily camouflaged motor torpedo boats. Mosquito HR629, piloted by Flight Lieutenant Raymond Rootes, with navigator Pilot Officer Stephen Blower, failed to return.

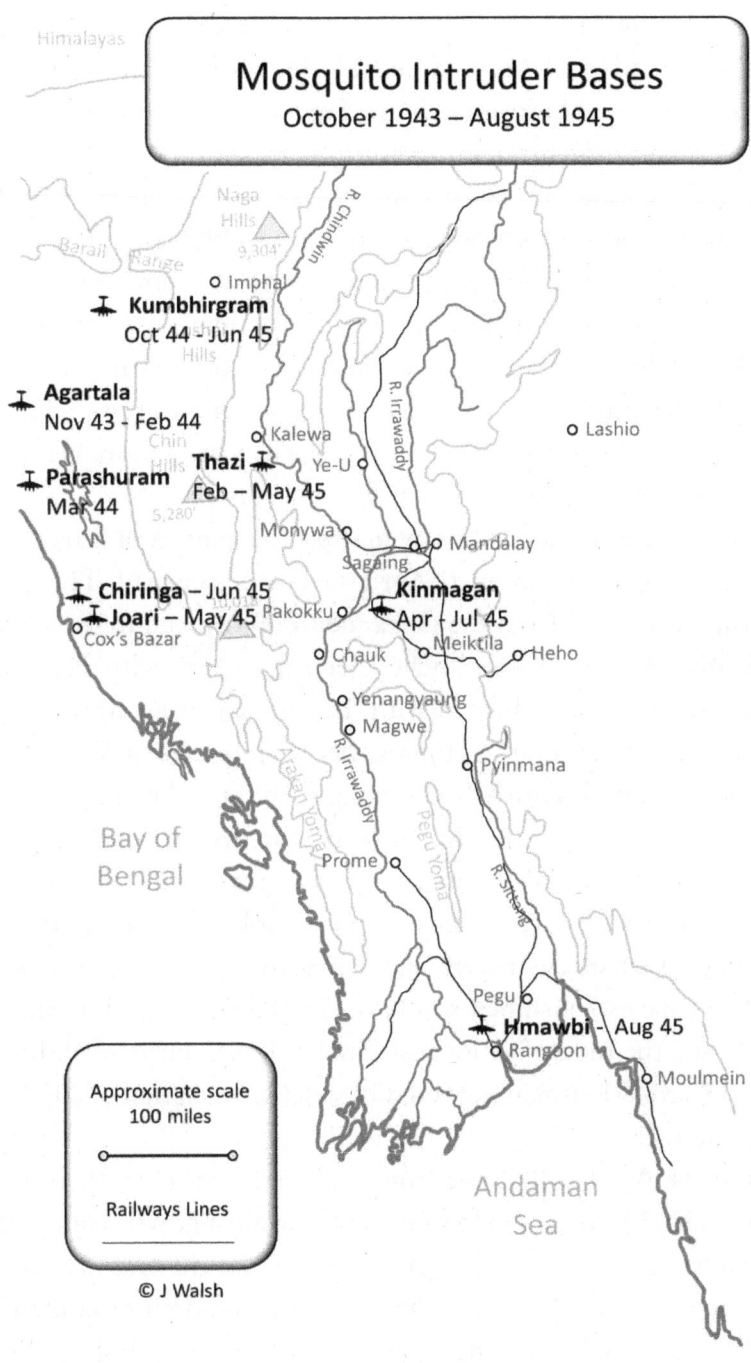

Mosquito Intruder Bases
October 1943 – August 1945

Himalayas

Naga Hills 9,304'

R. Chindwin

o Imphal

✈ **Kumbhirgram**
Oct 44 - Jun 45

Barail Range

Hills

✈ **Agartala**
Nov 43 - Feb 44

o Lashio

o Kalewa

Chin Hills

Thazi ✈

Ye-U o

R. Irrawaddy

✈ **Parashuram**
Mar 44

Thazi
Feb – May 45

5,280'

Monywa o

Sagaing

o Mandalay

✈ **Chiringa** – Jun 45

Kinmagan

✈ **Joari** – May 45

Pakokku o

Kinmagan
Apr - Jul 45

Cox's Bazar

o Chauk

Meiktila o Heho

o Yenangyaung

o Magwe

R. Irrawaddy

Arakan Yoma

o Pyinmana

**Bay of
Bengal**

Pegu Yoma

R. Sittang

Prome o

Pegu o

Approximate scale
100 miles

Hmawbi - Aug 45

o Rangoon

o Moulmein

Railways Lines

Andaman
Sea

© J Walsh

That same day, in preparation for the final assault on Rangoon, the commanders of both 45 and 82 Squadrons were advised of a move from Kumbhirgram to Joari. Two days later Duke Duclos flew to Joari to investigate the implications of the move. Whilst operations and daily Mosquito servicing would take place at Joari, the Repair and Inspection people would remain at Kumbhirgram.

There was little let up in the operations for both 45 and 82 at Kumbhirgram, even whilst packing for the move was taking place. Both squadrons were managing six or more operational sorties per day. New aircrew arrived and some experienced crews left. After three years with 45 Squadron, Wal McLellan and Jimmy Vernon left Kumbhirgram for their journey home to Australia.

With preparations underway to triple the number of Mosquitos at Joari, just after midday on 21 April the heavens opened. The 'terrific downpour of rain' from the chota monsoon resulted in the airmen's and officers' tents being 'inches deep in water', with many tents collapsing. Everyone helped with 'bailing out' prior to settling for the night. The runway, a fair-weather strip with a surface of rolled paddy, was unserviceable and remained so the following day.

Back in Rangoon, on 22 April, on the instructions of General Heitaro Kimura and without the Allies realising it, the Japanese quietly started leaving the city. Some troops were evacuated by sea, although British destroyers claimed several ships. Kimura's own HQ and the establishments of both the Burmese Head of State, Ba Maw, and the Indian Nationalist, Subhas Bose, started making their way towards Moulmein, covered by a defensive action of 105 Mixed Brigade at Pegu.

On 24 April, 110 Squadron launched eleven of their twelve serviceable Mosquitos in two operations against heavily camouflaged motor torpedo boats in Thonga. That same day the first 45 Squadron Mosquito arrived at Joari, followed by one hundred groundcrew in Dakotas on 26 April. The squadron had flown its last operations from Kumbhirgram the previous day – seven aircraft against three different targets. On 27 April eleven more 45 Squadron Mosquitos were flown to Joari, as well as fourteen 82 Squadron Mossies.

Compared to Kumbhirgram, the conditions at Joari were basic. There were concerns that the runway would not cope with three squadrons of Mosquitos, especially if it was hit by another downpour. Added to that, the domestic arrangements were rudimentary and there were no charpoys! Those with their own camp bed were fine but others had to make their own bed from bamboo. In addition to poor accommodation, it was hotter and more humid than Assam. Even though it was uncomfortable, they just got on with it. Food for the new arrivals was provided by 110 Squadron until their messes were established, with 82 and 45 Squadrons deciding to operate a communal officers' mess. They hadn't even settled in when 45 Squadron and the servicing echelon were told that they were to be withdrawn on 15 May to Chakulia, to be rested from operations.

On 27 April only 110 Squadron was operational, the other two still completing their move which would take two more days. That day, 110 Squadron launched ten aircraft on four different night operations, one of which was a recce by a Mosquito pair of the Bay of Martaban. One of the aircraft failed to return. Although their colleagues were hoping for favourable news, Flying Officer St. John Hawkins and Flight Sergeant Wilfred Louis Allen were posted as 'Missing believed killed'.

No. 47 Squadron had now completed its conversion to Mosquitos at Kumbhirgram. With the 14th Army pressing southwards, intruders were needed in central Burma to help prevent the Japanese from regrouping at Moulmein or retreating into Thailand. On 26 April, after completing an evening rhubarb along the Sittang River and railways north-east of Rangoon, two of 47 Squadron's Mossies landed at Kinmagan, which would be their new base.

RAF Kinmagan was an abandoned Japanese airfield fifty-five miles south-west of Mandalay. Whilst it had a 2,000-yard north-south uneven dirt strip and anti-blast shelters for the dispersed aircraft, most other facilities were primitive, with only tented accommodation. The monsoon season was starting, and it was clear that drainage would be a problem. Supplies would also be an issue because Kinmagan was nearly 400 miles away from the closest railhead and the established servicing facilities in Assam. Everything, including fuel, armaments, spare parts and food, required to keep the Mosquitos and crews operational had to be flown in by the ubiquitous Dakotas.

On 27 April, Billy Filson-Young and a further eight Mosquitos relocated to Kinmagan. The following day, they were immediately operational, sending four pairs against different targets, strafing and bombing. On landing from his sortie, Pilot Officer H.D. Milne suffered a brake failure. He overshot the airfield and his aircraft was written off.

Lewis 'Sandy' Osterfield, one of the armourers, had clear memories of living conditions at Kinmagan. 'We were four to six to a small ridge tent, sleeping on half a dozen bamboo poles roped together propped up on empty ammunition containers with one blanket for a mattress and a mosquito net. This was not exactly luxury accommodation! The food was, shall we say, just tolerable and, with the heat and humidity when the monsoon struck, "prickly heat" had to be kept at bay.'[240] It was not much better for the officers, according to pilot Bob Willis. 'It was a case of looking after oneself in a small ridge tent for two plus camp beds, canvas washstand, Tilley lamp and a few minor luxuries usually begged, borrowed or scrounged.'[241]

On 29 April, as IV Corps continued to close in on Rangoon, in preparation for Operation Dracula, Operation Freeborn was launched. Luckily, the early arrival of the monsoon season did not stop the airlifting of a battalion group from 9 Brigade to Pyuntaza airfield, about forty miles north of Rangoon and just north of Pegu, to cut off the Japanese escape route eastwards. Twenty-eight transports re-positioned the infantry and their support equipment. The troops immediately set about clearing Pegu of enemy, discovering in the process about 400 British and American prisoners of war being marched by the Japanese towards the Sittang River and into Thailand.

The deteriorating weather also caused concerns for Operation Dracula. The plan started with a force of paratroops neutralising seaward-facing heavy guns followed by a seaborne invasion, units of XV Corps entering the city from the Rangoon River estuary. Both operations were to be covered by extensive air support from 224 Group, with 221 Group maintaining pressure on any outlying Japanese formations. The Strategic Air Force had been preparing the way to take Rangoon by saturation bombing of strategic supply dumps, including using twenty of Bomber Command's Superfortresses.

The intruders continued to be tasked with communications and supply routes, in general coping reasonably well with the weather conditions, but sometimes it was impossible. On 30 April 1945, Arthur Maude flew as Babe Wambeek's navigator. 'We were briefed for a rhubarb on the Rangoon River and, after taking off from Joari where the squadron was now based, we encountered massive CuNimbus in the Bay of Bengal. We couldn't get under them or round them and finally had to admit defeat and return to Joari.'[242]

That same day, 47 Squadron flew eight Mosquito sorties against two targets. Billy Filson-Young led four aircraft against a reported Japanese concentration at Nammekon. Although the bashas that they bombed and strafed seemed deserted, 'a report later received from 221 Group that many Jap casualties were caused and a stores dump set on fire.'

Through the month of April, the four Mosquito intruder squadrons completed 483 operational sorties. March's 'maximum effort' had resulted in reduced serviceability in both 45 and 82 Squadrons. The early start to the monsoon season was not helping either, but Duke Duclos reported that 45 Squadron aircrews 'were as keen as mustard' that they should prove their worth in 224 Group. No. 110 Squadron lost six pilots and navigators, with two more deaths in 47 Squadron.

Billy Filson-Young reported that the change from bashas to tented accommodation for 47 Squadron had not presented any problems, and that the men had not complained about the primarily tinned food at Kinmagan, even though 'rations are only fair.' From reviewing the men's letters home, he reported that the move and conditions were 'accepted philosophically'. However, having been told that shortages at Kumbhirgram were due to providing for the men in the forward areas, there was 'great disappointment to many to find that the position is even worse in the forward areas than the back areas. There is also a widespread belief that all personnel serving in this theatre are forgotten and that their effort is not considered in its proper proportion.'[243]

Squadron	Mosquito Intruder Operations		Aircrew Losses Operations		Aircrew Losses Training	
	Month	Total	Month	Total	Month	Total
No. 45 Sqn	136	1,179	0	20	0	3
No. 82 Sqn	135	911	0	11	0	2
No. 47 Sqn	91	231	2	2	0	0
No. 110 Sqn	131	133	6	6	0	2
No. 27 Sqn	0	45	0	2	0	0
Other Units	0	0	0	0	0	9
Total	483	2,499	8	41	0	16

Chapter 16

Harsh Environment

May 1945

*'Rangoon Captured in Lightning Drive; Capital's Fall
Heralds Early Burma Liberation – British Move to Seal
Retreat Gaps. Major Burma Victory.'*
New York Times, *3 May 1945, Calcutta, India*

It was not only the early arrival of the monsoon that was being felt in Rangoon by mid–April. The Japanese, their prisoners and the Burmese locals knew that the Allies were approaching the city. Johnny Yanota, a POW since he and his pilot Cliff Emeny had been shot down on 9 November, recalled, 'Rumours started circulating as to how close our troops were, and air activity increased considerably. Mustangs and Thunderbolts were constantly overhead dive bombing and strafing in Rangoon town and along the rivers.'[244]

On 24 April the buzz around the jail was that the Japanese were preparing to leave. One of the prisoners, Don Lomas, an RAF warrant officer wireless operator, had found some scraps of paper and started writing notes, 'April 25th. Paraded to discover who was "fit" who was unfit. I and rest of crew placed in latter category. All Japs wearing new kit – gave us large bundles of used clothes, shoes, etc.' The Japanese officers and guards were leaving and had selected about 400 able-bodied prisoners to accompany them. 'Party moved off at 1600hrs. Raining heavily – all very wet – a dismal spectacle.' The next day Don wrote, 'New guards now in charge. Different types entirely – much more intellectual and sympathetic.' Then he noted, 'April 27th. Moved into dining hall upstairs – very nice indeed.' Still under guard, Don wrote, 'April 28th. Received more food including very large amount of meat and sugar. Meals really excellent now – also receiving lots of cigars, cheroots, etc, etc. Lots of fires still raging. Had good sing-song after lights out.'[245] For the POWs left in Rangoon jail, liberation was feeling close.

Johnny Yanota continued, 'On Sunday, 29 April at about 2030hrs, a member of our compound saw a truck loaded down with kit leaving the prison. This news, of course, spread among the prisoners instantly. We then noticed that there was no guard at the front of our compound, so we started shouting in an attempt to attract any guard who happened to be around. When no guard appeared, we yelled across to the Chinese compound and asked a prisoner named Anthony if he could see any guards. When he replied in the negative, Wing Commander Hudson, acting as our CO in place of the more-senior Wing Commander Hill, who was ill with dysentery, climbed over the fence to inform No. 6 Compound of the state of affairs. He went over to their gate and started chatting with the English prisoners, and suddenly Flight Lieutenant MacDonald noticed a note attached to the railings of the gate.'[246]

RANGOON 29 April 1945

Gentlemen,
Bravely you have come here opening prison gate. We have gone keeping your prisoner safely with Nipponese knightship. Afterwards we may meet again at the front somewhere. Then let us fight bravely each other. (We had kept the gate's keys in the gate room.)

Nipponese Army

The prisoners forced open the compound gate and did a recce. There were no guards on the main gate, so Johnny and other prisoners stood guard to prevent either the BDA or INA entering the prison. They also found paper and pencils, blankets and Japanese cigarettes, which were immediately distributed. Then they found a second note, attached to the main prison gate.

Rangoon
29th April 1945.

To the whole captured persons of Rangoon Jail.

According to the Nippon military order, we hereby give you liberty and admit to leave this place at your own will.

Regarding food and other materials kept in the compound, we give you permission to consume them, as far as your necessity is concerned.

We hope that we shall have an opportunity to meet you again at battlefield of somewhere.

We shall continue our war effort eternally in order to get the emancipation of all Asiatic Races.

Harvo Ato [Haruo Ito]
the chief officer of Rangoon Branch Jail

Realising that the new Japanese guards had left, the prisoners released everyone still in solitary confinement.

On 1 May the first phase of Operation Dracula was initiated as planned. Two pathfinder aircraft and thirty-eight transports of the 317th and 319th Troop Carrier Squadrons USAAF lifted off from Akyab carrying Gurkha paratroops, which they successfully dropped over their intended landing ground at Elephant Point, south of Rangoon at the mouth of the Rangoon River. The Gurkhas met little resistance from the Japanese rearguard.

Johnny was told what happened, 'Gurkha paratroopers, ahead of the naval force, had come upon thirty Japs and had wiped them all out, with the exception of one who they left for dead. The ears had been cut off of all of them, including the one survivor who was later picked up by our troops; ear-lopping was a Gurkha tradition.'

Gordon Thewlis, 82 Squadron navigator, recalled his twenty-sixth op. 'It was 2 May 1945, the first day of Operation Dracula, the invasion of lower Burma via the port of Rangoon. The task of 82 Squadron was to neutralise the gun positions, both ground artillery and anti-aircraft protecting an oil refinery situated at Syriam about five miles to the south of Rangoon. It was essential to put these guns out of commission. Royal Marine Commandos were coming up the estuary in landing craft which would have left them like sitting ducks. We were in two flights of four Mosquitos, each armed with two 500lb, eleven-second delay, fused bombs.

'Prior to take off on this operation from Joari, newsreel cameramen recorded our open-air briefing and continued to film as we climbed aboard and took off. The whole trip took five hours and fifteen minutes.'[247] Gordon's mother worked as a cinema usherette so, after post-op debriefing, he quickly wrote an air telegram to her advising her to look out for him on the *Movietone News*. He couldn't write any more, because of censorship restrictions.

The POWs were worried, as Johnny Yanota explained: 'It started at dawn; bombers and fighters spent all morning strafing along the river, and they really raised a rumpus. At 0930hrs a Mosquito of 110 Squadron overshot its run on an unoccupied gun post just outside of our prison, and its bomb hit the outer wall of the prison's eastern perimeter, just beyond No. 6 Compound. Luckily no one was hurt, but had that pilot been another fraction of a second delayed in releasing his bomb, half of the jail's occupants would have been maimed and killed. We couldn't figure this close bombing out, so, in anger, but also with genuine concern for our welfare, we painted another rooftop message, "EXTRACT DIGIT". Its meaning, "get your finger out", could not possibly be mistaken as a Japanese ploy.'[248]

Australians Flying Officer 'Russ' Cowley and Flight Sergeant Nev Jones of 45 Squadron were airborne in HR309 before dawn. Their ground controller, 'Boxwood', in a Visual Control Post (VCP) at the Irrawaddy, had no trade for them so they dropped their bombs on an opportunity target before setting off for base. Russ remembered 'the return flight was the most frightening I have ever experienced. For about an hour I had virtually no control over the aircraft as it was tossed up and down from about 200ft to 10,000ft with lightning flashes from all points. The most amazing thing is that the "wooden wonder" held together.'[249]

No. 110 Squadron despatched a Mosquito to Rangoon carrying an official photographer. Sadly, it failed to return. Flight Lieutenant Buchanan and war photographer Flight Lieutenant Sidney Woodcock were posted 'Missing presumed killed'.

Bob Willis and Tommy Thompson, 47 Squadron, were tasked with their first operation from Kinmagan on 2 May, flying HR518 in a formation of six Mosquitos. 'The monsoon weather was already upon us. Huge thunderstorms, with storm clouds rising well over twenty-five thousand feet, built up in the afternoon when the heavens opened. This monsoon weather forced our return to base with both the primary and secondary targets impossible to reach. Immediately on landing we enlarged the ditches around the tent which we had previously moved to a gently sloping site to give us better drainage. The rain came down in torrents, tent floors were awash and the open latrines overflowed.'[250]

Almost unnoticed, Wing Commander Eric James Brindley 'Nick' Nicolson VC was killed that day when the Liberator in which he was flying as an observer crashed into the Bay of Bengal. Nick had flown the first Mosquito FB VI intruder operation over Burma on 25 December 1943. Some of the current intruders had flown with him in 27 Squadron but it took some days for word to spread across the squadrons.

That afternoon, a 110 Squadron intruder Mosquito flew low over the centre of Rangoon. The pilot was 110's CO, Soapy Saunders. He had decided that he needed to personally verify what was painted on the roof of Rangoon jail. Seeing the words 'JAPS GONE' and 'EXTRACT DIGIT', Soapy knew that he had to land and investigate further. Their radio transmitter had developed a fault during their flight so they couldn't inform anyone of their intentions. On arriving overhead at the nearest Japanese airfield to the north, Mingaladon, and seeing just three people waving a white flag, they landed. Soapy was extremely lucky because, although the Mosquito was damaged when its tail wheel failed to fully extend, he had chosen to land on part of the runway which the Japanese hadn't mined before they departed. Soapy and his navigator, Flight Lieutenant James Stephen, hitched a lift into Rangoon and made for the jail where they were greeted by Bill Hudson. Back at Joari, as time passed without news, fears increased and they were posted as 'Missing'.

After attempting to radio back to his base from the prison, that evening Soapy set off with James to stop Operation Dracula in its tracks. Under the cover of darkness, the flotilla of ships approached the coast and the Indian 26th Division set off in landing craft towards Rangoon. The liberation of Rangoon was underway! Against the odds, Soapy met up with them and, by dawn the following morning, had persuaded them not to use force.

Hopeful that Operation Dracula had been postponed, early on 3 May 1945 Bill Hudson took Cliff Emeny, Eric Osboldstone and Flying Officer Bellingen to Mingaladon with orders to make it safe for Dakotas to land to evacuate their fellow POWs. Bill appointed Cliff as temporary station commander of the newly liberated RAF Mingaladon. Meanwhile, at Joari, Warrant Officer Murkin and Charles Carruthers of 82 Squadron took off at 0800hrs in their FB VI. In the early hours they had been tasked to support Operation Dracula by rhubarbing south of Rangoon. Charles recalled, 'We were issued with a detailed map of Rangoon and its surrounds, delineating the area of each particular rhubarb of this day. Many aircraft were involved in this operation. It was called off after the famous sign

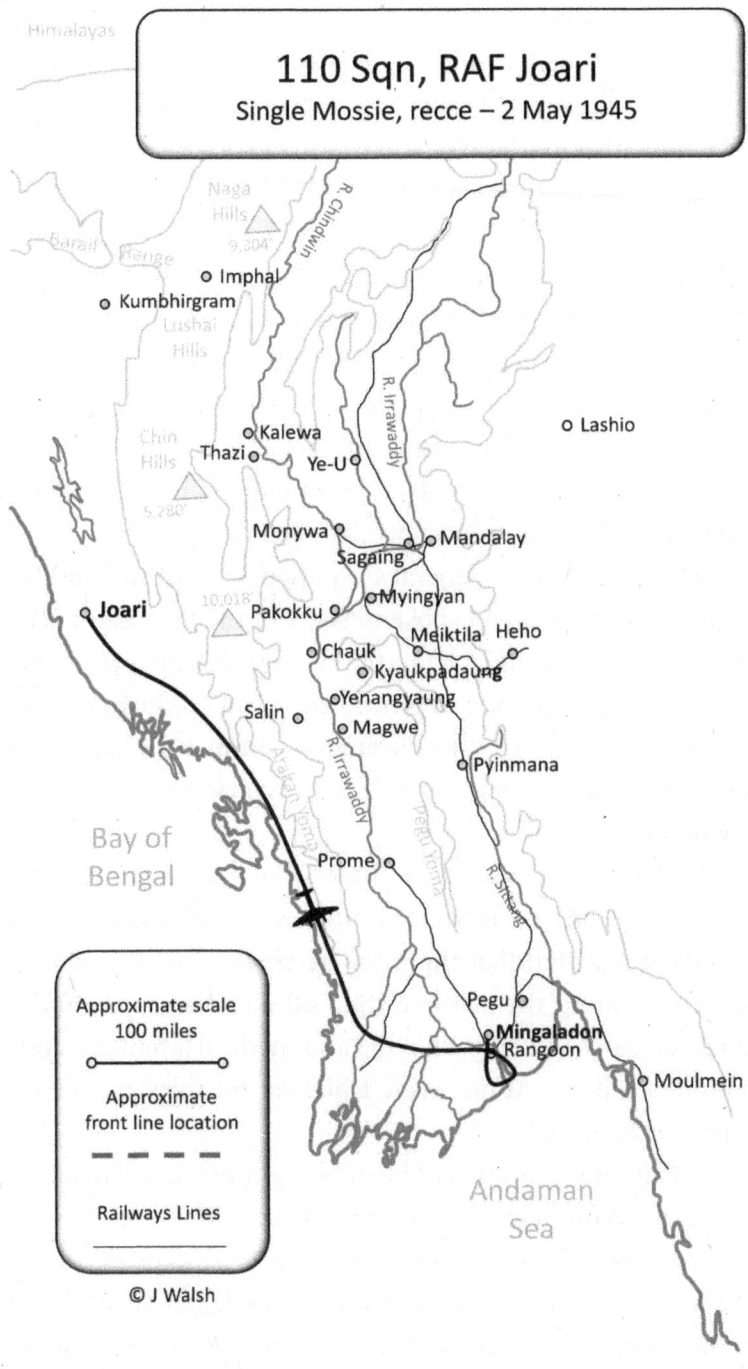

110 Sqn, RAF Joari
Single Mossie, recce – 2 May 1945

© J Walsh

"JAPS GONE, EXTRACT DIGIT" was discovered on the prison roof. We were airborne for five hours twenty minutes – our longest operation [of the] tour.'[251]

The now-liberated POWs still didn't know what was happening, as Johnny explained. 'At 1430hrs an RAF Liberator approached at low-level with its bomb bays open and showered us with what we initially feared were 1,000lb. bombs. At just about fifty feet from the ground, however, parachutes opened to gently deposit numerous containers within the prison walls. The Liberator then circled around taking pictures of the prison. Over the next twenty minutes, two more RAF Liberators made similar parcel-dropping runs. We were thrilled to receive twenty-two containers, in total, filled with delicious K-rations and much-needed medical stores.'[252]

That evening Major General Chambers of 26th Indian Division met with Bill Hudson and spoke to some of the liberated POWs. By the next day army medics had arrived to triage the prisoners. The following day Group Captain John Gandy landed the first Dakota at Mingaladon to be greeted by its 'station commander', an emaciated Cliff Emeny wearing a loin cloth. The POWs' war was over and their evacuation could start in earnest.

Details quickly emerged of the POWs' treatment. Conditions had been harsh and beatings for minor indiscretions commonplace. Bill Hudson reported that the Japanese treated aircrew as 'criminal prisoners', treating them worse than others. They were forbidden such privileges as washing, shaving and medical attention, and were kept on half rations. At one stage Bill went for three weeks without washing his hands.[253]

After Cliff and Johnny had been brought down in Japanese-held territory on 9 November 1944, they made their way to a village where they were robbed of anything useful to the Burmese villagers. They were then held by the local police until the Japanese arrived. Cliff said they were made to stand in the 'at ease' position in the boiling sun and at the mercy of flies by day and of cold and mosquitoes by night.[254] They were subjected to repeated questioning and beatings before the Japanese moved them to Rangoon.

As aircrew, Cliff was not given any medical care for his leg injuries or the burns to his head. By chance, neither the villagers nor the Japanese took the first-aid kit which he had taken with him when he escaped from the crashed Mosquito. At Rangoon, the Japanese guards had a complete indifference towards the sick, so Cliff took on the role of running the airman's hospital. He had virtually no experience but, 'I was thankful for the time I spent in hospital after several "prangs". The knowledge I gained there proved invaluable while in prison. Providing adequate nutrition was my main difficulty. The diet mainly consisted of rice with very few vegetables.'[255] Malaria was commonplace, which Cliff treated by making them drink water, covering them with sacks and forcing them to sweat it out.

The liberation of Rangoon was just a stepping-stone, albeit an important one, towards the objective of the complete rout of the Japanese from Burma, Thailand and South-East Asia. The work of the intruder squadrons continued.

The Mosquito crews from 47 Squadron were now really pushing. On 1 May eleven Mossies bombed Battery Point; the next day twelve aircraft provided 'cab ranks' over the Rangoon River for VCP controllers, with weather forcing their early return to base in the afternoon; on 3 May, eleven aircraft took part in four operations – two rhubarbs and two bomb and strafes; the following day, twelve aircraft were tasked, the morning 'bomb and strafe' was completed but the afternoon op was abandoned due to deteriorating weather, with all aircraft returning to base. On 5 May, eight aircraft took part in two rhubarbs and a 'bomb and strafe' and on the next day six aircraft, working very closely with Allied ground forces, bombed and strafed a Japanese troop concentration and rest point.

With up to a dozen sorties per day, maintaining 47 Squadron's Mosquitos with the sparse facilities at Kinmagan was a real challenge, especially since daytime temperatures were usually over 90°F [30°C]. As Sandy Osterfield explained. 'You may be an armourer but servicing a Mosquito had to be a real team effort. How do you cope when an engine change was needed? There was no lifting tackle, no metal stands, but there was plenty of manpower! Together with some bamboo poles and rope, with the whole team lifting, a Merlin engine was lifted out and a serviceable one put in its place. It took six men to carry one Merlin engine.

'Bombing up with 500lb bombs was in many ways no easier. Around the strip there was little cover to protect bombs, rocket heads and fuses from the hot sun. How do you cope when they are too hot to handle? We often parked the bombs under the aircraft wings as being the best shelter. How many regulations did we break? Sitting on top of the nose of the Mosquito loading the Browning machine guns, and with sweating groundcrew stripped to the waist refuelling and bombing up at the same time, how did we feel? Perhaps we were on a tinder box – it only needed some spilt fuel and a spark!'

The operational tasking was similar for the three squadrons on the coast. It was clear why they had been repositioned, as Gordon Thewlis, an 82 Squadron navigator, explained. 'Joari allowed us to fly due south over the coast, then on a due east course to the Irrawaddy estuary, then north–east to Rangoon. This route allowed us to miss the highly dangerous monsoon clouds building up further inland in Burma.'[256] However, with the early monsoon starting, the weather was deteriorating, and extensive thunderstorms were affecting operations. Flight Lieutenant C.L. 'Twitch' Turner recalled. 'It was always piddling down with rain. It was very uncomfortable, particularly when one hit a monsoon cloud, which was diabolical; I hit one once and found myself upside down.'[257]

On 4 May 110 Squadron despatched three Mosquito pairs to patrol roads, rivers and railways. RF586, piloted by Flight Sergeant Sid Hemingway, with navigator Warrant Officer Phil Turner, failed to return.

The weather thwarted 45 Squadron on both 3 and 4 May, forcing them to return to base. They operated successfully the next two days but then, together with 82 and 110, they moved to Chiringa, with an all-weather strip, due to the anticipated approach of heavy rain. It was very crowded at Chiringa, with six operational squadrons based on the airfield, but on 7 May, 45 Squadron managed to complete two operations each of four aircraft. Importantly, the weather over the targets was acceptable for bombing, strafing and rhubarbing.

Although Group had authorised a rest day due to Victory in Europe, only 45 Squadron in Joari and the servicing echelons at Kumbhirgram could take theirs on 8 May. The others would enjoy a celebration in due course but continued with operational tasking. However, notwithstanding the momentous news in Europe, the importance of liberating Rangoon was acknowledged by Prime Minister Winston Churchill in a signal to Admiral Mountbatten on 9 May 1945:

'I send you my most heartfelt congratulations upon the culminating victory at Rangoon of your Burma campaigns. Pray convey to everyone under your command, or associated with you, the sense of admiration and gratitude felt by all at home at the splendid close of the Burma campaign.'

The pace of operations continued at Chiringa – cab-ranks, bomb and strafe, bridges, troop concentrations, and rhubarbs – through to the expected 'resting' of 45 and 82 Squadrons. On 12 May, having completed 1,261 operational intruder sorties, 45 Squadron was rested and Duke was told that they would no longer be moving to Chakulia and to await further instructions.

Looking back on their operational time, Bill Taylor summarised, 'Our job was mainly low-level air to ground firing and bombing day and night. We attacked Japanese airstrips, bombed bridges and occupied towns, fired at trains and fuel dumps. In fact, we shot anything that moved in Japanese territory. We lost a number of crews and especially at night it was most disturbing as no one knew what happened to them. Even when training, quite a number were killed.'[258]

Aircrews from 82 Squadron flew its final two operations of the war that same day, the last one being a two aircraft rhubarb along the road and rail line from Kyaikto along the Saleen River to Mawachi. After 979 operational intruder sorties, Freddy Snell was told they would remain on standby until the squadron was rested.[259]

It had already been decided that 110 Squadron should join 47 Squadron at Kinmagan, so it also flew its last ops from the coastal sites on 12 May. However, their new challenge was moving their support equipment and supplies by road to Cox's Bazar now that the rainy season had begun. The move took longer than expected, especially with squadron personnel now in three locations. Eventually the squadron's move would be completed in ten days.

That night, Chiringa was hit by a destructive storm. When dawn broke on 13 May, the full impact was apparent. Due to their insubstantial construction, most of the domestic bashas were badly damaged, with some in total ruins. The men from 45 and 82 would be happy to relocate to a new base.

Both 45 and 82 Squadrons had a few non-operational aircraft and crews still at Kumbhirgram, as well as some servicing echelon personnel. Unfortunately, even though 45 Squadron had stopped operational flying, avoidable fatalities continued. Freddie Fortune and Gordon 'Tiny' Lauder were killed in an accident in the squadron's Harvard on 14 May when Freddie lost control during a low-level inverted fly-past over Monierkhal Tea Estate, Paianghat.

Their deaths were deeply felt by the owners of the plantation and, two days after the crash, the plantation owner's wife, Olive

Smith, wrote to Tiny's mother. 'At this sorrowful time for you all, my husband and I feel we must write for the sake of your son Gordon, whom we liked so much, to express our sincere sympathy. The ill-fated plane crashed not far from here and we got to the scene of the crash in record time, I should think, little knowing who we would find there. Both boys were killed instantaneously, that is the only consolation; they couldn't have known a thing about it. Tiny looked so natural I couldn't believe he was dead.' Having explained that Freddie and Tiny were medically examined on the spot, laid in the plantation hospital and then moved to Silchar, Olive wrote, 'The shock of his sudden death has left us in a daze.' She then described attending his funeral. 'The funeral was held at Silchar cemetery at 10a.m. yesterday. We were there to see Tiny gently laid to rest by his pals. The service was nicely carried out by a young padre. All his pals were at the funeral and after the service they went up one by one and saluted the graves in turn. They all thought the world of Tiny, as they called him, and that is the name by which we have always known him. Tiny came and spent a fortnight's leave with us in March. It was a happy time for us all.'[260] Tiny was only twenty years old. His death impacted the lives of his parents William and Edith, his brother Tom, his sister Bess and, not least, his wife Olive.

Having paid their respects to Freddie and Tiny in the morning, in the evening the officers from 45 Squadron who were at Kumbhirgram threw a farewell party to thank Mr and Mrs Smith for their hospitality. They had been generous hosts to 45 Squadron. Olive Smith wrote a spontaneous poem concluding with:

But we'll think of you often, now you have gone,
And follow your progress with keen interest.
And remember you always – the Best of the Best.
The time is now here for saying Good-Byes.
And Good Luck to you all – you guys of the skies.

You'll always be welcome; knowing you has been fun.
Do haste ye back often.

                                        Your Favourite Blonde

Eight 47 Squadron crews from were tasked on 15 May with attacking a supply point and river crossing at Lagunbyo, on the east bank of the Bilin River. Lagunbyo was a key point in a Japanese escape route from the Sittang River valley south towards Thaton, Moulmein and thence Malaya. The Mosquitos were flown in two four-ship formations, led in RF700 by their CO, Billy Filson-Young. The CO's regular navigator, Flight Lieutenant McGlory, had just completed his tour, so Billy, who was also 'tour expired', was accompanied by Flying Officer Waters.

Before the raid, Billy walked over to the squadron's fire crew for a quick chat, then got into his aircraft, RF700. Warrant Officer Bill Powell, with his navigator, Maurice Jones, flew as Billy's No. 2, recalling, 'The weather was reasonable, and we found the target without much difficulty. Lagunbyo was situated in a valley and each of us was to drop our two 500 pounders in a dive-bombing attack. The CO waved to me in the No. 2 position and then peeled off to the left diving on to the target area at an angle of 45°. I followed suit and, as I looked down halfway through my diving turn, saw to my horror the CO's aircraft crash and explode in a colossal fireball. My navigator's view must have been partly obscured by the angle and partly perhaps by me... Maurice was completely unaware of what had happened.

'I must have been in something of a daze as I made my attack, dropping both bombs in the target area and then carrying out a strafing attack with cannon on the buildings which came into the gun sight as I pulled out of the dive. Only then was I able to switch on the intercom and let the other two crews in the first flight and the leader of the second flight, which was now close to the target, know what had happened.'

Bill continued, 'Much later the news filtered through to us that the headman of the village of Lagunbyo had been questioned by some of our guerrilla friends shortly after our attack. He said that at the time many Japanese troops were in the village and they had been defending themselves with 40mm anti-aircraft guns and machine guns. The obvious conclusion was that the CO's aircraft had been shot up as he dived towards the target area giving him and his navigator no chance to bale out.'[261]

Wing Commander Billy Filson-Young DFC* was only twenty-five years old and had completed 232 operational sorties. Bob Willis later wrote, 'Filson-Young, as a successful commander, had always led the squadron by example. It was a great tragedy that this quality proved to be his undoing. He will always be remembered with great affection by all who knew him and served with him on the ground and in the air. He had courage, competence and compassion in abundance.'[262] One of the last people on the ground to see him alive, LAC John Eurwyn Williams, part of the fire crew with whom Billy spoke before the flight, echoed these thoughts.[263]

That same day, after ten days of uncertainty, it was finally decided that both 45 and 82 Squadrons would relocate to Cholavaram, near Madras, to prepare for the invasion of Malaya. On 17 May, 45 Squadron started packing up. Some of the commissioned aircrew flew from Kumbhirgram to Cholavaram but, with a depleted establishment of aircraft, the remaining aircrew were consigned to the tediously slow train journey with the other squadron personnel. They finally arrived at Cholavaram on 31 May, having set off ten days earlier.

With the loss of Billy Filson-Young and 45 Squadron being rested, Group decided that Duke Duclos should take command of 47 Squadron. Flight Lieutenant Aykroyd, 45's senior Flight Commander, was given command of 45 Squadron.

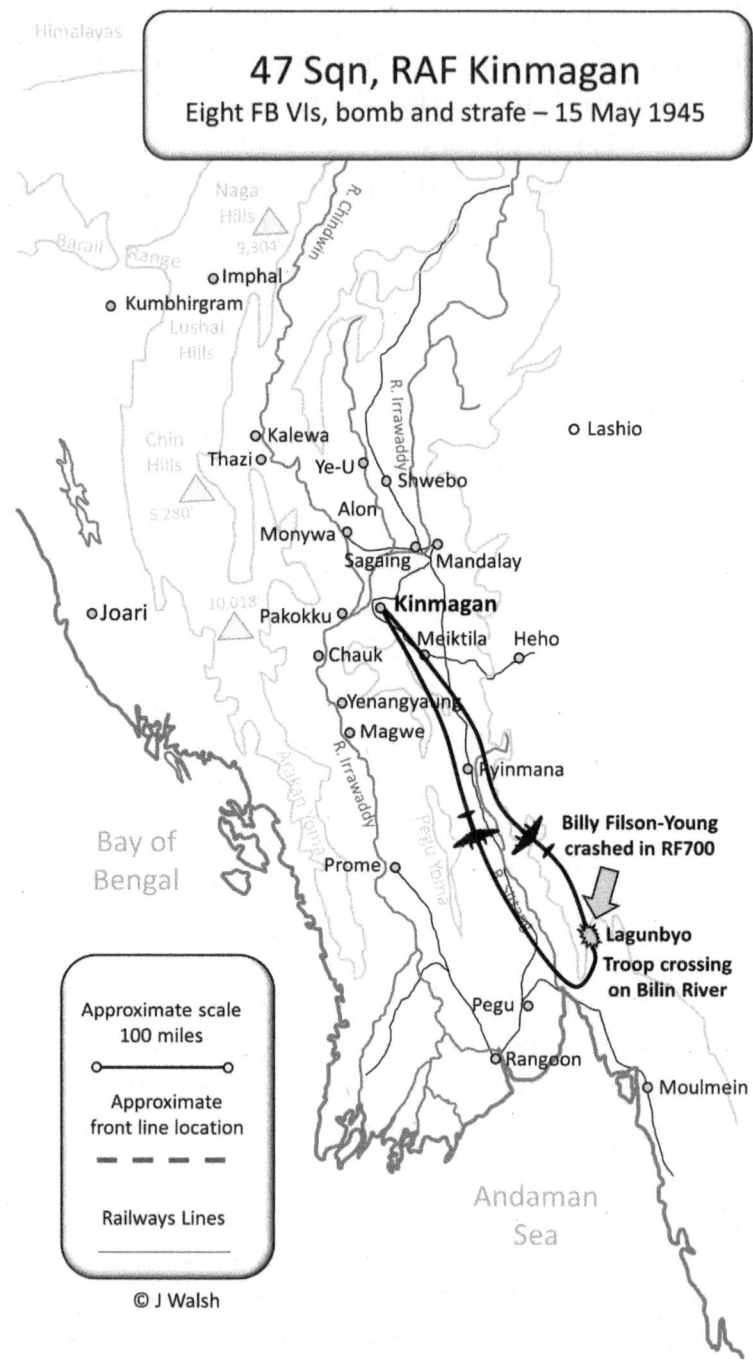

47 Sqn, RAF Kinmagan

Eight FB VIs, bomb and strafe – 15 May 1945

Himalayas

Naga
Hills
9,304'

Barail Range

o Imphal

o Kumbhirgram

Lushai
Hills

R. Chindwin

R. Irrawaddy

o Lashio

Chin
Hills

5,280'

o Kalewa

Thazi o
Ye-U o
o Shwebo

Alon

Monywa o

Sagaing Mandalay

10,018'

o Joari

Pakokku o **Kinmagan**

o Chauk Meiktila Heho o

o Yenangyaung

o Magwe

o Pyinmana

Bay of
Bengal

R. Irrawaddy

Arakan Yoma

Pegu Yoma

Prome o o

**Billy Filson-Young
crashed in RF700**

**Lagunbyo
Troop crossing
on Bilin River**

Pegu o

o Rangoon

o Moulmein

Andaman
Sea

Approximate scale
100 miles

o———————o

Approximate
front line location

— — — —

Railways Lines

———————

© J Walsh

Aung San, leader of the BNA, had been given a 'safe pass' by Force 136 and on 15 May he met with Lieutenant General William Slim, commander of the British 14th Army. Aung San and Thakin Soe proposed that the BNA be accepted as 'Allied Forces' and the Anti-Fascist Organisation acknowledged as the provisional government of Burma. Slim refused to accept the AFO as a government and insisted that the BNA submit to being disarmed by the British in areas where the fighting was over. The AFO accepted this in return for recognition as a political movement and promises that the BNA's officers and men would be incorporated into the new Burma Army.

There were also changes in leadership with 110 Squadron. Having 'liberated Rangoon', Soapy Saunders and navigator James Stephen were transferred to duties with Group. On 17 May, 110 Squadron was ordered to relocate to Kinmagan and its senior Flight Commander, Peter Clarence Joel DFC, was given command of the squadron, with promotion to Wing Commander. He flew to Kinmagan to start making arrangements.

That day, 47 Squadron despatched three Mossie pairs at different times. The first rhubarbed river craft from Aungban to Saween, striking sampans. The second pair rhubarbed the railway and river to Kemapyu, scoring hits on four boxcars and noting a new 40ft high 'tripwire' designed to take down low-flying intruders at Shwegun. The third pair were despatched at 1345hrs to bomb and strafe 'Japs dug in at junction. Strafe fox holes along east edge of track of village.' The result was 'Bashas destroyed and multiple strafing runs completed.'

The next day 47 Squadron launched two Mosquito pairs and a four. The first pair identified their target but did not attack – 'Pilots considered whole area clear of Japs.' The second pair bombed and strafed a ferry near Duyinzeik and identified another 'tripwire', this time at 80ft, near Zathagyin. In the late afternoon, four Mosquitos were despatched to 'bomb and strafe 500 Japs harbouring in Anyapwa and Yantahya'. Their bombs were on target.

Having been unable to fly ops for ten days, on 22 May, 110 Squadron Mosquitos arrived at Kinmagan to coincide with the arrival of their groundcrew, engineers, support and stores. Four aircraft were immediately in action that afternoon. Two pairs were tasked with rhubarbing from Toungoo to Kanmamaung. A few vehicles and ten bashas were attacked but the roads appeared waterlogged.

The next ops for 110 were on 24 May when, having bombed and strafed Kyuaktan, just north of Yinyon, South African Captain Montgomery and his wingman, Flight Lieutenant Brown, saw 'a column of Japs (100–150) . . . marching in threes. They immediately dived into 20 yards of scrub on roadside.' Montgomery made four runs and Brown made three, 'the whole plastered by cannon fire – believed many casualties.'[264]

After a few days of 'bomb and strafe' sorties, on 26 May one of the four pairs despatched by 47 Squadron was tasked with checking out some drop zones before making the sorties look like standard rhubarbs. They reported that Area A had 'thirty Japs seen' in region, Area B was not seen, Area C was marshy, but that Area D was suitable.

That same day, 82 Squadron entrained at Chiringa and Kumbhirgram for Cholavaram. They noted the usual problems of initially dirty carriages, then the journey was dogged by 'confusion and lack of authorisation'. It was another long, slow journey.

The last few days of the month for 47 Squadron were completed with determination, flying ten sorties on 27 May, thirteen over the next two days before a stand-down, then eleven on 31 May.

The intruder Mosquitos completed nearly 500 sorties in May. Two squadrons, 45 and 82, were transferred to 901 Wing, 224 Group and were on their slow journeys to Cholavaram, having completed over 2,200 operational sorties between them. The two remaining squadrons, 47 and 110, both with new COs, were now operating from Kinmagan in central Burma, hindering Japanese troops trying to escape.

Squadron	Mosquito Intruder Operations		Aircrew Losses Operations		Aircrew Losses Training	
	Month	Total	Month	Total	Month	Total
No. 45 Sqn	82	1,261	0	20	2	5
No. 82 Sqn	68	979	0	11	0	2
No. 47 Sqn	217	448	2	4	0	0
No. 110 Sqn	127	260	4	10	0	2
No. 27 Sqn	0	45	0	2	0	0
Other Units	0	0	0	0	0	9
Total	494	2,993	6	47	2	18

Chapter 17

Mopping Up

June – July 1945

'ENEMY CASUALTIES IN BURMA. SITTANG RIVER BATTLE. More Than 6,000 Are Killed. Building Up Allied Force For Next Stage.'
Associated Press, *London, 31 July 1945*

T he weather at Kinmagan continued hot and humid. The tented accommodation could be stifling. Tasking for 47 Squadron continued to be bomb and strafe, usually attacking under the direction of VCP ground controllers – '100 Japs dug in on hilltop,' 'Concentration of 700 Japs with MG at Mingon.' They managed to launch six or eight aircraft each day and sometimes worked in partnership with 110 Squadron.

On 1 June, 110 Squadron despatched four aircraft to attack targets in Natkyi. During the attack, at 1002hrs RF589's starboard engine and V.H.F. radio were hit by machine-gun fire. Twitch Turner, who was leading the operation, accompanied the damaged aircraft to Mingaladon where the pilot, Flight Lieutenant Alan John, attempted an emergency landing at 1020hrs. The aircraft crashed, killing the pilot and seriously injuring the navigator, Sergeant Norman Keighley. Twitch landed a few minutes later and, after attending to formalities, returned to Kinmagan that afternoon.

On 2 June, four Mossies from 47 and two from 110 attacked gun positions at Pauggyi, and then strafed camp areas at Duyinzeik and

Pan-an, north of Moulmein. The monsoon was never far away, as 47 Squadron's Bob Willis recalled, 'Flying often involved going through heavy rain with the reduced visibility making it far from easy in trying to judge the way forward through towering masses of cloud. The windscreen wiper worked overtime.'[265]

On 5 June, four 47 Squadron Mosquitos attacked 500 Japanese troops near a wireless station at Nyaungbo. Bob Willis, flying RF713, was very satisfied with the outcome, 'Our aircraft fired 450 20mm shells and 1,000 rounds of .303 machine gun bullets. As with other occasions, a later report indicated we had very effectively dispersed the Japanese troop concentration, inflicting many casualties. Returning from this operation in loose formation at about 10,000ft, between the most picturesque cloud formations towering over the mountains to the east and with the River Salween glistening below, it was difficult to believe that behind us was a Burmese village that, having sheltered the enemy, was now quite devastated after being heavily bombed and then blasted by our cannon fire.'[266]

On 6 June, 110 Squadron despatched four aircraft on an early morning 'bomb and strafe' raid on a Japanese headquarters at Kunzeik. The cloud base enroute was only 500ft but Warrant Officer Alan Rendell, like the other three pilots, dropped his four 500lb eleven-second delay bombs on target. Between them they completed twenty strafing runs on the target area. Later, the squadron received a 'strawberry' from the Army, 'A ground source states that the attack on Kunzeik by 110 Squadron on June 6th resulted in many Japs being killed.'[267]

On 7 June the monsoon hit hard, with heavy rain closing Kinmagan's airstrip for seven days.

On 13 June, Flight Lieutenant Tonks and Flight Sergeant Cook, newly arrived at 45 Squadron in Cholavaram, were killed during training when their Mosquito hit a cable across a ravine.

The next day, with the ground drying, 47 Squadron just managed to launch two operational sorties from Kinmagan. On 15 June the weather was not good enough for operations, but Mountbatten still held the planned Victory parade in Rangoon. Led by 47's temporary CO, Squadron Leader Etherington, twelve Mosquitos (eight from 110 and four from 47) defied the weather to participate in the parade's fly-past. Most other invited aircraft didn't make it, apart from some Spitfires based near Rangoon. The weather was also good enough for Duke Duclos to be flown into Kinmagan from Cholavaram to take command of 47 Squadron. Sadly, having survived sixty ops with 45 Squadron, Flying Officer Ron Wilcock, who had flown Duke by Mosquito from Cholavaram, failed to return to base and was posted 'Missing believed killed.' Several replacement crews from the UK also arrived at Kinmagan before the airstrip was closed again on 16 June.

On 17 June, 47 Squadron managed to launch six Mossies on two 'bomb and strafe' ops, and 110 launched seven against two targets. Bad weather prevented 47's Mossie pair from reaching their primary target, so they diverted to their secondary, a bridge. Success! One of their bombs removed the centre span.

The next day 47 despatched nine aircraft against three targets, whilst 110 launched nine, four of which returned to the previous day's primary target, a large Japanese staging post, only to be beaten again by the weather, with the 'cloud down in the valleys'.

Squadron Leader Ira Sutherland, a New Zealander who was 110's senior flight commander, led five aircraft against an enemy concentration around a sawmill in Nutka. Between them they dropped fourteen 500lb bombs, two of which fell short in the river. The other twelve were on target. After twenty-three strafing runs from all directions, they returned to Kinmagan.

Wing Commander Duke Duclos led his first 47 Squadron operation on 20 June – four FB VIs on a 'bomb and strafe'. With the cloud base at 200ft over their primary target, they diverted to their alternative, a transit camp under construction. Eleven of their twelve bombs landed on target in the bashas, the other undershot. The crews completed eleven strafing runs before returning to base.

Weather conditions were poor but the tasking continued. Completing a successful op on 21 June, the starboard undercarriage of Flying Officer Saunders' Mosquito collapsed on landing at Kinmagan. The aircraft was a write-off but both Saunders and Wise were unhurt.

On 25 June, six aircraft from 47 Squadron successfully damaged their primary target, a bypass bridge, as well as dropping six- and twelve-hour delay bombs to hinder rebuilding. Then, during a rhubarb on the Moulmein railway, after following a colleague attacking a 'three-tonner', Warrant Officer Ken Illingworth and Flight Sergeant George Tuck crashed. Their aircraft was seen 'burning on the ground'.

Meanwhile, 110 Squadron had cranked up its daily sorties. On 21 June, with en route weather 'cloud on deck, heavy rain', their targets in the Duyinzeik area had a 1,500ft cloud-base and six aircraft successfully completed a 'bomb and strafe'. The next day, Squadron Leader Ira Sutherland led eight Mosquitos against a concentration of Japanese. On 23 June, two flights of four aircraft were despatched. The four aircraft attacking a pontoon at Duyinzeik had to contend with 'low stratus 100ft-500ft heavy rain, vis. 1,000yds' in the target area. Nine of 110's Mosquitos were despatched on 26 June, when the weather at the three targets was noted respectively as '8/10 s/cumulus base 300ft', 'clouds on hilltops but clear in valleys' and '8/10 s/cumulus on deck, visibility 500ft to nil.' The attack on the third target was aborted. On 27 June, CO Wing Commander Peter Joel led seven aircraft on a bridge attack ('10/10 stratus, base 500/700ft heavy rain'), whilst two aircraft completed an offensive recce on the Moulmein railway.

On 27 June, with his departure for his next posting in the UK imminent, Ira Sutherland flew alone in Mosquito RF582 to Akyab to bid farewell to friends. The next morning, Ira took off at 1150hrs to return to Kinmagan but was never seen again. No trace was found during searches over the following days. On 12 July the wreckage of the Mosquito was found on the side of a chaung (valley) about twenty miles east of Akyab. The accident investigators decided that Ira's aircraft had probably disintegrated in mid-air, noting that, because of its poor condition, RF582 had already been withdrawn from operational flying.

For the final few days in the month, 110 Squadron continued to attack fuel and ammunition dumps, as long as the weather permitted. Meanwhile, 47 Squadron attended to Japanese troop concentrations, as well as the railway lines.

July brought more of the same for both 110 and 47 Squadrons, with 47 focusing on 'bombing and strafing' Japanese troop concentrations which were making their way through the mountains east from the Sittang River towards Thailand.

The speed of the 14th Army's advance had trapped what remained of Japan's Twenty-eighth Army in central Burma. Large groups were hiding in the ravines of the Pegu Yoma, intent on crossing the Sittang River to escape to Thailand. On 3 July, the Japanese Thirty-third Army came to their aid by trying to secure Sittang Bend. It was badly mistimed since the Twenty-eighth Army wasn't ready. British forces, having captured their plans, blocked their path and attacked with artillery, Spitfires and Thunderbolts. The Japanese finally withdrew after four days of pummelling from the ground and air. The Allies knew that they would try again.

That morning 110 Squadron had launched six aircraft against 'four Jap held villages in Kyauktaung area'. Unfortunately, RF600 hit a bump during take-off, bounced, and a wing hit the ground. Flying Officer Van der Pol couldn't save it. Both he and Flight Sergeant Gordon were killed in the crash. The other five aircraft bombed on target and strafed but noted that strafing runs were 'difficult due to the nature of the terrain'.

The pressure continued and, over the next six days, 110 Squadron completed thirty-nine intruder sorties in ten ops. On both 8 and 9 June they were directly involved in the battle of Sittang Bend. On 10 July the CO noted, 'It is becoming increasing evident that our aircraft are being overworked and serviceability is suffering. We are reduced to eight available aircraft.' Over the same period 47 Squadron despatched thirty-four aircraft on eight operations, primarily bombing and strafing Japanese troop concentrations, supporting the Army. Strawberries were coming in virtually daily for both squadrons.

On 11 July, Wing Commander Arthur 'Soapy' Saunders and his navigator Flight Lieutenant James Stephen set off to transit from Baigachi to Kinmagan, via Feni, in a Beechcraft Expeditor HB158, flown by 3 TAF Communications Squadron. The weather was bad and they failed to arrive at Feni. They were reported 'Missing' and were later declared 'Missing believed killed'.

On Thursday, 12 July, 110 Squadron despatched three Mosquitos to bomb 'a Jap ration dump' in the centre of Shwehle. Unfortunately, RF672 crashed into paddy fields 800yds north of the target, the aircraft disintegrating. Flying Officer Leo O'Neill and Flight Lieutenant David Cookson were killed on impact.

Both squadrons continued to accept tasking for all operational aircraft. Even collecting replacement Mosquitos could be challenging, as 47 Squadron's Flying Officer Reg Davis found out. He was asked by Duke Duclos to fly HR705 to Barrackpore and exchange it for a new aircraft, RF523. When Reg and his navigator, Flight Sergeant Bert Reich, checked HR705's Form 700 they noted that it stated 'serviceable for S & L flight only' with an altitude limitation of 13,000ft. Bert immediately planned a route to avoid the peaks of Arakan Yoma and they thought they would be back the following day. With the weather deteriorating, they set off towards Prome, then crossed the Arakan Yoma in cloud. When they believed they were over the coast, 'Bert gave me a more northerly course and we inched down with a view to getting below the base of the cloud. This seemed to take forever, but we finally caught sight of the sea through the rain and wispy cloud and continued on a northerly heading at an uncomfortable level below the fluctuating cloud base.' Reg and Bert decided to divert to Akyab and called up for a heading. Whilst listening out on Akyab's frequency, they heard one of the 'Songbirds', one of the Dakotas which flew up and down the coast providing real-time weather, reporting a cloud base of 300–500ft with heavy showers. They were relieved when they landed at a very wet Akyab where they were told that the weather was 'clearing further north.' With this information, they decided to continue but the weather was so bad it forced them to return to Akyab. After two hours flying, they were little more than forty minutes from Kinmagan!

The next day they completed the transit to Barrackpore where they were told that RF523 was actually at Kanchrapara. Rather than fly HR705 any further, Reg and Bert were offered seats on a transport aircraft, which did not materialise. They overnighted in their respective messes. The following morning, when they met up, in addition to his parachute bag, Bert also now had a parakeet which he had decided to take back to Kinmagan as a 'squadron mascot'. After a discussion, Bert assured Reg that the parakeet would not be free in the cockpit 'as he proposed to tie it to the loop aerial.' Air transport again did not materialise, so they endured a rather grim train journey.

Reg commented, 'There appeared to be many American servicemen in clean neatly pressed uniforms at Kanchrapara who seemed indifferent to the needs of two untidy looking, sweat stained members of the RAF, plus a parakeet, and had no wish to help us find RF523.' Eventually they found a flight sergeant who had the necessary paperwork and, with signatures in place, he arranged for groundcrew to start the new aircraft. With everything checked and the parakeet safely perched and securely tied to the loop aerial, they were given permission to take off. As soon as they were airborne, they realised that their radio didn't work but decided to press on towards Chittagong, then follow the coast towards Akyab. The parakeet seemed quiet and content. Rather than landing at the usually busy Akyab, they continued to Ramree, which turned out to be little more than a relief strip with no one to help with the radio. They decided to fly back to Akyab, but the starboard engine refused to start. Begrudgingly they stayed overnight in 'one of the wettest parts of the planet.'

The next morning, with the parakeet securely in place, the starboard engine once again failed to start. 'Being very hot and sticky in the cockpit, we almost gave up but, talking it over, we felt the "helpful" airman may not have primed the engine as much as required, so Bert offered to do so. This required him to climb down the flight ladder, pump the priming lever located in the wheel bay, secure it once the engine had started then climb back up the ladder, behind the arc of the moving propeller, and return to the cockpit.' The engine fired and Reg watched nervously as Bert climbed back into the cockpit. The port engine immediately started, and they were off, headed south with the new mascot chirping away merrily behind Reg's head. After finding a break between the cloud masses at 8,000ft to cross the Arakan Yoma, Bert informed Reg that the bird had fallen off its perch and was hanging upside down, still tied to the aerial. They assumed it had died of anoxia. Luckily, after descending to a lower level over the Pegu Yoma, the parakeet came back to life and Bert duly replaced it on its perch. The mascot had survived!

On arrival at Kinmagan, RF523 was duly handed over to the engineers and Reg and Bert retired to their respective accommodations. Reg added, 'And the mascot – the parakeet – sad to relate that during the following morning, as it had been tethered to one of the lines on Bert's tent, it was reported to have been attacked and devoured by a mongoose!'[268]

On 15 July, the Japanese Twenty-eighth Army began their attempt to break-out from the Pegu Yoma, still unaware that the British knew their plans. The British created two killing fields on either side of the main highway. The first was for artillery and the second was for ground attack aircraft. Burmese guerrillas helped co-ordinate air attacks from the east bank of the Sittang River, ambushing escaping Japanese forces and 'cutting them to pieces'. The plan and its execution were highly effective, as shown in a message to the RAF from one of the guerrilla leaders during the battle. 'You are killing hundreds of Japs,' he said, 'and your perfect co-ordination and patience in reading our crude signals is saving the lives of many thousands of defenceless civilians.'[269] The battle continued for days. For the Japanese, it was a bloodbath.

On 17 July, four 110 Squadron Mosquitos were tasked with 'bombing and strafing' the railway at Apalon. During the attack, RF705 was damaged by bomb-blast, possibly from an instantaneous bomb. Its main fuel tanks were losing petrol so Flying Officer Locke, with Warrant Officer Nicolson, immediately headed for Rangoon, accompanied by aircraft HR438. Locke was eventually forced to ditch in shallow water on mudflats, but RF705 broke its back. He was picked up by an Air-Sea Rescue boat, but no trace was found of Nicolson, who was posted 'Missing believed killed'.

For the next week both 47 and 110 Squadrons continued 'bombing and strafing' Japanese troop concentrations, providing ground support, with many of the operations part of the extended Battle of Sittang Bend. Sometimes the weather prevented them reaching their primary targets and often their bombing runs were flown at 50-80ft due to the low cloud-base.

Winston Churchill resigned as Prime Minister on 26 July after a humiliating electoral defeat to Labour's Clement Atlee. Now that the war in Europe was over, the British people wanted change. That same day, the Allies issued the Potsdam Declaration calling for unconditional Japanese surrender. If the Japanese did not accept, they warned that there would be 'prompt and utter destruction'. Ten days previously, the Manhattan Project to develop the atomic bomb had successfully completed its live test, the Trinity Test in New Mexico. The Americans now committed to preparing Little Boy and Fat Man bombs to bring an end to the conflict.

The intruder Mosquitos continued to 'bomb and strafe'. Their aircraft were now really showing the strain and replacements had dried up again.

It did not come as a surprise to Allied High Command when Japan rejected the Potsdam Declaration on 29 July. They had been trying to broker a more advantageous surrender through the Russians, without success. The Allies continued with their plans.

On 31 July 1945, Flying Officer Reg Davis with Flight Sergeant Bert Reich in HR500, Flight Lieutenant Powell with Flying Officer Busby in RF695, and Warrant Officers Byatt and Horn in HR523, all from 47 Squadron, were briefed for a 'bomb and strafe' operation, with the customary primary, secondary and alternative targets. Each Mosquito was armed with four 500lb eleven-second delay bombs. A line of thunderstorms forced the three crews to divert from their primary target to their secondary target, a hospital area in Moulmein which the Japanese were using as a barracks. They had been briefed to expect 'a higher concentration of flak'.

'Only one attack was made, from south to north, which course lay at right-angles to a range of hills beyond the target and allowed a clear break away to the west. The aircraft flew at roof-top height in echelon starboard and at a speed of 280mph, bombed simultaneously in sticks of four. 20mm and L.M.G. flak were experienced and the leader saw what appeared to be cannon strikes just in front of him. It was discovered at de-briefing however that No. 2 and No. 3 had not fired their guns up to this point – the fire must have therefore come from the range of hills behind the target.

'No. 2 also carried out cannon and machine-gun attacks on two [two-masted ships] being unloaded in the harbour and one basha believed to be a flak position.

'A Force 136 report, dated 2 August 1945, stated that nine direct hits and two near misses were scored on the buildings and one direct hit on a flak position. Over 400 bodies were recovered from the debris.'[270]

The rout of the Japanese was nearing completion, but they continued to fight determined rearguard actions. Together, 47 and 110 Squadrons completed 344 operational sorties during the month at the cost of a further fourteen aircrew's lives.

Squadron	Mosquito Intruder Operations		Aircrew Losses Operations		Aircrew Losses Training	
	Month	Total	Month	Total	Month	Total
No. 45 Sqn	0	1,261	0	20	3	8
No. 82 Sqn	0	979	0	11	0	2
No. 47 Sqn	217	665	2	6	0	0
No. 110 Sqn	127	387	7	17	2	4
No. 27 Sqn	0	45	0	2	0	0
Other Units	0	0	0	0	0	9
Total	**344**	**3,337**	**9**	**56**	**5**	**23**

Chapter 18

Finals

August 1945

'Even the inevitable end of a great war cannot wholly lift from men's hearts the burden that was laid upon them last Sunday by the dropping of an atomic bomb on the Japanese city of Hiroshima. By their own cruelty and treachery our enemies had invited the worst we could do to them.'
New York Times, *12 August 1945*

On the first two days of August, 47 Squadron launched six aircraft on 'bomb and strafe' operations against troop concentrations; 110 Squadron managed to despatch seven and nine aircraft on similar raids. Then heavy rain made the dispersals unserviceable for three days.

On 6 August, the Americans dropped the Little Boy atomic bomb on Hiroshima, with devastating effect. Japan did not immediately capitulate. However, 47 and 110 Squadrons could now get from the dispersals to the airstrip, so a few operations were completed.

On 9 August, the Americans increased the pressure on Japan by dropping the Fat Man atomic bomb on Nagasaki. Again, the impact was awesome. They had delivered 'prompt and utter destruction.' It was estimated that between 130,000 and 225,000 people were killed by the two atomic bombs. Some aircrew had concerns about its impact and 110 Squadron noted that, 'There has been a great deal of discussion on the subject of the new atomic bomb and general opinion seems to be a little fearful of the possibilities opened up by this discovery. However, it is felt that this, coupled with the entry of Russia in the war against Japan is likely to cause capitulation at an early date.'[271]

Waterlogged dispersals at Kinmagan prevented operations on 10 August, allowing time to prepare to move the squadrons further south to Hmawbi airfield.

In London, on 11 August 1945, Vernon Brown, the Chief Inspector of Accidents, RAF Accident Investigation Branch, presided over another meeting to discuss Mosquito airframe failures. The minutes, classified as secret, concluded:

> *'The susceptibility of the Mosquito to break up during a pull-out shows that, considering the manoeuvrability and stability characteristics, the aircraft is weak structurally. The high fatality rate may be attributed to the cramped accommodation and the extreme difficulty in leaving the cockpit once the aircraft structure has failed.'*[272]

The team had investigated sixty-nine structural failures in Mosquitos, including some in Australia, but none of the failures in India or Burma.

Operations were beginning to wind down, but on 12 August Duke Duclos led four 47 Squadron Mossies to bomb Ba Maw's residence south of Moulmein. Five Burma 'ministers' were known to be there. One aircraft went unserviceable and needed to be escorted back to Hmawbi, leaving only two for the operation. There were heavy thunderstorms over the target and their bombs overshot slightly, although they had some success with strafing runs.

Six days after Nagasaki, on 15 August 1945, the people of Japan heard for the first time the voice of their Emperor, when Hirohito spoke on the radio to announce the unconditional surrender of Japan's armed forces.

The next day, 47 and 110 Squadrons started their relocation to Hmawbi, with the serviceable aircraft, their aircrew and some groundcrew flying there as the advance party. Everyone else set off by road. Reg Davis, a 47 Squadron pilot, was given charge of their rear party and navigator Lewis 'Lew' Pepper was the officer-in-charge for 110's rear party. With the monsoon continuing, they knew their convoys of three-ton trucks would take several days to complete the journey.

Having completed twenty-one ops, Lew found it interesting to see the roads and railway bridges they had flown over and tried to destroy. They had an incident-free journey, even though there were reports of continuing raids by groups of Japanese, in denial that the war was over, trying to escape to the east.

Both squadron's aircrew, aircraft and some groundcrew quickly started settling into their new tented accommodation. Everyone was in a celebratory mood due to the Japanese surrender. Having over-imbibed most of the day, 'Twitch' Turner, recently promoted to Squadron Leader and 110 Squadron 'B' Flight Commander, had spent the evening relaxing with some fellow officers hosted by the squadron's doctor, Flight Lieutenant Harbinson. Twitch finally took a 'rain check' and returned to his nearby tent to sleep.

Warrant Officer Jimmy Gibson and his navigator Pete Rostance were both asleep on their charpoys when they were woken by 'all hell braking loose'. Jimmy explained, 'Coming from the officers' lines was the sound of gunfire and explosives. We just thought that some of the crazy officers were celebrating victory a little too enthusiastically. Not to be, the officers' lines were under attack from approximately eighty Japanese who had no intention of surrendering.'[273]

Twitch continued, 'I had not long been stretched out on the charpoy under the mosquito net when I heard, literally, the patter of feet, then "bang, bang" as the bullets flew. Since our side arms had been handed over on the Jap surrender and being no hero under such circumstances, I dived (starkers!) out of the back of the tent in the conveniently dug monsoon trench at the rear, just as there was a mighty explosion in the Doc's tent.'[274] Luckily, no one was killed by the grenade, although two people suffered burst ear drums and the Doc's pet collie received head cuts and lost an eye.

Syd Parker, a 47 Squadron pilot, was also caught in the attack. 'Lying on my camp bed half asleep, I became aware of explosions, shouts and other noises. On raising myself on one elbow to look through the open flap of my tent I was just in time to see a running figure of a Japanese soldier about 20ft away. He stopped, bent down, released the pin of a grenade which he then lobbed into our tent. As I watched the figure disappear there was a blinding flash, a ferocious explosion and the next thing I remember is picking myself up from the monsoon ditch outside the remains of the tent with an aching head and back and a very loud agonising silence in my ears. Some hours later in a military hospital with both eardrums burst, a massive bruise from calf to shoulder and having bits of metal picked out of my back ...'[275] The disapproving army medical officer called out of bed believed he was treating the effects of celebratory excesses at an RAF Mess.

Bob Milne, another 47 Squadron pilot, was also injured in the attack, having been blown out of his charpoy suffering shrapnel wounds to his hand. 'It was the sober type who suffered,' he recalled. From a hail of hand grenades and Molotov cocktails, six officers of 47 Squadron and two of 110 Squadron received 'minor injuries' and were taken to hospital. Fortunately, most of the officers were still celebrating VJ Day in the Officers' Mess, which escaped attack. One Mosquito was written off and much personal baggage destroyed.'[276]

The next day, Twitch Turner heard that the Gurkhas had caught some Japanese infiltrators and 'a bit later I met with a Gurkha officer (British) and asked him about it. His reply – "What Japs?" I often wonder what happened to them if the report was true.'[277]

The Hmawbi incident was by no means unique. A significant number of the retreating Japanese forces refused to accept that the war was over. A couple of days later, *Associated Press* quoted a SEAC news release, 'It is officially stated today that there are still no signs in Burma of any formal surrender. Nor has there been any response to nearly a million leaflets.'

Even now, the war was not over. 'On 20 August 1945, out of the blue came an SOS for help from a section of our guerrilla Force 136 who were being attacked by Japs who would not accept surrender. I led the raid which put paid to this problem,' recalled Twitch Turner, 110 Squadron. They were tasked to provide close support to Force 136 at Tikedo to deal with some Japanese forces who were completely disregarding Japan's unconditional surrender four days earlier.

Under Twitch's command, eight 110 Squadron Mosquitos took off in two groups of four between 1423hrs and 1438hrs, heading for three separate targets near Tikedo. The first four attacked their target just after 1457hrs, returning to Hmawbi by 1554hrs. Then, one pair bombed their target at 1517hrs and landed back at base at 1604hrs. The final Mosquito pair were piloted by Flight Lieutenant Ron Prankerd, with Flying Officer George Richards navigating, in RF731 nicknamed 'Rum and Coke', and Warrant Officer Alan Rendell, with navigator Warrant Officer Bell, in HR562. Their target was bashas surrounded by trees at reference QG426815. HR562's undercarriage wouldn't retract after take-off, so Alan fell behind resolving it. Ron arrived over target at 1510hrs and loitered for more than ten minutes until Alan arrived. Both aircraft completed their attacks at 1525hrs, with Ron releasing its bombs first, followed by Alan. The two aircraft arrived back at base at 1606hrs.

For the RAF, the Second World War was now finally over. Twitch added, 'It was established later that on this raid the last bomb of the war was dropped by the RAF (the pilot who actually dropped it was W/O Rendell).'[278] Later, Alan Rendell, without boastfulness, was known to relate how technical problems with his aircraft had resulted in him accidentally dropping the last bomb of the war.

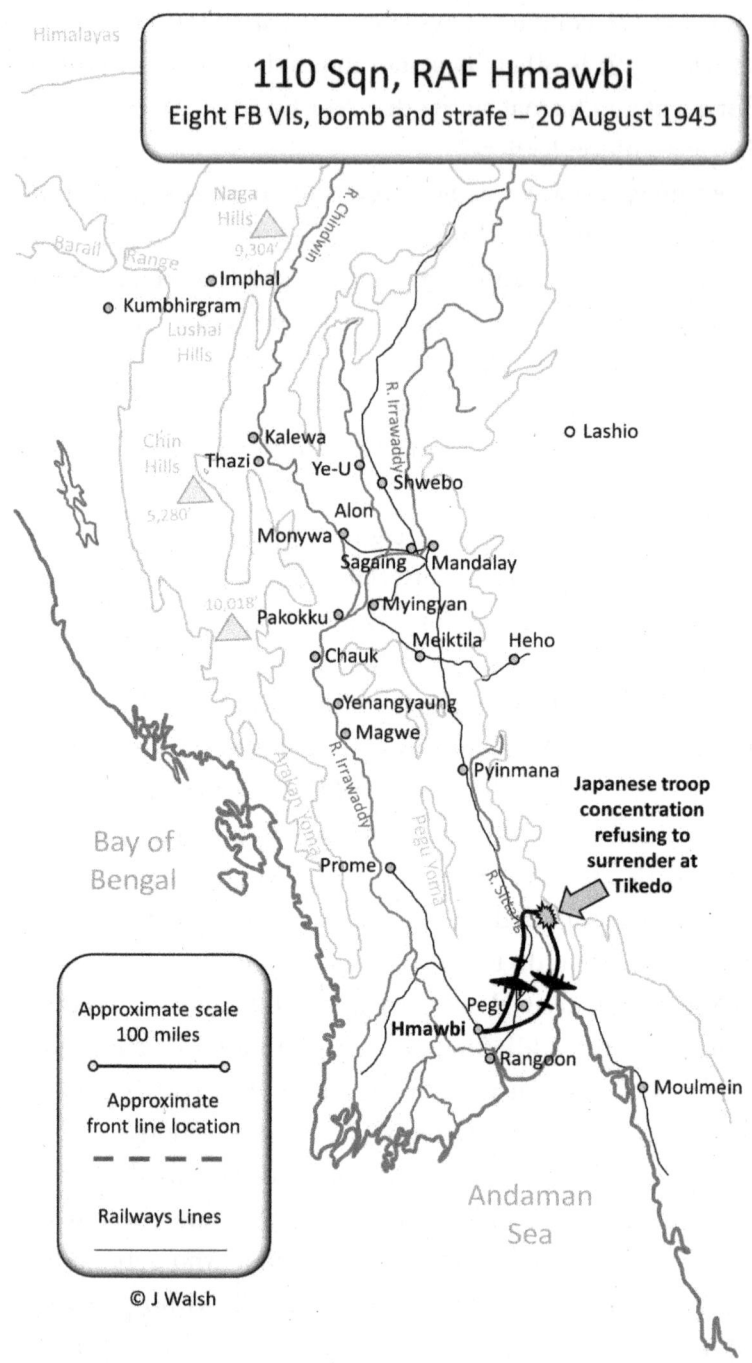

110 Sqn, RAF Hmawbi

Eight FB VIs, bomb and strafe – 20 August 1945

Himalayas

Naga
Hills
9,304'

Barail Range

R. Chindwin

o Imphal

o Kumbhirgram

Lushai
Hills

Chin
Hills
5,280'

o Kalewa

Thazi o

Ye-U o

o Shwebo

o Lashio

Alon

Monywa o

R. Irrawaddy

Sagaing   Mandalay

10,018'

Pakokku o

o Myingyan

o Chauk

Meiktila   Heho
o   o

o Yenangyaung

o Magwe

R. Irrawaddy

Arakan Yomas

o Pyinmana

Pegu Yoma

**Japanese troop
concentration
refusing to
surrender at
Tikedo**

Bay of
Bengal

Prome o

R. Sittang

Pegu o

Hmawbi o

o Rangoon

o Moulmein

Approximate scale
100 miles

o━━━━━━o

Approximate
front line location

‐ ‐ ‐ ‐

Railways Lines
───────

© J Walsh

Andaman
Sea

Purely by chance, this created some real symmetry in the Second World War, since No. 110 (Hyderabad) Squadron dropped both the RAF's first and last bombs of the conflict. The first Allied offensive operation of the war was on 4 September 1939. Five 110 Squadron Blenheims were sent on a low-level bombing raid to Wilhemshaven for which Flight Lieutenant Kenneth Doran was awarded the DFC. His citation read, 'this officer led an attack against an enemy cruiser. In face of heavy gunfire and under extremely bad weather conditions he pressed home a successful low attack with great determination'.

On 22 August the rear parties' convoys finally arrived at Hmawbi. Reg Davis was not impressed with first impressions, 'It was a large spread-out camp with lots of air traffic. Having driven all day in rain, it was grim to find the camp very definitely under water. Even the metal strip had been put u/s for Mossies due to the accumulation of water.'

Needless to say, Reg was updated by his colleagues on the 'incident' a few days earlier. 'In the Mess that night I learned of the Jap attack on the camp, injuring six of our officers. Fortunately, seven Jap bombs failed to go off, saving a lot more injuries – so bods were very much on alert.'[279] Lew Pepper also arrived with his 110 Squadron convoy and saw the impact of that incident. 'We would sit in the Mess with loaded revolvers on the table in front of us.'[280]

On 26 August the Japanese surrender delegation finally arrived at Hmawbi airfield. Ray Hicks and Jack Goodwin of 47 Squadron immediately flew the 'surrender documents' to HQ SEAC in Ceylon. On arriving late in the afternoon, no one wanted to take the papers so late in the day, so Ray had to retain them overnight and hand them in the following morning!

It was not until 2 September 1945, just one day short of six years since the British declared war on Germany in 1939, that the official documents confirming the surrender of the Japanese forces were signed in Tokyo Bay.

The war had been over for several months now in Europe and most of the European theatre combatants had already returned home. The British had even elected a new post-war government, adding to the feeling of those still in Burma that they were part of a forgotten war. Many of their families still had no real idea where they were or what they had been doing.

Over the following months many of the men who flew, serviced and supported the Mosquito FB VIs over Burma started to return to their homes. Others were required to stay on in the region until their tour was completed.

Squadron	Mosquito Intruder Operational Sorties		Aircrew Losses Operations		Aircrew Losses Training	
	Month	Total	Month	Total	Month	Total
No. 45 Sqn	0	1,261	0	20	0	8
No. 82 Sqn	0	979	0	11	0	2
No. 47 Sqn	25	690	0	6	0	0
No. 110 Sqn	41	428	0	17	0	4
No. 27 Sqn	0	45	0	2	0	0
Other Units	0	0	0	0	0	9
Total	66	3,403	0	56	0	23

Chapter 19

Fast and Furious

Victory, 1945

*'Japan Surrenders, End of War! Emperor Accepts
Allied Rule; M'Arthur Supreme Allied Commander;
Our Manpower Curbs Voided.'*
New York Times, *14 August 1945*

Once properly underway, the Mosquitos' intruder campaign over Burma was fast and furious. By day and on moonlit nights, in often inhospitable weather, they skimmed over the jungle, villages, airfields and rivers, dive-bombed critical targets, strafed transport, degraded infrastructure and denied airspace. They even counter-attacked the Japanese fighters. Their commitment and courage were recognised with many intruders being awarded DFCs. At times, the operational pressures were so intense for both aircrew and ground support that they had to back off, to refresh and rebuild. The Mosquito intruders' legendary status seems to be fully justified, but their achievements came at a cost.

When the Mosquito made its maiden flight, de Havilland knew that they had designed a winner! It was fast, with an impressive payload. Fifty years later, Ralph Hare, the designer responsible for its wing loads and stresses (who later became British Aerospace's Chief Structural Engineer and worked on the wings for Airbus), described its lightweight composite wood construction as 'probably man's highest engineering achievement in timber.'[281] It was beautifully balanced, confirmed by Wing Commander Bill Hudson. 'We used

Distinguished Flying Cross
Flight Lieutenant Peter Norman Ewing

HONOURS AND AWARDS

DISTINGUISHED FLYING CROSS

FLIGHT LIEUTENANT PETER NORMAN EWING

(406523)

C I T A T I O N

Flight Lieutenant Ewing is an exceptionally able and resolute pilot who has completed more than 100 sorties including many low-level attacks on various enemy targets.

Throughout he has shown the greatest determination to inflict loss on the enemy and has set a fine example to all.

On a recent occasion in an attack on an enemy airfield Flight Lieutenant Ewing was wounded in the hand, arm and body but despite this he completed the attack and afterwards flew back to base.

These West Australians each hold a D.F.C. (left to right) P/O Peter Black, F/L Victor Ferry, F/L Ray Hutchinson, F/L Peter Ewing.

© R Ewing

to say no woman could be as sensitive as a Mosquito. You flew it with the tips of your fingers on the control column, delighting in the response.'[282]

Senior staff in the RAF, the Air Ministry and de Havilland must have known that the RAF was either expecting or tacitly allowing aircrew to operate the Mosquito at or beyond the boundaries of its performance envelope. This seems especially true in India, where climatic conditions and poor workmanship could have restricted the Mosquitos' tasking. However, operational imperatives took precedence. The task was more important than the individuals and it was important that the aircrew did not lose faith in the Mosquito's impressive capabilities.

At the start of 1945, when the airframes were demonstrating their fragility, the payload of the already fully stressed FB VI was increased. The crews were often expected to deliver their increased ordinance by dive-bombing, creating maximum airframe stress during pull-out. As Wing Commander Johnny Walker wrote. 'The work that this squadron is doing is more dangerous than most and we have not been without our losses. This is a terrible war, but never so terrible as when it strikes so closely as this.'[283] Possibly the facts that the pilots loved the Mosquito, that its capabilities seemed almost endless and that accurate bombing with the FB VI could only really be achieved through dive bombing contributed to its high airframe failure rate in the theatre. As Vernon Brown, the Chief Inspector of Accidents, concluded, 'The susceptibility of the Mosquito to break up during a pull-out shows that, considering the manoeuvrability and stability characteristics, the aircraft is weak structurally.' Dedicated, skilled and seemingly fearless, the aircrew made the most of the aircraft's performance and its intruder capabilities. To some degree, the Mosquito was complicit since it was so beautifully balanced and a delight for the aircrew to fly. It seemed to give whatever was asked of it!

Of course, the aircrew understood the Mosquito's weaknesses but still flew it to the limit. No. 47 Squadron even created a new squadron song, laced with black humour and sung with enthusiasm to the tune of 'My Darling Clementine'. The first verse sums up their relationship with the Mosquito:

47, 47, 47 is the name
We fly Mosquitos,
Bits of plywood, fastened down with glue and twine,
Though on take-off, wings may break off,
It's a wonderful design.
47, 47, 47 is the name,
All the aircrew and the groundcrew slowly going down the drain.[284]

The Mosquito FB VI was flown operationally over Burma for just fourteen months between September 1943, when the first arrived in theatre, and the end of hostilities in August 1945. During that time, 113 pilots and 118 navigators from only five squadrons flew a total of 3,403 operational sorties. No. 45 Squadron flew thirty-seven per cent of the operational sorties and also delivered the highest monthly squadron operations' tally of 352 ops during March 1945. Flight Lieutenant Bob Barclay DFC RAAF, a navigator with 45 Squadron, flew sixty-three Mosquito intruder operations, believed to be the highest individual tally. Many pilots and navigators flew over fifty Mosquito intruder ops.

The human cost was significant. At least eighty-two Mosquito aircrew (effectively the establishment of two complete squadrons), one engineering officer and one photographer gave their lives during this short campaign – ferrying, during training, during operations, in transit and whilst testing FB VI aircraft in India and Burma. They shall not be forgotten.

Abel, Flight Sergeant Victor, RAAF, 82 Sqn navigator, 13 September 44 – probable structural.

Allen, Flight Sergeant Wilfred Louis, RAF, 110 Sqn navigator, 28 April 45 – operations.

Ashworth, Flight Sergeant Gordon Herbert, RAF, 45 Sqn pilot, 17 February 45 – operations.

Austin, Flight Sergeant William Arthur, RAF, 45 Sqn navigator, 26 March 45 – operations.

Bargh, Sergeant George William, RAF, 45 Sqn navigator, 3 October 44 – operations.

Best, Warrant Officer Robert, RAF, 82 Sqn pilot, 2 March 45 – operations.

Black, Sergeant Ronald Erskine, RAF, 82 Sqn navigator, 29 March 45 – operations.

Blower, Pilot Officer Stephen Hugh, RAF, 110 Sqn navigator, 18 April 45 – operations.

Botterill, Flying Officer Keith, RAF, 45 Sqn navigator, 12 October 44 – operations.

Bourke, Squadron Leader Norman Leslie, RAF, 45 Sqn pilot, 16 October 44 – operations.

Buchanan, Flight Lieutenant John George, RNZAF, 110 Sqn pilot, 2 May 45 – operations.

Butler, Flight Lieutenant Norman Grenville, RAF, 47 Sqn pilot, 17 April 45 – operations.

Campbell, Flight Lieutenant Richard Gladstone, RCAF, 143 R.S.U. pilot, 10 October 44 – structural.

Cargill, Flying Officer Harry James Scutchings, RAAF, 45 Sqn navigator, 17 December 44 – operations.

Cook, Flight Sergeant Geoffrey, RAF, 45 Sqn navigator, 13 June 45 – training.

Cookson, Flight Lieutenant David, RAF, 110 Sqn navigator, 12 July 45 – operations.

Davis, Flight Sergeant John Ashby, RAF, 301 FTU pilot, 24 July 43 – ferry transit.

Dorricott, Flying Officer Kenneth John, RAF, 82 Sqn pilot, 26 December 44 – operations.

Draper, Flight Lieutenant Brian Vincent, RAF DFC, 45 Sqn pilot, 28 February 45 – operations/structural.

Dumas, Flying Officer Keith Russell, RAF, 45 Sqn navigator, 16 October 44 – operations.

Edwards, Squadron Leader Donald Stuart, RAF AFC, 45 Sqn pilot, 20 October 44 – probable structural.

Edwards, Warrant Officer William Prince, RAF, 45 Sqn navigator, 3 January 45 – operations/engine.

Felsenstein, Flight Sergeant Basil Saul, RAF, 82 Sqn navigator, 15 January 45 – operations.

Filson-Young, Wing Commander William David Loraine, RAF DFC*, 47 Sqn pilot, 15 May 45 – operations.

Findlay, Flight Lieutenant Patrick Bernard, RAF, 110 Sqn pilot, 6 April 45 – operations.

Flatt, Warrant Officer William Francis, RAF, 82 Sqn navigator, 19 February 45 – operations.

Fortune, Flying Officer Frederick Charles, RAF, 45 Sqn pilot, 14 May 45 – transit.

Goldstone, Sergeant Albert Abraham, RAF, 301 FTU pilot, 1 August 43 – ferry transit.

Goodall, Flight Sergeant Richard Anthony, RAF, 301 FTU navigator, 24 July 43 – ferry transit.

Goodwin, Flight Lieutenant Charles Ronald, RAF, 45 Sqn pilot, 15 January 45 – operations.

Gordon, Flight Sergeant James, RAF, 110 Sqn navigator, 3 July 45 – operations.

Gunn, Pilot Officer William Alexander, RCAF, 27 Sqn pilot, 12 January 44 – operations.

Hawkins, Flight Lieutenant St. John, RAF, 110 Sqn pilot, 28 April 45 – operations.

Hayes, Flying Officer Gwilim Griffiths, RAF, 82 Sqn pilot, 29 March 45 – operations.

Hayward, Warrant Officer William Sidney, RAF, 45 Sqn navigator, 12 January 45 – operations.

Hemingway, Flight Sergeant Anthony Sidney, RAF, 110 Sqn pilot, 4 May 45 – operations.

Holmes, Warrant Officer Alan, RAF, 45 Sqn pilot, 26 March 45 – operations.

Hurst, Flying Officer Lawrence Goddard, RAF, 110 Sqn navigator, 6 April 45 – operations.

Illingworth, Warrant Officer Kenneth, RAF, 47 Sqn pilot, 25 June 45 – operations.

James, Warrant Officer Peter Roesch, RAF, 45 Sqn navigator, 28 February 45 – operations/structural.

John, Flight Lieutenant Alan, RAF, 110 Sqn pilot, 1 June 45 – operations.

Kinnell, Flying Officer David, RAF, 82 Sqn pilot, 1 March 45 – operations.

Lambert, Warrant Officer Harry Allen, RAF, 82 Sqn navigator, 1 March 45 – operations.

Lauder, Flying Officer Gordon, RAF, 45 Sqn navigator, 14 May 45 – transit.

Levey, Flight Lieutenant James Maxwell, RAAF, 45 Sqn pilot, 17 December 44 – operations.

Lorimer, Flight Sergeant Andrew Symon, RAF, 82 Sqn navigator, 2 March 45 – operations.

Luff, Sergeant William Charles, RAF, 27 Sqn navigator, 12 January 44 – operations.

McKerracher, Flight Lieutenant Walter, RAAF DFM, 22 A.P.C. navigator, 13 May 44 – structural.

McQueen, Warrant Officer John Sawers, RNZAF, 45 Sqn pilot, 3 January 45 – operations/engine.

Nicolson, Warrant Officer Donald John, RAF, 110 Sqn navigator, 17 July 45 – operations.

O'Neill, Flying Officer Hugh Leo, RAF, 110 Sqn pilot, 12 July 45 – operations.

Parker, Flying Officer Allan Edward, RAAF, 82 Sqn pilot, 20 October 44 – probable structural.

Pinkerton, Warrant Officer Robert Leonard Cecil Conrie, RAF, 45 Sqn navigator, 17 February 45 – operations.

Potts, Flying Officer Samuel, RAF, 45 Sqn navigator, 15 January 45 – operations/engine.

Proctor, Flight Lieutenant Gordon Hayter, RAF, 45 Sqn pilot, 3 October 1944 – operations.

Prout, Flying Officer Leonard Gordon, 45 Sqn navigator, 11 September 44 – possible structural.

Quinn, Warrant Officer Norman Lawrence Peter, RAF, 110 Sqn navigator, 18 February 45 – training.

Randall, Sergeant Harry, RAF, 301 FTU navigator, 6 September 43 – ferry transit.

Randall, Flying Officer Maurice Dean, RAAF, 82 Sqn navigator, 20 October 44 – probable structural.

Reeves, Flight Lieutenant John Harper, RNZAF, 45 Sqn pilot, 11 September 44 – possible structural.

Rimell, Flight Lieutenant Douglas William, RAF, 143 R.S.U. engineer, 10 October 44 – structural.

Robson, Flight Sergeant Frank, RAF, 47 Sqn navigator, 17 April 45 – operations.

Rootes, Flight Lieutenant Raymond, RAF, 110 Sqn pilot, 18 April 45 – operations.

Sandifer, Flying Officer Eric Leonard, RAF, 45 Sqn navigator, 20 October 44 – probable structural.

Saunders, Wing Commander Arthur Ernest OBE, RAF, 110 Sqn pilot, 11 July 45 – transit.

Scott, Squadron Leader Alward Elmer, RCAF, 47 Sqn pilot, 14 April 45 – operations.

Sims, Flight Sergeant Sidney Ashton, RAF, 301 FTU pilot, 6 September 43 – ferry transit.

Smith, Flight Sergeant Norman Alfred, RAF, 45 Sqn navigator, 6 February 45 – accident.

Stephen, Flight Lieutenant James Bryden RAF, 110 Sqn navigator, 11 July 45 – transit.

Stumm, Wing Commander Harley Charles, RAAF DFC, 45 Sqn pilot, 13 May 44 – structural.

Sutherland, Squadron Leader Ira Allison, RNZAF DFC, 110 Sqn pilot, 28 June 45 – structural.

Thynne, Pilot Officer Edward Andrew, RAAF, 82 Sqn pilot, 19 February 45 – operations.

Tonks, Flight Lieutenant Geoffrey John, RAF, 45 Sqn pilot, 13 June 45 – training.

Tuck, Flight Sergeant George Edward, RAF, 47 Sqn navigator, 25 June 45 – operations.

Tufnell, Flying Officer William Clark, RAAF, 82 Sqn pilot, 13 September 44 – probable structural.

Tullett, Flying Officer William Melville, RAF, 110 Sqn pilot, 18 February 45 – training.

Turner, Warrant Officer Philip Edward, RAF, 110 Sqn navigator, 4 May 45 – operations.

Van der Pol, Flying Officer Hendrick John, RAF DFM, 110 Sqn pilot, 3 July 45 – operations.

Waters, Flight Lieutenant Roger Claud Vaughan, 47 Sqn navigator, 15 May 45 – operations.

Watts, Sergeant Cyril Henry William, RAF, 301 FTU navigator, 1 August 43 – ferry transit.

Wilcock, Flying Officer Roland John, RAF, 45 Sqn pilot, 17 June 45 – operations.

Wilson, Flying Officer Hank, RAF, 82 Sqn navigator, 26 December 44 – operations.

Wilson, Pilot Officer John Robert, RAF, 45 Sqn pilot, 12 January 45 – operations/engine.

Woodcock, Flight Lieutenant Sidney Leslie, RAF, 110 Sqn photographer, 2 May 45 – operations.

In addition, the following Mosquito intruder aircrew became prisoners-of-war:

Emeny, Flight Lieutenant Cliff Stanley, RNZAF, 45 Sqn pilot, 9 November 44 – operations.

Hudson, Wing Commander Lionel Vivian, RAAF, 82 Sqn pilot, 19 December 44 – operations.

Shortis, Warrant Officer Jack, RAF, 82 Sqn navigator, 19 December 44 – operations.

Yanota, Warrant Officer John Joseph Stephen, RCAF, 45 Sqn navigator, 9 November 44 – operations.

Chapter 20

Survivors' Breakfast

Post War

'I yield to none in my desire to see preserved this splendid weapon of the Royal Air Force, upon which our safety and our freedom depend, but, for this great purpose, it is all the more necessary to get the life of the nation working again, and not to squander our remaining treasure in keeping a large number of men in the Royal Air Force – who are not really wanted either for immediate needs, or for the permanent organisation – and to keep them lolling about at great cost to the public and vexation to themselves.'
Winston Churchill, Demobilisation debate, Houses of Parliament, London, 22 October 1945

What of the intruders who returned? Did their experiences have lasting impact on their health? Wal McLellan's daughter, Barbara Boon, realised that the war had long term effects on her father.

'In hindsight, I feel so disloyal to Dad in realising that he certainly had PTSD but, when I talk to other children about their fathers, I realise that we mostly had the same experience of being children of those men. They were kind, peaceful, compassionate and private. They were the strong silent types so often, good citizens and gave much of themselves in service to community and others. But there were the rare and completely unexpected flashes of intense anger. Dad was helping me with my maths homework and I just couldn't grasp a concept of algebra – he suddenly blew sky high, slammed the book shut and stormed off as he shouted that "I couldn't be that stupid." To this day, I feel the tears prickle at the memory. I had never seen Dad angry. He was eternally patient about anything and this shook me to the core. Truly I have PTSD from his PTSD!

'Some years later he blew up again, completely out of context to the situation and left me devastated with grief. Of course, I didn't know about PTSD – I had great uncles who regularly went mad and the adult conversations were always so sympathetic because they were ex-WW1 soldiers. But it was never part of Dad's vernacular for himself. The clue of course was in his nightmares, which were terrifying. I would hear him screaming and calling out in the middle of the night and then the footsteps down the hall of him and Mum and the quiet clinking of cups as they sipped their tea. Low conversations and on the occasion that I crept down the hall to see what was going on, Dad with his head in his hands saying over and over again, "Jesus wept, Jesus wept" with Mum standing behind him with her arms around him and her head on the back of his neck till he recovered. Wow, I haven't thought of this for a long time. I'm rather emotional now. But, the one time that I asked about it, he laughed and said, "Oh the Heeby Jeebies got me" and that was the end of that!'[285]

And finally, what sort of civilian lives did they lead?

Alf Pridmore, Warrant Officer RAF, navigator 45 Squadron, about forty Mosquito ops over Burma. After he had been demobbed, Alf settled in Bletchley, took a job as an accounts clerk and married Rachel whom he had met during his training at RAF Weston on the Green where she was an ATS typist/stores orderly. Later, after a family tragedy, they moved to Wiltshire where Alf worked in the audit office of the local water company until he took early retirement. Alf died in 2007, less than two years after Rachel.

'Babe' Wambeek, Squadron Leader RAF DFC, pilot 82 Squadron, fifty-five Mosquito ops over Burma. Ronald Stuart Wambeek was born in Quetta, India in 1922 and in 1939 started studying medicine in

London, before volunteering as a pilot in 1941. Post-war, Ron married Joan Ross. He qualified as a doctor and then specialised in aviation medicine, flying most of the early jet fighters and becoming Flying Principal Medical Officer at the RAF Institute of Aviation Medicine at Farnborough. In 1972 Ron and Joan emigrated to Australia, where he died in 2005.

Benny Walsh, Warrant Officer RAF, pilot 27, 82 & 45 Squadrons, forty-three Mosquito intruder ops over Burma. One of the youngest intruder pilots, Benjamin Walsh returned to the UK suffering from 'the twitch'. He was demobbed in July 1946, aged just twenty-two, with over five years' service and seventy-five ops in total. In 1947 he married Patricia Coombe. Ben resumed his education, qualified as a pharmacist and became a Fellow of the Royal Pharmaceutical Society. Ben and Pat had two children (one being the author). During 1996 the company he had founded in 1971 went public on NASDAQ in the United States. Ben died in 2008, eight years after his wife, Pat.

Bill Hudson, Wing Commander RAAF, pilot and CO of 82 Squadron, one Mosquito intruder op over Burma. Lionel Vivien Hudson was freed from Rangoon Jail on 3 May 1945. He returned to journalism becoming a war correspondent in Korea, Malaya and Vietnam. Having studied Ancient Chinese History at Harvard, he became a news executive before moving into wildlife documentaries. Bill was eighty-five when he died in 2001.

Bill Taylor, Flying Officer RAAF, pilot 45 Squadron, forty-four Mosquito intruder ops over Burma and sixty-five ops in total. William Taylor departed India on 27 September 1945. On arrival in Sydney, he was met by his mother and sister-in-law. He secured a job as a switch operator with Country Producers Selling Company, a wool merchant in Sydney. In 1950 he married Una and they had two children. Bill remained with the wool merchant, becoming a wool auctioneer and eventually the Sydney manager until he retired in 1983. Bill died at the age of ninety-eight in 2019.

Bob Willis, Flight Lieutenant RAF DFC, pilot 47 Squadron, nineteen Mosquito intruder ops over Burma. George Robert Thomas Willis returned to the UK in July 1945, married Joan in November and they raised four children. Demobbed in June 1946, Bob joined his family's wholesale food business and headed its development until he retired in 1991. During retirement, he assisted start-up companies and was awarded an MBE for service to training in 1996.

Cliff Emeny, Flight Lieutenant RNZAF, pilot 27 and 45 Squadrons, eleven Mosquito intruder ops over Burma. On his return to New Zealand, Cliff Stanley Emeny married Joan, naming their first son of their six children John, after Johnny Yanota. Post-war Cliff had some health issues and moved into alternative medicine, becoming a qualified iridologist. He died in October 2000.

'Duke' Duclos, Wing Commander RAF CBE DFC AE, pilot 45 and 47 Squadrons, about fifty Mosquito intruder ops over Burma. Victor Sydney Henry Duclos remained in the RAF after the war and married Lois Cash. In 1969 he was Station Commander at RAF Bicester. One of his minor duties was to present swimming certificates to visiting schoolboy members of the Combined Cadet Force. When the author showed his certificate to his parents, his father, Benny Walsh, was reduced to tears on seeing Duke's signature. Duke retired as a Group Captain and remained in the Bicester area.

'Freddy' Snell, Wing Commander RAF DFC, pilot 27 and 82 Squadrons, thirty-six Mosquito intruder ops over Burma. Vivian Robert Snell was appointed CO of 125 Squadron, RAF Church Fenton, in October 1945. The squadron was disbanded soon after and he was discharged from the RAF in 1946. 'Freddy' died in August 2007.

'Jock' Torrance, Squadron Leader RAF DFC, pilot 27 and 45 Squadrons, nearly thirty Mosquito intruder ops over Burma. Alexander Torrance was repatriated to the UK from Singapore on 12 November 1945. He continued in aviation, initially with

Scandinavian Airlines at Prestwick and later as flight operations chief with British Caledonian at London Airport. In July 1971 he acted as 'flight despatcher' for Sheila Scott when she became the first person to fly solo in a single engine aircraft over the true North Pole.[286]

'Johnny' Walker, Wing Commander RAF DSO, pilot 45 Squadron, fifty-three Mosquito intruder ops over Burma. Robert James Walker did not fly operationally after he was injured on 25 March 1945. Having returned to the UK at the end of the war, he was reunited with his wife, Margaret, whom he had married in 1939. Robert remained in the RAF post-war, retiring as a Group Captain in 1964. In civilian life he was a director of James Walker and Sons, Mirfield and Dewsbury, a textile company, and also served as a magistrate. Johnny died in Shrewsbury in 2001.

Johnny Yanota, Warrant Officer RCAF, navigator 27 and 45 Squadrons, seventeen Mosquito intruder ops over Burma. John Joseph Stephen Yanota was evacuated on the hospital ship *Karapara*, returning via the UK to his hometown, Blairemore, in Alberta, Canada. After a short time working in the local coal mines, he started a career in the Canadian Unemployment Agency. Johnny married Helen Pozzi in 1948 and they raised seven children. He changed to working with the Canadian Postal Service, retiring in 1983. Johnny remained friends with Cliff Emeny throughout his life, meeting with him on several occasions. Johnny died in 2011.

Wal McLellan, Flight Lieutenant RAAF DFC, pilot 45 Squadron, thirty-nine Mosquito intruder ops over Burma and eighty-five ops in total. Walter Maclellan arrived back in Australia and returned to the rural accountancy firm with which he worked prior to the war. In 1947 he married Joan Matthews and they raised two daughters. In later years he became the deputy Town Clerk for Greater Cessnock. Wal died aged seventy-two in 1988.

All were warriors who dared to fly to the limit!

Chapter 21

Glossary of Terms

For consistency, all times are local and shown as a 24-hour clock.

AA (ack-ack) – Anti-aircraft gun or fire, also see Flak.

Anti-Fascist Organisation, a Burmese political and resistance movement formed in August 1944 by the leaders of the Communist Party of Burma, the Burma National Army (BNA) led by General Aung San, and the People's Revolutionary Party (later renamed the Socialist Party).[287]

Airscrew – Propeller.

Army Zero Fighter – See Nakajima Ki-43 Hayabusa fighter.

ASI – The airspeed indicator tells the pilot how fast the aircraft is flying. The instrument works by measuring the difference in pressure between the side of the fuselage (static point) and the pitot head, pointing directly into the airflow.

ATP – Air Transport Pool; a unit which allocated pilots and other aircrew to tasks or squadrons.

Bar – When associated with a decoration for gallantry, Bar means that the gallantry medal has been awarded to the individual for a second time.

Basha – An Assamese hut typically made of bamboo and grass.

Blenheim – The Bristol Blenheim was a British twin-engine light bomber aircraft first delivered to the RAF in 1937. After extensive use in the first two years of the war, it was increasingly relegated to training roles.

Bofors – Automatic 40mm anti-aircraft canon, known as Bofors guns, used by both the Allies and Axis forces.

Boulton Paul Defiant – A British interceptor aircraft that served with the RAF. It was designed and built as a 'turret fighter', without any fixed forward-firing guns.

Burmese National Army (BNA) – The BNA had its roots in the Burma Independence Army (BIA). Formed just after Japan entered the war in 1941, the BIA fought alongside Japan against the British 7 Armoured Brigade in the Battle of Shewdaung in March 1942. After Japan conquered Burma, it disbanded the BIA and created the Burmese Defence Army (BDA). With nominal Burmese independence in 1943, the BDA transitioned into the BNA under General Aug Sang in 1944 and started making contacts with other groups in Burma, including Force 136. Recognising the likely outcome of the war, in late 1944 the BNA contacted the Allies. On 27 March 1945, it openly declared war on the Japanese, aligning itself with the Allies.

Cab-rank – A type of operation where aircraft are despatched to a holding area to await target instructions from a Visual Control Post.

Cannon – A cannon fires larger shells than a machine gun (typically 20mm or larger) and uses heavier explosive or incendiary shells which explode upon contact. They deliver more destructive power.

Chance Light – A mobile directional floodlight, which could be positioned beside the threshold of an operational runway. Universally known as Chance Lights after their manufacturer, Chance Brothers, which made lighthouse equipment.

Charpoy – (Or charpai) An Indian bed consisting of a frame strung with light rope or tapes.

CMU – Central Maintenance Unit; a unit that repaired and rebuilt aircraft, as well as completed major services and overhauls.

CO – Commanding Officer, usually of a squadron.

DFC – The Distinguished Flying Cross is a military decoration awarded to warrant officers and commissioned officers of the Royal Air Force and other Empire services, for 'an act or acts of valour, courage or devotion to duty whilst flying in active operations against the enemy'.

Dhobi Wallah – An Indian washerman.

Dive Bombing – In dive bombing the pilot aims the plane towards a stationary target at an angle of sixty degrees or more and, in the Mosquito, uses the idling engines as an 'airbrake' to keep the aircraft's speed constant in the dive. The pilot judges the aircraft's forward movement towards the target and uses this to decide when to release the bombs. In a steep dive, with the bomb released between 6,000ft and 2,000ft, the time of flight is short and air resistance, wind and target motion are small. Given the Mosquito FB VI's compromise gun/bomb sight, dive bombing delivered reasonably accurate results with the pilot's assessing release using rule-of-thumb and experience. The disadvantage with dive bombing is that the aircraft makes a good AA target, especially when pulling out of its dive.

DSO – Distinguished Service Order, awarded to members of all three services for exceptional valour.

Elevators – Flying control surfaces usually at the tail of the aircraft which are used to make the aircraft climb or descend.

ENSA – Entertainments National Service Association, set up in 1939 to provide entertainment for the armed forces personnel during the war.

Flak – German anti–aircraft gun (from the word *Fliegerabwehr-kanone*), used generically for AA fire.

Flaps – Moveable panels on the trailing edge of an aircraft's wing which allow the same lift to be safely generated at a lower speed and nose attitude, permitting better visibility on the approach, a slower touch down and shorter landing run.

Flarepath – A row of lights (either kerosene gooseneck flares or electric) that mark the boundary of the runway for taking off and landing.

Flight Lieutenant – RAF officer rank equivalent to an army Captain.

Flying Officer – RAF officer rank equivalent to an army Lieutenant.

Flying Tour – A period of active duty for an individual with an operational (as opposed to training) unit which would be denoted in Europe by the number of operational sorties (usually 30 or 35 for intruders) but in the Far East was defined as three years or 250 hours of operational flying.

F/O – Abbreviation for Flying Officer.

Force 136 – A cover name for Britain's Special Operations Executive working in South-East Asia, providing intelligence from behind the Japanese lines. Although commanded by British officers and civilians, most of Force 136 in Burma were indigenous people, often working with Burmese-speaking former plantation and forestry managers. It tended to work with the Chins, Karens and Kachins.

FTU – Ferry Transport Unit.

Glide bombing – Similar to dive bombing except that the attack angle is less than sixty degrees. This technique is better adapted to fighter aircraft which tend to develop excessive speeds in steep dives. Glide bombing is a high-speed attack and bombs are generally released at an altitude of between 2,000ft and 3,000ft. Advantages include surprise and quick getaway. The disadvantages are that the bomb velocity is less than in dive bombing and AA vulnerability is greater than in dive bombing.

Goolie Chit – (Or 'blood chit') A Goolie Chit, so called because it protected an airman's most personal items, was a message of vital importance, often in several languages, which promised a reward for anyone who aided an airman trapped behind enemy lines. Printed on material, they were first issued in the First World War and continued in use in various forms through to the Iraq conflict.

Group Captain – RAF officer rank equivalent to an army Colonel.

HE – High explosive.

hp – Horsepower, a measure of power.

IAS – Indicated Air Speed is speed which the air speed indicator displays.

Indian National Army (INA) – The INA was a collaborationist armed force formed by Indian collaborators and Imperial Japan on 1 September 1942. Its aim was to secure Indian independence from the British Empire.

Jap, Japs – Second World War term used by the Allies for the Japanese military.

Kutcha Strip – An emergency landing strip alongside the main runway, allowing a belly-landing without blocking the runway itself.

LAC – Leading Aircraftman in the RAF.

Machete – A large knife that was issued to aircrew as both a jungle escape tool and a defensive weapon.

Mae West – A personal life preserver flotation jacket, which was nick-named after the popular American movie star.

Mossie – Aircrew term for a DH Mosquito.

M/T – (Or MT) Motor transport vehicle: car, truck, or troop carrier.

MO – Medical officer.

mph – Miles per hour.

Nakajima Ki-43 Hayabusa (Japanese fighter aircraft) – Known as the Oscar by the RAF (and Army Zero by US Forces), the Ki-43 was a relatively slow, lightly-armed land-based tactical fighter plane which became legendary due to its success in East-Asia in the early war years. Its primary strengths were its extraordinary manoeuvrability and climb rate.

NCO – Abbreviation for Non-Commissioned Officer. Lance Corporal, Corporal, Sergeant, Chief Technician and Flight Sergeant. (Frequently Warrant Officers are included with Sergeants and Flight Sergeants as senior NCOs.)

Observer – The aircrew role now known as Navigator.

OC – Officer Commanding, usually of a station or Group.

Ops or Operations – Flights intended to actively engage the enemy in some way. The same term was used widely by all Allied Forces and had a number of meanings depending on context. For RAF aircrew it signified a flight of greater hazard which they would record in their logbooks, usually counting towards their 'flying tour' total.

Oscar – See Nakajima Ki-43 Hayabusa fighter.

O.T.U. – Operational Training Unit; the RAF unit which provides role training for aircrew, sometimes also on the operational aircraft (thus becoming an Operational Conversion Unit or OCU).

Pilot Officer – RAF officer rank equivalent to an army Second Lieutenant.

P/O – Abbreviation for Pilot Officer.

POW – Prisoner-of-war.

Prang – RAF aircrew jargon for a crash or to hit.

Prop – Abbreviation of propeller.

PRU – Photographic reconnaissance unit, which could include specialists in photographic processing and interpretation.

psi – pounds per square inch, a measure of pressure.

Quarter attack – A high energy attack manoeuvre, positioning the aircraft in an advantageous 'quarter' to attack an enemy aircraft – forward, abeam or rear.

RAAF – Royal Australian Air Force.

RAF – Royal Air Force.

RCAF – Royal Canadian Air Force.

Rhubarb – A type of operation over enemy-held territory when individual, or groups of fighters, or fighter-bombers, often taking full advantage of low cloud, poor visibility or darkness, search at low-level for opportunity targets such as railway locomotives and rolling stock, aircraft on the ground, enemy troops and vehicles on roads.

RNZAF – Royal New Zealand Air Force.

RSU – Regional Support Unit; a maintenance team providing aircraft maintenance and repair support to the front-line squadrons.

R/T – Radio telephony. Using the radio.

S/L – (Or S/Ldr) Abbreviation for Squadron Leader.

Sortie – A sortie is a combat mission of an individual aircraft, starting when the aircraft takes off and ending on its return. Sir Archibald Sinclair, Secretary of State for Air 1940–1945, defined it as 'one flight by one aircraft' in Parliament on 29 March 1944.

Squadron Leader – RAF officer rank equivalent to an army Major.

Strafing – Attacking ground targets from low-flying aircraft using aircraft-mounted automatic weapons, namely machine guns and cannon (not bombs or rockets).

Undercart – Undercarriage.

U/S – Unserviceable.

USAAF – United States Army Air Force; the precursor to the independent United States Air Force which was formed on 18 September 1947.

VCP – Visual Control Post, often an RAF controller, wireless operator and an RAF Regiment driver, working with Army liaison and/or Force 136.

VHF – Very High Frequency, a type of radio.

V_{MC} – The minimum control speed of an aircraft is the speed that specifies the calibrated airspeed below which directional or lateral control of the aircraft can no longer be maintained, after the failure of one or more engines.

VNE – Velocity Never Exceed. The maximum speed at which the aircraft should fly.

Warrant Officer – An officer holding a royal warrant, the most senior non-commissioned rank.

W/C – Abbreviation for Wing Commander.

Wing Commander – RAF officer rank equivalent to an army Lieutenant Colonel.

WO – Abbreviation for Warrant Officer.

Yanks – British military slang for Americans. At the time not perceived as derogatory, the Americans in turn referred to the British as 'Limeys'.

References

General abbreviations:

AWM   Australian War Memorial

MAA   Mosquito Aircrew Association, Second World War Experience Centre, UK

SORB   Squadron Operations Record Book, National Archives, UK

Notes

1. Air 27/861-3 110 SORB
2. Ibid
3. AWM, photograph PO2491.079
4. Hudson, L., *The Rats of Rangoon*, Leo Cooper, London, 1987, p. 184
5. Ibid
6. Air 27/861-3 110 SORB
7. Hudson, op. cit., p. 185
8. Ibid, p. 186
9. Ibid, p. 188
10. Ibid
11. Ibid, p. 189
12. *The Mosquito 50 Years on*, Royal Aeronautical Society, Hatfield, Symposium Proceedings 24 November 1990, GMS Enterprises, Peterborough, 1991, Ramsden, M., p. 34
13. Ibid, Fillingham, P., p. 66
14. Ibid
15. de Havilland, G., *Sky Fever*, Hamish Hamilton, UK, 1961
16. *The Mosquito 50 Years on*, op. cit., Fillingham, P., p. 66
17. Ibid, p. 67
18. Ibid, Summerville, T., p. 74
19. Ibid, Fillingham, P., p. 68
20. Hilliard, H., *The Mossie No. 36*, MAA, September 2004, p. 27
21. *The Mosquito 50 Years on*, op. cit., Fillingham, P., p. 67
22. Ibid, p. 68-70
23. Ibid, p. 70
24. Service Accident Report No. Misc, 23, Mosquito Structural Failures, RAF Accident Investigation Branch, 25 January 1943
25. Air 23/2135, Far East Operations: AOC-in-C, Air Marshal Sir Richard Peirse; personal signals to and from the Air Ministry, 1942.

26. Innes, D.J., *Beaufighters over Burma*, Blandford Press, Poole, UK, 1985, p. 49
27. Ibid, p. 64
28. Ibid, p. 65
29. Ibid, p. 67
30. Service Accident Report No. Misc, 23A, Mosquito Structural Failures, RAF Accident Investigation Branch, 14 June 1943
31. Mosquitos fitted with a single stage supercharged Merlin engine had only five stub ejector exhausts per bank, since the two rear cylinders shared an exhaust preventing it fouling the ducted radiator in the wing's leading edge.
32. George, P., *The Mossie No. 19*, MAA, April 1998, p. 29-31
33. Air History internet site, DH98 Mosquito production.
34. Ibid
35. Walsh, B., Personal memories 2004
36. Ibid
37. Ibid
38. Pridmore, A., Letter to J. Jefford
39. Pridmore, A., *The Mossie No. 10*, MAA, April 1995, p. 15
40. Ibid
41. Howland, M., *The Mossie No. 21*, MAA, January 1999, p. 26
42. www.lordmountbattenofburma.com/burma
43. Service Accident Report No. Misc, 23C, Mosquito Structural Failures, RAF Accident Investigation Branch, 25 October 1943
44. Chadburn, P., *Death Whispers over Burma*, Parade Magazine, March 1944
45. Pridmore, A., *The Mossie No. 11*, MAA, August 1995, p.25
46. Maude, A., *The Mossie No. 29*, MAA, September 2001, p. 16
47. Stonehouse Heritage Group, UK, Newsletter 14
48. Innes, op. cit., p. 62
49. AIR 27/327 27 Squadron ORB
50. Innes, op. cit., p. 85
51. Shortis, J., Letter to Matt Poole in 1991
52. RAF Historical Society and RAF Staff College, *The RAF and the Far East 1941-1945*, Symposium Proceedings 24 March 1995, p. 39
53. AIR 27/327 27 SORB
54. Ibid

55. Bowman, M.W., *The Men Who Fly the Mosquito*, Pen & Sword Books, UK, 2003, p. 208

56. Maude, A., *The Mossie No. 29*, MAA, September 2001, p. 16

57. API, 3 Feb 1944

58. Walsh, B., Newspaper cutting in logbook

59. Service Accident Report No. Misc, 23D, Mosquito Structural Failures, RAF Accident Investigation Branch, 25 February 1944

60. Mason, P.D., *'Nicolson V.C.'*, Geerings of Ashford Limited, UK, 1991, p. 95

61. Ibid, quoting one of 27 Squadron's pilots, Ron Thorogood

62. Lewis, D., *The Mossie No. 29*, MAA, September 2001, p. 36

63. AIR 27/457-12 45 SORB

64. Wing Commander Stumm's DFC Citation

65. Day, A.F., *Air War over the Arakan*, Unpublished collection, AWM, p. 342

66. Boon, Barbara, Email 3 November 2022

67. Taylor, W., Notes on wartime experiences, 2004

68. Aviation Safety internet site (aviation-safety.net)

69. Jefford, C.G., *The Flying Camels. The History of No. 45 Squadron RAF*, High Wycombe, Bucks: C.G. Jefford, UK, 1995, p. 268

70. Cox, S., Bill Taylor's eulogy by his daughter, Sue.

71. Service Accident Report No. Misc, 23, Mosquito Structural Failures, RAF Accident Investigation Branch, 25 January 1943

72. Jefford, op. cit., p. 270

73. 29 June 1938, 72 Squadron, mid-air collision during formation flying, 1m south of Selby. Gladiator I K6139, Flight Lieutenant W.F. Pharazyn killed; K6138 Pilot Officer R.J. Walker unhurt in K6138.

74. AIR 27/457 45 SORB

75. Jefford, op. cit., p. 269

76. Service Accident Report No. Misc, 23E, Mosquito Structural Failures, RAF Accident Investigation Branch, 7 June 1944

77. Yanota, J., Unpublished personal account

78. AIR 27/457 45 SORB

79. Jefford, op. cit., p. 272

80. AIR 27/457 45 SORB

81. Odgers, G., *Australia in the War of 1939-1945. Series Three, Air, Volume II. Air War Against Japan 1943-1945*, AWM, 1957, p. 417

82. Hudson, op. cit., p. 56
83. Sweeting, A.J., *No 'line-shooting' in flyer's memoirs*, *The Canberra Times*, 6 Feb 1988, p. 5
84. Service Accident Report No. Misc, 23F, Mosquito Structural Failures, RAF Accident Investigation Branch, 23 August 1944
85. AIR 27/683 82 SORB
86. Hudson, op. cit., p. 53
87. AIR 27/457-12 45 SORB
88. AIR 27/683 82 SORB
89. Willis, G.R.T., *No Hero, Just A Survivor*, Robert Willis Associates, Huddersfield, UK, 1999, p. 181
90. AIR 27/457-12 45 SORB
91. Bill Taylor's logbook
92. AIR 27/457-12 45 SORB
93. Commonwealth War Graves Registery
94. Pridmore, A., *The Mossie No. 10*, MAA, April 1995, p. 15
95. Willis, op. cit., p. 162
96. Ibid, p. 163
97. Stephan Wilkinson on the Mosquito.
98. Thomas, A., *Combat over Burma. Flypast*, Key Publishing, Stamford, UK, November 2015, p 56
99. Wambeek, R., *The Mossie No. 26*, MAA, Late Summer 2000, p. 13
100. Day, op. cit., p. 341, quoting Ralph Whitworth
101. Maude, A., *The Mossie No. 29*, MAA, September 2001, p. 16
102. AIR 27/683 82 SORB
103. Thomas, op. cit., p. 57
104. AIR 27/457 45 SORB
105. Ibid
106. Chabot, Charles James, *Oral History*, Imperial War Museum, UK, April 1973, Reel 11
107. AIR 27/683 82 SORB
108. Ibid
109. AIR 27/457 45 SORB
110. RAF Historical Society and RAF Staff College, op. cit., p. 36
111. Ibid, p. 38
112. Jefford, op. cit., p. 279
113. Willis, op. cit., p. 165

114. Norridge, C., *The Mossie No. 10*, MAA, April 1995, p. 18
115. RAF Historical Society and RAF Staff College, op. cit., p. 92
116. AIR 27/683 82 SORB
117. Yanota, op. cit.
118. Day, op. cit., p. 344
119. Yanota, op. cit.
120. Day, op. cit., p. 344
121. Yanota, op. cit.
122. Day, op. cit., p. 344
123. AIR 27/457 45 SORB
124. Yanota, op. cit.
125. Woods, T., *The Three Wings; Cliff Emeny's Story*, Zenith Publishing, New Plymouth, NZ, 2004, p. 195
126. Yanota, op. cit.
127. Woods, op. cit., p. 195
128. Ibid
129. Yanota, op. cit.
130. AIR 27/457 45 SORB
131. Ibid
132. Ibid
133. It seems quite clear that Geoffrey de Havilland visited the Mosquito squadrons in India in early November 1944. Ronald Wambeek, 82 Squadron, mentions the 'Chairman of de Havilland' visiting in early November and having dinner with him (although he does refer to him as Major, not Captain). Benny Walsh, 45 Squadron, said that he had briefly met Geoffrey de Havilland when he came out to inspect the Mosquitos. Ralph Whitworth, an 82 Squadron rigger, said that when Geoffrey de Havilland came out, he collected Parker's wing and sent it back to England. 45 Squadron's ORB mentions Geoffrey de Havilland by name (on 11 November), as does Alf Pridmore. Wal McLellan, 45 Squadron, told his daughter that he had met Geoffrey de Havilland. Additionally, on 26 November 1944, Major Hereward de Havilland, Geoffrey's brother, visited to try to wrap up the investigation and report back.
134. Pridmore, A., *The Mossie No. 10*, MAA, April 1995, p. 15
135. AIR 27/457 45 SORB
136. Jefford, op. cit., p. 280

137. Day, op. cit., p. 341
138. Wambeek, R., *The Mossie No. 26*, MAA, Late Summer 2000, p. 13
139. Day, op. cit., p. 342
140. AIR 27/683 82 SORB
141. Thomas, op. cit., p. 57
142. Willis, op. cit., p. 169
143. Ibid, p. 168
144. Service Accident Report No. Misc, 23G, Mosquito Structural Failures, RAF Accident Investigation Branch, 20 November 44
145. AIR 27/457 45 SORB
146. Bowman, op. cit., p. 212
147. Wambeek, R., *The Mossie No. 26*, MAA, Late Summer 2000, p. 13
148. Warwick, N.W.M., *Constant Vigilance; The RAF Regiment in the Burma Campaign*, Pen & Sword Aviation Books, UK, 2007, p. 107.
149. Thomas, op. cit., p. 57
150. Ibid
151. Hudson, op. cit., p. 5
152. Ibid, p. 6
153. Ibid, p. 8
154. Thomas, op. cit., p. 57
155. Norridge, C., *The Mossie No. 10*, MAA, April 1995, p. 17
156. Taylor, W., Interview with Rockdale Council, undated
157. Taylor, W., Notes on wartime experiences, 2004
158. Taylor, W., Interview with Rockdale Council, undated
159. Taylor, W., Notes on wartime experiences, 2004
160. Walsh, op. cit.
161. AIR 27/457 45 SORB
162. Walsh, B., *The Mossie No. 12*, MAA, April 1996, p. 18
163. Barbara Boon, the daughter of Australian 45 Squadron pilot Wal McLellan said that he always referred to the effects of 'g' at the bottom of the dive as 'the squash'.
164. Jefford, op. cit., p. 285
165. AIR27/684 82 SORB
166. Elliott, Bryn, *Charles Chabot*, www.brynelliott.co.uk, 2017, p. 13, accessed November 2022
167. Ibid
168. Norridge, C., *The Mossie No. 10*, MAA, April 1995, p. 18

169. Willis, op. cit., p. 183
170. Walsh, op. cit.
171. Jefford, op. cit., p. 275
172. AIR 27/457 45 SORB
173. Ibid
174. Ibid
175. Day, op. cit., p. 345
176. AIR27/684 82 SORB
177. Ibid
178. Spinks sale of Ron Goodwin's medals,
     https://www.spink.com/lot/17001000223, accessed on 8 May 2022
179. Ibid
180. Willis, op. cit., p. 193
181. Walsh, B., *The Mossie No. 12,* MAA, January 1996, p. 18
182. AIR 27/457 45 SORB
183. AIR27/861 110 SORB
184. Day, op. cit., p. 345
185. Bowman, op. cit., p. 213
186. AIR27/684 82 SORB
187. Ibid
188. Jefford, op. cit., p. 289
189. AIR 27/457 45 SORB
190. Warwick, op. cit., p. 126
191. https://weaponsandwarfare.com/2017/01/09/race-for-rangoon-i/
192. Air Ministry, *Wings of the Phoenix. The Official Story of the Air War in Burma,* His Majesty's Stationary Office, London, UK, 1949, p. 123
193. Gotch, G.L., *The Mossie No. 26,* MAA, Late Summer 2000, p. 26
194. Warwick, op. cit., p. 136
195. Bowman, M., *Mosquito Fighter/Fighter-Bomber Units of World War 2,* Osprey (Combat Aircraft Series), Oxford, UK, 1998, p. 86
196. Jefford, op. cit., p. 289
197. Air Ministry, *Wings of the Phoenix,* op. cit, p. 123
198. https://military.wikia.org/wiki/Battle_of_Pokoku_and_Irrawaddy_River_operations
199. AIR 27/457 45 SORB
200. RAF Historical Society and RAF Staff College, op. cit., p. 92
201. Pridmore, A., *The Mossie No. 11,* MAA, August 1995, p. 15

202. AIR27/684 82 SORB
203. F/L Wal McLellan's logbook, details supplied by Barbara Boon
204. Thewlis, G., *The Mossie No. 25*, MAA, May 2000, p. 19
205. Ibid
206. Willis, op. cit., p. 208
207. Signal, 24 February 1945, from Group Captain L.E. Whitley, CO of 908 Wing to 221 Group
208. Willis, op. cit., p. 209
209. Carruthers, C., *The Mossie No. 28*, MAA, May 2001, p. 15-6
210. Service Accident Report No. Misc, 23H, Mosquito Structural Failures, RAF Accident Investigation Branch, 24 February 45
211. AIR27/684 82 SORB
212. Willis, op. cit., p. 211
213. Day, op. cit., p. 343
214. Jefford, op. cit., p. 288
215. Storey, W.A., *The Mossie No. 31*. MAA, May 2002, p. 40
216. AIR27/684 82 SORB
217. Jefford, op. cit., p. 291
218. AIR27/684 82 SORB
219. Ibid
220. Thomas, op. cit., p. 58
221. Wambeek, R., *The Mossie No. 26*, MAA, Late Summer 2000, p. 35-6
222. RAF Regiment Heritage Centre website, *Battle for Meiktila*, www. rafregimentheritagecentre.co.uk Accessed on 2 Apr 2022
223. Smith, M., *Burma - Insurgency and the Politics of Ethnicity*, Zed Books, London and New Jersey, 1991, p. 60–1
224. Carruthers, C., *The Mossie No. 28*, MAA, May 2001, p. 16
225. McLellan, W., *North West and Hunter Valley Magazine*, Vol. 14, issue No. 1, April 1985
226. Day, op. cit., p. 344
227. AIR27/861 110 SORB
228. Thompson, H.L., *New Zealanders with the Royal Air Force (Volume III)*, Historical Publications Branch, Wellington, NZ, 1959, p. 362
229. AIR27/684 82 SORB
230. Pridmore, A., *The Mossie No. 11*, MAA, August 1995, p. 26
231. Walsh, B., *The Mossie No. 13*, MAA, April 1996, p. 20

232. AIR 27/457 45 SORB
233. Ibid
234. AIR27/684 82 SORB
235. Walsh, B., *The Mossie No. 13*, MAA, April 1996, p. 20
236. Ibid
237. My father described Ossie's response several times, including when we were at the RAF Museum under the Mosquito.
238. Jefford, op. cit., p. 506
239. http://www.dehavilland.ukf.net/_DH98%20prodn%20list.txt
240. Osterfield, L., *The Mossie No. 25*, MAA, May 2000, p. 25
241. Willis, op. cit., p. 193
242. Maude, A., *The Mossie No. 29*, MAA, September 2001, p. 18
243. AIR27/465 47 SORB
244. Yanota, op. cit.
245. Poole, M., The Diary of Donald Lomas, Royal Air Force, 29 November 2008
246. Yanota, op. cit.
247. Thewlis, G., *The Mossie No. 26*, MAA, Late Summer 2000, p. 5
248. Yanota, op. cit.
249. Jefford, op. cit., p. 299
250. Ibid, p. 242
251. Carruthers, C., *The Mossie No. 30*, MAA, January 2002, p. 27
252. Yanota, op. cit.
253. AWM, SEA0240
254. *New Zealand Herald, Japanese Torture New Zealand Airman, Experience in Rangoon.* 17 July 1945
255. R.N.Z.A.F. Official News Service, Eastern Air Command, *Airman in Burmese Prison, Extraordinary Experience*, 9 May 1945
256. Thewlis, G., *The Mossie No. 26*, MAA, Late Summer 2000, p. 5
257. RAF Historical Society and RAF Staff College, op. cit., p. 82
258. Taylor, W., *The Notes of a 45 Squadron Pilot*, Mossie Bites, Autumn 2022
259. Thomas, op. cit., p. 61
260. Letter from Mrs Olive Smith to Mrs Edith Lauder, 16 May 1945, Via Penny Hunt
261. Powell, G.W., *One "Op" too many*. Richarddnorth.com website accessed 10 May 2022

262. Willis, op. cit., p. 250

263. Williams, Nevin, Unpublished notes about his father's wartime experiences, 19 April 2022

264. AIR 27/861-5 110 SORB

265. Willis, op. cit., p. 252

266. Ibid, p. 253

267. AIR 27/861-5 110 SORB

268. Davis, R., *The Squadron Mascot ... Almost*, www.aircrew.org.uk accessed 19 February 2023

269. Thompson, H.L., New Zealanders with the Royal Air Force (Volume III), Historical Publications Branch, Wellington, NZ, 1959, p. 364

270. Davies, R., *The Mossie No. 15*, MAA, January 1997, p. 22

271. AIR 27/861-5 110 SORB

272. Service Accident Report No. Misc, 23I, Mosquito Structural Failures, RAF Accident Investigation Branch, 11 August 1945

273. Gibson, J., *The Mossie No. 23*, MAA, Summer/Autumn 1999, p. 8

274. Turner, C.L., *The Mossie No. 25*, MAA, May 2000, p. 35-6

275. Parker, S., *The Mossie No. 24*, MAA, January 2000, p. 25

276. Gibson, J., *The Mossie No. 23*, MAA, Summer/Autumn 1999, p. 8

277. Turner, C.L., *The Mossie No. 25*, MAA, May 2000, p. 36

278. Turner, C.L., *The Mossie No. 25*, MAA, May 2000, p. 36

279. Davis, R., *The Mossie No. 37*, MAA, January 2005, p. 12-3

280. Bowen, G., *The Mossie No. 12*, MAA, January 1996, p. 34

281. *The Mosquito 50 Years on*, op. cit., Ramsden, M., p. 32

282. Hudson, op. cit., p. 5

283. Spinks sale of Ron Goodwin's medals, https://www.spink.com/lot/17001000223 Accessed on 8 May 2022

284. Willis, op. cit., p. 268

285. Boon, Barbara, 1 May 2022

286. Stonehouse Heritage Group, UK, Newsletter 14

287. Hensengerth, O., *The Burmese Communist Party and the State-to-State Relations between China and Burma, Leeds East Asia Papers*, 2005, p.10-2

Index

Kunlon airfield, Burma (now
    Myanmar), 139-40
Kutcha strip, 26, 127, 244
Kyaukpadaung, Burma (now
    Myanmar), 172

Lambert, Warrant Officer Harry
    Allen, 157, 231
Lashio, Burma (now Myanmar),
    133, 151
Lauder, Flying Officer Gordon
    'Tiny', 198-9, 231
Levey, Flight Lieutenant James
    Maxwell 'Max' (RAAF), 82,
    88, 112, 232
Little Boy atomic bomb, 215, 217
Little, Wing Commander James
    Hayward 'Jimmy' DFC
    AFM, 17-8
Lorimer, Flight Sergeant Andrew
    Symon, 158, 232
Luff, Flight Sergeant William
    Charles 'Bill', 43, 50, 56
Lushai Hills, Burma (now
    Myanmar), 53-4, 121, 175

Magwe airfield, Burma (now
    Myanmar), 144, 176
Malaria, 126, 195
Mandalay, Burma (now Myanmar),
    114, 125, 128, 133, 135, 141, 143,
    147-8, 150-1, 159, 165-6, 169, 184
McKerracher, Flight Lieutenant
    Walter (RAAF) DFM, 69, 232
McLellan, Flight Lieutenant
    Walter Scott 'Wal' (RAAF)
    DFC, 66-7, 141, 147, 155,
    166-7, 182, 235, 239

McQueen, Warrant Officer John
    Sawers 'Mac' (RNZAF),
    125, 232
Meiktila airfield and town, Burma
    (now Myanmar), 28, 53, 86,
    88, 101-2, 111, 120-1, 128-32,
    135, 140, 149, 154, 157-9, 161,
    163-5, 169, 171, 176
Merlin engine:
    See Rolls-Royce Merlin engine
Mitchell aircraft:
    See North American B-25
    Mitchell aircraft
Monsoon, 1, 3, 21, 27, 98, 107, 109,
    125, 157, 174, 182, 184-5, 187,
    191, 196, 207, 219-20
    Chota monsoon, 182
Monywa airfield and town, Burma
    (now Myanmar), 55, 111, 128,
    132, 148, 176-7
Mosquito aircraft, 'Mossie':
    See De Havilland DH.98
    Mosquito aircraft
Moulmein, Burma (now
    Myanmar), 21, 60-1, 182-3,
    200, 207, 209, 215
Mountbatten, Admiral Lord
    Louis, 49, 52-3, 197, 208
Myers, Mr F.G., de Havilland
    company representative, 27,
    74, 96-7, 105-6, 109, 124
Myingyan, Burma (now
    Myanmar), 53
Myitnge, Burma (now Myanmar),
    139

Naga Hills and tribe, 51, 54, 114,
    121, 171